P9-ELX-711

RADICAL RELIGION
COMMUNITY FOR RELIGIOUS
RESEARCH AND EDUCATION
P. O. BOX 9164
BERKELEY, CALIF. 94709

Jesus Christ Liberator

For my friends
in Rio and in Petrópolis
and for all those
who seek Christ with a sincere heart

JESUS CHRIST LIBERATOR

A Critical Christology for Our Time

LEONARDO BOFF, O.F.M.

Translated by Patrick Hughes

ORBIS BOOKS
Maryknoll, New York 10545

Library of Congress Cataloging in Publication Data

Boff, Leonardo.
  Jesus Christ liberator.

  Translation of Jesus Cristo libertador.
  Includes bibliographical references.
  1. Jesus Christ—Person and offices.
I. Title.
BT202.B5313   232   78–969
  ISBN 0-88344-236-1 pbk.

First published as *Jesus Cristo Libertador. Ensaio de Cristologia Crítica para o nosso Tempo*, Copyright © 1972 by Editora Vozes Ltda., Rua Frei Luís, 100, Petrópolis, RJ, Brazil

This translation copyright © 1978 by Orbis Books, Maryknoll, NY 10545

The Catholic Foreign Mission Society of America (Maryknoll) recruits and trains people for overseas missionary service. Through Orbis Books Maryknoll aims to foster the international dialogue which is essential to mission. The books published, however, reflect the opinions of their authors and are not meant to represent the official position of the Society.

Contents

Preface

This book was first published in 1972. It was put together in Brazil at a time when severe political repression was being exerted against broad segments of the church. The word "liberation" was forbidden to be used in all the communications media. Thus the book did not say all that its author wanted to say; it said what could be said. Nevertheless the liberation message was understood by Christians, justifying successive printings, editions, and translations into many modern languages.

In this English translation an Epilogue has been added. It is written in the same spirit as the earlier chapters; its intent is to underline the liberative dimensions present in the life, message, and practical activity of the historical Jesus. But an atmosphere of greater tolerance now permits the author to introduce a more open and straightforward type of socio-analytical thought.

It is my hope that the reading of this book will help more privileged Christians to join in fellowship with those who are more oppressed, to commit themselves to the messianic task of liberating human beings completely from everything that diminishes them and offends God.

1

The History of the History of Jesus

"Who do people say that I am?" Posed by Christ, this question has been given the most diverse answers down through the centuries: the answers of faith, of critical science, of philosophy, of psychology, of sociology, and of turbulent youth in search of a radical meaning for life. In this chapter we will study the complexities and difficulties that our critical and demanding spirit encounters today while attempting to situate itself responsibly before Jesus Christ. No one can study Christ and remain indifferent. With Christ, the fate of each person is decided.

"Who do people say that I am?" Christ's question to his disciples resounds through the centuries to this day and possesses the same relevance as when it was first posed in Caesarea Philippi (Mark 8:29). Anyone who at some time has become interested in Christ cannot avoid similar questioning. Each generation must answer within the context of its own understanding of the world, of the human person, and of God.

1

THE ANSWER OF IMPERTURBABLE FAITH

To imperturbable faith the answer is quite clear: Jesus of Nazareth is the Christ, the only begotten and eternal Son of God, sent as man to liberate us from our sins; in him are fulfilled all the prophecies made to our fathers; he executed a preordained plan; his sorrowful death on the cross was a part of this plan; he fulfilled, even unto death, the will of the Father; though dead, he arose, thereby making it clear that his claim to be the Son of Man, the Son of God, and the Messiah was substantiated and genuine. Ordinary Christians have felt secure about all this because it is the message witnessed by the New Testament itself. In this Christ they deposited their confidence in life and in death. In this kind of answer there is no preoccupation with distinguishing between a historical fact and an interpretation of a fact conditioned by some perspective, be it philosophical, religious, historical, or social. Indiscriminately all is affirmed, content and form, as the inspiration of the Holy Spirit, consigned in the divinely inspired Scriptures. This is the image of the dogmatic Christ.

ANSWERS IN THE ERA OF CRITICISM

The eighteenth century, however, saw the breakthrough of critical reason. People began to question the social and religious models of interpretation. Historical studies, based on a serious research of original sources, unmasked dominant myths and ideologies. The questioning did not stop when faced with the New Testament. People saw immediately that in the case of the Gospels we are not dealing with historical biographies about Jesus but with the witness of faith, the fruit of preaching, the pious and self-interested meditation of the primitive community. The Gospels are above all a theological *interpretation* of the events rather than an objective and disinterested description of the historical Jesus of Nazareth. This discovery operated like a fuse setting a fire that even today is not yet fully extinguished. There were multiple reactions ranging from one extreme to the other. The question imposes itself: Should we look for the historical Jesus which is at the base and root of the dogmatic Christ?[1]

How Do We Know that Jesus Existed?

The first extreme answer appeared at the end of the eighteenth century. Whereas imperturbable faith had affirmed all to be historical without a shadow of doubt, now all is negated: Christ never existed;[2] he is a myth,[3] created by the human unconscious longing for liberation, a phenomenon observable in all religions.[4] Perhaps one can even say that Jesus Christ is a projection originated by a social movement of slaves and poor en route to social liberation and in the process of developing a consciousness of their alienation.[5]

This position was discredited at an early date. As Bultmann said: "The doubt as to whether Jesus really existed is unfounded and not worth refutation. No sane person can doubt that Jesus stands as founder behind the historical movement whose first distinct stage is represented by the oldest Palestinian community."[6] The Gospels are interpretation, but the interpretation of events that really took place. Moreover, extrabiblical witnesses, be they Roman (Pliny, *Ep.* 10, 96, 2; Suetonius, *Claudius*, 25, 4; *Nero*, 16, 2; Tacitus, *Annals* 15,44);[7] or Jewish (Flavius Josephus and the Talmudic literature)[8] cannot be conjured away. Evidently, this problem can always be posed not only in reference to Christ; it also applies to Buddha, Caesar Augustus, or Charlemagne. Using the method that some authors applied to Christ, one could prove that Napoleon did not exist; this was done by the historiographer R. Whateley (1787–1863), a contemporary of Napoleon himself.[9]

There Is Not, Nor Can There Be,
a Single Biography of Jesus

In questioning the dogmatic Christ of imperturbable faith, an attempt was made, employing the instruments and methods of modern scientific historiography, to get at the true image of Jesus of Nazareth, independent of dogmas and the interpretations of faith. The preoccupation of the historians and rational theologians was to arrive at a Jesus not yet interpreted as Christ and Son of God and not chained to cult or dogma. *The Christ of faith* ought to be well distinguished from the *historical Jesus.* Hundreds of Lives of Christ were written from Reimarus (d. 1768) to Wrede (d. 1904), with such well known names as Renan, D. F. Strauss, and M. Gognel in between. Each scholar sought to distinguish and discard the gospel texts regarded as nonhistorical or as dogmatic interpretations of the communities and thereby get at the really historical figure of Jesus. Albert Schweitzer, the then renowned theologian and exegete, later the famous physician of Lambarene, Africa, wrote a classic "history of research on the life of Jesus,"[10] showing the debacle resulting from such intentions. He characterized the Lives of Christ written with the historicist mentality of the nineteenth and early twentieth centuries in the following manner: "Each successive epoch of theology found its own ideas in Jesus and in this way alone could they give him life. Not only were the epochs reflected in him; each one in particular created him in the image of its own personality. There is no historical enterprise more personal than writing a life of Jesus."[11]

It is impossible to write a full biography of Jesus, to get at his personality, by focusing on his words, acts, behavior, and the great tendencies and trends of his epoch. The Gospels furnish the critical historian with an accumulation of traditions (at times very divergent and only exteriorly united with one another), witnesses of faith made in worship, and summaries of preaching given to a wide audience, especially to the Gentiles. The problem becomes even more difficult when we employ the texts of the New Testament to get at the historical awareness of Jesus. Did he consider himself Messiah and Son of God? Did he announce himself as the Son of Man who would shortly come upon the clouds? To this day purely historical research has not yielded a secure answer.

Moreover, another factor, which we will develop later, enters in at this point: the so-called hermeneutic circle. Can we reconstruct a history without at the same time already interpreting it? Historians approach their objects with the eyes of their epoch, with the interests dictated by, for example, the concept of scientific scholarship that they and their time possess. No matter how much they attempt to abstract from themselves as subjects, they can never escape the self and arrive at the object. For this reason every life of Jesus will necessarily partly reflect the life of its author. There will always be interpretation. It is a circle from which no one can escape. This can be demonstrated by the evangelists themselves.

In the case of Mark (who probably wrote between A.D. 65 and 69), Jesus is above all the hidden Messiah-Christ and the great liberator. He exorcises the earth wherever he appears. Therefore, rather than refer to the words and parables of Jesus, Mark emphasizes his actions and miraculous deeds. Jesus is the cosmic victor over death and the devil, liberating the earth of its alienating forces and inserting a divine peace, though he refuses to reveal himself explicitly and publicly as the Messiah.

Matthew, preaching to Jewish Christians and Greeks of Syria (circa 85–90) sees in Jesus the Messiah-Christ, prophesied and awaited, the new Moses who instead of bringing an improved law and an ever more rigorous pharisaism gave us a new gospel. Jesus is the one who demonstrates the will of God better than anyone and in a definitive manner—where to find it and how to realize it.

In Luke, evangelist to the Gentiles and the Greeks (who wrote circa 85–90), Jesus is presented as the liberator of the poor, the sick, sinners, the socially and religiously marginalized. He is Man revealed; at the same time he is the Son of God who revealed the filial nature of all human beings. In following the example of Christ people know themselves to be radically transformed and located within the kingdom of God.

John (writing in about 90–100) sees in Jesus the eternal Son of God, the Logos, who pitches his tent in the midst of the people in order to be the way, the truth, the life, bread and living water. The image of Jesus that emerges from the Gospel of John is hieratic and transcendent, moving always in the divine sphere. More than any other, John is the theologian for whom the facts exist in function of a theology, to the point where kerygma becomes history. His Jesus is already the Christ of faith.

Paul, who did not know the historical Jesus, is the proclaimer par excellence of Christ resurrected by faith as the new humanity, as the new heaven and new earth already present in this world, as the only mediator and savior for the totality of history. The author of the epistle to the Colossians and Ephesians (certainly a disciple of Paul) uses the categories of Stoic and Gnostic thought to answer the question: What is the function of Christ in the redemption of the cosmos? Christ is called therefore the head of all things (Eph. 1:10), the centralizing force wherein everything has its existence and consistence (Col. 1:16–20).

As readily appears from these brief indications, each author seeks within his pastoral, theological, apologetic, and vital preoccupations to respond in his own way to the question: "Who do men say that I am?" Each sacred writer sees the same Jesus—but with his own eyes. With such material transmitted to us through the intermediary of the New Testament we cannot construct a biography of Jesus that would be historically and scientifically clear.

The Primacy of the Christ of Faith over the Historical Jesus, of Biblical History over History, of Interpretation over Bare Fact

From the fact that historical exegesis failed to reconstruct a precise historical Jesus of Nazareth Rudolf Bultmann draws an ultimate consequence: We should definitively abandon such attempts and concentrate exclusively on the Christ of faith.[12] Yes, the methods of historical criticism have given us some secure information about the historical Jesus even though they do not allow us to reconstruct a biography. But such information is irrelevant to faith, because it presents Jesus as a Jewish prophet who preached a radical obedience, demanded conversion, and announced the pardon and proximity of the kingdom. Jesus is not a Christian but a Jew, and his history does not pertain to Christianity but to Judaism: "The message of Jesus is a presupposition of the theology of the New Testament rather than a part of that theology itself."[13] His teaching is one presupposition among others such as Gnosticism and Stoicism, that is, the pagan world of the day with its myths and hopes.

Bultmann insists on a distinction between "the so-called historical Jesus and the Christ of biblical history."[14] It is taken from his master Martin Kähler whose celebrated book (1892) was programmatic for all later discussions. He urges that we distinguish between plain historical *(historisch)* data and interpreted historical *(geschichtlich)* data, between Jesus and Christ. "Jesus" refers to the man of Nazareth, whose life critical historiography attempted in vain to reconstruct. "Christ" is the Savior, the Son of God announced by the church through the Gospels. The term *historisch* designates the facts of the past that can be demonstrated by documents and critically analyzed by the methods of scientific history; *geschichtlich* refers to the meaning that a fact assumes for an epoch or a group of people within history. According to this distinction only the latter Jesus is of interest to the faith because preaching alone (that is, the New Testament) made him the Savior of the world—and we can establish this historically. Therefore, according to Bultmann, the renunciation of the historical Jesus is based fundamentally on two considerations:

1. It is not possible to write a life of Jesus because we lack disinterested sources. What we can establish as historically certain is the figure of a Jewish prophet whose message consists in the radicalization of the faith of the Old Testament. These two facts are without major importance for the faith.
2. The task of theology ought not to consist in wasting time looking for the historical Jesus—he cannot be found but in the interpretation and translation into the language of our own day of the apostolic teachings that announced Jesus as the Christ, the Savior, the Son of Man, and the Son of God. We ought to demythologize the message of its syncretistic overlay belonging to the Greco-Roman culture.[15]

The difference between the historical Jesus and the Christ of faith can be summarized in the following points made by Bultmann:

1. Instead of the historical person of Jesus, the mythical figure of the Son of God entered into the apostolic teachings *(kerygma)*.

2. Instead of the eschatological preaching of Jesus concerning the kingdom of God there entered into the *kerygma* the proclamation of the Christ who died crucified for our sins and was marvelously resurrected by God for our salvation. Jesus preached the kingdom; the church preaches Christ. The preacher is now preached.

3. Instead of the radical obedience and total living out of love demanded by Jesus there now entered the doctrine about Christ, the church, the sacraments. What Jesus put in first place now comes second: ethical parenesis.[16]

Confronted with this division between Jesus and Christ one may ask: What christological value can be attributed to the historical humanity of Jesus? It is irrelevant, responds Bultmann. "Concerning the life of Jesus the *kerygma* (preaching) need only know *that* Jesus lived, and *that* he died on the cross. That there is no need to go beyond this is demonstrated by Paul and John each in his own way."[17] The only aspect of interest to faith is that he existed. What really occurred, the historically objective facts, is of no interest.

According to such theses, to believe in Jesus does not mean to believe in his person but in the preaching concerning him preserved in the Gospels. It is not Jesus who saves but Christ preached. Through preaching he touches each one personally. Now this preaching is done by the church. Thus there is no faith in Christ without faith in the church, because there is no Christ without the preaching announced by the church. The study of traditions and form criticism's *(Formgeschichte)* research of the Gospels make concrete the theological, literary, and editorial work of the primitive communities.

What then is Christology? "Not a doctrine concerning the divine nature of Christ, but an announcement, a call of faith inviting me to believe, to take up the cross of

Christ, and thus justified, to participate in the resurrection."[18] Christology is the Word of God that affects me today, now. To believe in Christ as the Gospels preach him is to experience and achieve redemption. Nevertheless, we ought to demythologize the evangelical formulations and see their meaning for our existence. For example, what does it mean to believe in the cross of Christ? It does not mean to believe in some bygone fact that happened to Jesus. Rather it means "making the cross of Christ one's own cross, that is, letting yourself be crucified with Christ."[19] To believe in the Crucified is to wrench oneself away from oneself. Salvation is to be found in this. Christology is thus reduced to soteriology. Christology is "the explanation of the Christian understanding of being,"[20] "an explanation of the understanding that faith has of new being";[21] the remainder consists of "mythological representations and cultic concepts from Hellenic syncretism."[22]

As is evident, here we have discovered a new radicalization. If theologians and historians seeking the historical Jesus went to one extreme, setting aside the Christ of faith and later dogmatic interpretations, Bultmann went to the other extreme, seeking only the Christ of faith, setting aside the historical Jesus, and reducing him to the mathematical point of mere existence.[23]

THE RETURN TO THE HISTORICAL JESUS: JESUSOLOGY AND CHRISTOLOGY

Bultmann's position, no matter how fascinating it may seem, leaves the faith open to serious problems. From whence emerged the faith? What is the basis of the *kerygma?* How do we distinguish preaching concerning Jesus from an ideology built around the figure of Jesus by a group of people? What force is behind, propelling the preaching? An idea or a historical person? Can a rupture between the historical Jesus and the Christ of faith be sustained? Are the redeeming death and resurrection of Jesus mere interpretations of the community that can be dismissed today? Or are we talking about something that was truly realized in Jesus?[24] Can we equate, as Bultmann does, preaching, Jesus, the church, the New Testament, and the Holy Spirit? If we identify Jesus with the teaching of the church, then we lose every critical element and the possibility of legitimate protest. It takes away from us the criterion by which we can judge Mark, Luke, Matthew, John, Paul, and other scriptural authors and see to what extent they interpreted and developed the original message of Jesus when confronted with the new necessities of their respective communities. From what point of departure can we maintain a critical attitude toward the church if Christ, as Bultmann says, is created by the faith of that same church? Moreover, Bultmann's Christology deprives the incarnation of all substance. Christ is not primarily an idea, a theme for preaching. He was above all a historical being—conditioned, datable. In Bultmann's theology Christ is not the Word that was made flesh but flesh that was made Word.

In the discussion of problems raised here two very clear orientations were developed. One strong current of Bultmann's followers did not accompany the master in his radical thesis. It took a step backward; it reassumed the problem of the historical Jesus. This is well summarized by J. M. Robinson: "The question concerning the historical Jesus is a necessary one because the *kerygma* seeks to conduct the disciple to an existential encounter with a historical person, Jesus of Nazareth."[25] The post-Bultmannian problematic transposed the terms of interest. As Bultmann himself testified in 1960, "In the past the great theme consisted in establishing the difference between Jesus and the preaching concerning Jesus. Today we have the inverse: The interest lies in revealing the unity between the historical Jesus and the Christ of faith."[26]

This return to the search for the historical Jesus was

critical in nature. All agree that a biography of Jesus can never be written. Nevertheless, in spite of the christological, interpretive, and confessional character of the Gospels, the figure of Jesus they describe is that of a born original, unmistakable and unchangeable; the historical concreteness and the specificity of Jesus show through in spite of all the interpretations made by the primitive communities. It was precisely the qualities of greatness and sovereignty perceived in the historical Jesus that motivated the christological process and the multiple interpretations. As we shall explain better below, a whole current of post-Bultmannian theology and exegesis proceeds along this line.

Another current of thought carried Bultmann's program to demythologize the gospel message to its ultimate consequences. The result, as we shall see, is an atheistic Christianity, a position not shared by the master.

The Continuity Between Jesus and Christ:
Indirect Christology

What is the basis of the continuity between the historical Jesus and the Christ of faith? To a large extent, both Catholic and Protestant theological-exegetic research in recent years concentrated on the analysis and elaboration of this problem.[27] Such research revealed a very important fact already referred to above: Jesus' mode of acting, his demands that related participation in the kingdom and in the coming of the Son of Man to adhesion to his person (see Luke 12:8–10), his claim that in him the last chance of salvation is offered and that in him the poor shall be consoled and sinners reconciled—all this implies a latent, implicit, and indirect Christology.[28]

Robinson, Käsemann,[29] Bornkamm,[30] Mussner,[31] Geiselmann, Trilling, Pannenberg,[32] and many others have made it very clear that the authority and sovereignty with which Jesus comported himself when confronting legal traditions, and even the understanding of the Old Testament, transcend by a wide margin what a rabbi might be permitted. He invades the divine sphere and speaks as one who is in the place of God. Even the most demanding historian could not but observe that here is someone who breaks through human categories. Jesus possessed a messianic conscience, even if he did not express it by means of some traditional eschatological title such as Messiah, Son of man, or Son of God. The continuity between the historical Jesus and the Christ of faith consists therefore in the fact that the primitive community made explicit what had been implicit in the words, demands, attitudes, and comportment of Jesus. They called Jesus by such titles as the Messiah, the Son of God, the Lord, to decipher the authority, the sovereignty and the claims that emerged from his mode of being.

Research now began to distinguish between two things: a "Jesusology" (how Jesus understood himself and allowed others to understand him by his words and attitudes) and a Christology (the clarification done by the community afterwards). Christology is nothing other than going beyond that which emerged in Jesus. What emerged in Jesus was the immediacy of God himself. As G. Bornkamm, one of the greatest scholars of Jesus in this century, admirably noted: "Making present the reality of God is the basis of the special mystery of Jesus."[33] If this is true, then the most adequate position from which we should approach the historical Jesus is that of faith, because it is only within this perspective that the attitudes and behavior of Jesus acquire their natural connotations and corresponding clarification. Within this perspective an encounter with the witnesses of faith (the Gospels) signifies an encounter with Jesus himself. The historical Jesus is the Jesus of faith, not only because the Gospels are witnesses of faith, but because Jesus himself was a person of faith and a witness of faith.[34]

In the light of these studies interesting books concerning Jesus were written wherein history, shorn of the rigid preconceptions belonging to the liberal criticism of historicism, offered enough certified historical material —even though it be insufficient for a biography—for a schematized description of Jesus of Nazareth. Evidently, here too there were exaggerations, practiced especially by E. Stauffer, who in the euphoria of the new critical return to the historical Jesus tried to reconstruct a life of Jesus strictly within the confines of positivist criteria.[35] The method involved a minuscule and erudite analysis of the indirect sources concerning Jesus: old reports; prosopographical, political, juridical, moral, numismatic, and archeological documents of the time; and added knowledge of Qumran literature, the apocalyptic writers, and the rabbinical polemic against Jesus (especially the Midrash and the Talmud).

Stauffer's intention is to arrive at the clear, primitive message and self-consciousness of Jesus himself. From this standpoint he can judge the various theologies and Christologies elaborated by the communities and contained in the Gospels. With this in mind he performs the impious task of debunking all elements judged by him not to pertain to Jesus. The results of his research can be summarized as follows: God revealed himself in Jesus. The expression of divine self-revelation is to be found in the sovereignty of Jesus communicated in the various "I am" passages (see Mark 14:62). Consequently, the core of Jesus' message consists in a new morality, one of love, counterposed to the morality of obedience introduced at a later date by Paul and the church. The present Gospels are the products of a re-judaization of Christianity. The special task of Christology ought to consist in getting beyond the ethic of obedience, which has brought about so much evil in

Christian history, and in de-judaizing the Jesus tradition. The critics received Stauffer's program badly.[36] Although demonstrating an impressive erudition and an apostolic fervor, his studies represent the anachronistic fruit of classic historiography of the life of Jesus.

Christological Concentration and Reduction: Theologians of the Death of God

Some of Bultmann's disciples, such as H. Braun, D. Sölle and P. Van Buren among others, further radicalized the Bultmannian positions. Their demythologization touches not only the content of the New Testament but also the most fundamental concepts of religion, such as the image of God.

For example, H. Braun, the renowned exegete and theologian of Mainz, thought that after Kant we ought once and for all to exclude any objectification of God, even the designations "spirit" and "person." God is not an object of knowledge. Neither does God simply exist like the rest of realities. God happens within human life. God is that happening which allows for the emergence of love and in which the sinner and the desperate receive hope and future.[37] Consequently God does not constitute a superior entity, a divine essence that caused the world, that rewards and punishes in accordance with the merits of each person. To think of God in this manner would be to enclose God within the categories of a metaphysical or linguistic frame of reference and leave oneself prisoner to the structures of outmoded, mythical, and pre-critical thinking. Thus Braun, as well as the Protestant theologian Dorothee Sölle, affirms: The acceptance of the divinity is not a necessary presupposition for being a Christian. One can be an atheist and a Christian.[38]

Ernst Bloch, going one step further, formulated the following paradox in the title of a book: "Only a good

Christian can be an atheist and only a good atheist can be a Christian."[39] Van Buren suggested that the name of God should be definitively eliminated.[40] Evidently these radical authors are not preaching a vulgar atheism. God continues to have a *function:* God is the symbol of the comportment that Christ demanded of all—unrestricted love and disinterested obedience to the appeals of unlimited reciprocity. Wheresoever this may occur, there God is present (Braun).[41]

The theology of the death of God realizes a christological concentration without parallel in the history of Christian theology. Jesus suppresses the God who died and substitutes for him. Jesus is the true God. The God of transcendence, of creation, of divine attributes died within our empirical, experiential, pragmatic, and immediatist culture. The God who identified with our condition, with our darknesses and anxieties, is the divine God and he is called Jesus of Nazareth. Jesus fills the immense emptiness and the tremendous vacuum created by the death of God. Because God neither intervenes nor makes his cause triumph in the world, Christ takes his place. "He consoles those whom God abandoned. He cures those who do not understand God. He satiates those who earnestly desire God."[42]

Jesus is God's protagonist. He plays God's role in the world, makes him present, and makes his absence less dramatic. God speaks no more. He ceased to be transparent to us. Nevertheless we have God's lieutenant—Jesus Christ. In Jesus, God made himself weak and impotent in the world.[43] In this manner he resolved the problem of pain and evil, the permanent stumbling block and basis of argument for atheism. The God questioned by atheism in the name of the evils of the world was the omnipotent, infinite God, creator of heaven and earth, cosmic Father and Lord. In Jesus Christ, God took upon himself the evil and the absurd. By identifying with the problem he resolved it, not theoretically but through life and love. Consequently, this God alone is the God of the Christian experience. He is no longer the eternal and infinite loner but one with us, in solidarity with our pain and anguish caused by the absence and latency of God in the world.

The reader will have noticed that in all this there is not only a christological concentration, but also a reduction of the reality of Jesus Christ. The Jesus to whom the Gospels give testimony cannot be adequately understood without some explicit reference to God. It is true that Jesus also experienced the death of God. But this does not mean that he had suppressed God or even liberated human beings from all divinity. He acted in God's name. He announced the kingdom as the kingdom *of God*, taught us to call him Father, and have a sense of ourselves as his beloved sons. To deny this would be to reduce Christology to mere phraseology.

The Christology of Word, Silence, and Faltering Speech

What is the real problem that lurks behind the questions considered above, questions that many regard as academic, the fruit of a much too rigid concept of history elaborated since the eighteenth century in European, especially German, circles? The basic problem can be reduced to this: Faith says that Jesus is the future of human beings and the world, that he is the maximum realization of our religious desire to be in communion with the divine, that he is God himself incarnate. But is this a reality of history or a mere projection for the world of ideas and an idealistic interpretation of human existence forever inquiring of itself? Which is the savior? The word and the interpretation of human existence or the historical man, Jesus of Nazareth, who gave origin to the word and a new interpretation of existence?

What the Gospels wish to announce is the presence of

a new reality: Jesus as resurrected, victor over death, sin, and all that alienates the human person. Because of this they proclaim the presence of a new hope in the heart of history. It is not their primary intention to announce a new doctrine and a new interpretation of our relations with God. Basically they seek to demonstrate the reality of the human person, so that from this standpoint all people can have hope concerning our condition before God and the future that awaits us: that we will have a full life in communion with the life of God; that flesh has a future; a divinization; and that death with all that it signifies will not have its day. This historical optimism assumes a universal and eternal character because it represents a future within time. To many this is a scandal. Can the word transmit such positiveness? Or is the word merely a fragile vase that contains but cannot be identified with the precious essence? The New Testament and the preaching of the church present themselves as a word full of authority and power, a word that contains and communicates the positiveness of the *fact* of Jesus, the Christ. But can this word born in an old world adequately express the new? Rather, is it not primarily a question of faltering speech in the presence of a mystery? Is it not primarily a human answer and one full of faith rather than the answer of Christ and of God to humankind.

One current of theology affirms that silence is a greater communicator than the word. It is from silence that the fertile word is born. The wisdom of the word consists in carrying us back to the silence of the mystery. But is it not precisely in love that the maximum realization of God and of the human person resides? Love is silence and word. Love is not only word because the ineffable exists in each and every one and in God. Love is also not silence alone, since love communicates itself and demands another, a Thou, an otherness and a reciprocity. The human person can know the value both of silence and of the word.

However, faltering speech is even more natural to the human person when confronted with the mystery of our own self, of Christ, and of God. St. Bonaventure saw the task of the theologian and of theology in this. This power of faltering speech is called faith, not faith as a deficient mode of knowing but as a way of comporting oneself positively before the ultimate questions of human life, of the world, and of God. By faith we transcend one dimension of knowing, that is, scientific questioning. We have entered another domain wherein free decision is the determinant factor founding another universe of comprehension concerning human reality. Faith and scientific reason are not posited one against the other. They are two different dimensions within the same domain and not two modes of knowing.

Consequently, any attempt to reconquer or reclaim a historical Jesus at the cost of a dogmatic Christ merely confuses the dimensions and erroneously understands the faith as an inadequate and imperfect form of knowing. Can the historical Jesus himself be understood outside of the dimension of faith, if he himself, Jesus of Nazareth, understood his entire life as a life of faith? Is it not precisely faith itself that gives the proper atmosphere and perspective that enables us to understand the historical Jesus? It was not without reason that the primitive community identified the fleshly historical Jesus with the Christ risen in glory. History always comes to us in unison with faith and consequently any docetist watering down, be it reducing Jesus to mere Word (*kerygma*, preaching) or to a mere historical being that ceased to exist in death, ought to be rejected a priori.

The Word was made flesh. This means there is a history of a new and eschatological being, inaugurated with full, global clarity, in an epochal and unique manner, in the person of Jesus of Nazareth. This is the fundamental nucleus of the Christian message. Having this starting point, the nature of faltering speech concerning this reality will vary throughout history as it varies in the New Testament itself. Thus we see that this discussion concerning the historical Jesus and the Christ of faith involves the fundamental problem of Christianity: Has the *homo revelatus* already emerged, completely divinized and inserted into the mystery of God or are we still in a state of anxious expectation (cf. Luke 3:15), lost in an old world and an alienated being? The New Testament is unanimous: Salvation has already appeared and calls itself Jesus Christ; he is the new humanity, the first to arrive at the goal; we will follow him.

OTHER CONTEMPORARY CHRISTOLOGICAL POSITIONS

Along with the positions referred to above, there are still others that mark the horizons of reflection concerning Jesus and his religious activity. We will refer briefly to several.

The Philosophical-Transcendental Interpretation of Jesus

This theological current, popular among Catholic theologians, stems also from the problem of demythologization.[44] To us, they say, many of the most fundamental affirmations with regard to Jesus have the sound of archaic myths: that Jesus of Nazareth is at the same time God; that he was born of a virgin, etc. What does it mean to us when you say that Jesus is the Word incarnate? How can we mediate this fact so that it becomes intelligible within the horizons of our comprehension? Many people understand the incarnation of God in a mythical and erroneous manner: as if human activity were totally dispensed with; as if Jesus had not really participated in our human condition with all that that implies in terms of groping, hoping, growing, comprehending, relating to God and the necessity of believing. If Jesus were really God, what then is the basis and precondition in human nature that makes its assumption by God possible? If Jesus-man can be the incarnation of the Word, it is because there already existed this possibility within human nature.

Jesus is a man like us. Therefore human nature as such contains this transcendence and ability to relate to the Absolute. It can identify with it and be a part of its history. Thus Christology presupposes a transcendental anthropology: People are by nature suited for the Absolute; people are anxious for it and hope to unite themselves with it as the ultimate meaning of their full humanization. The most radical demand of their existence consists in the possession of a radical sense of unity with the Infinite. People find in themselves such a force and movement in the direction of the Transcendent. They accept it freely. They recognize that this force exists in them in fact, as a condition, so that the Infinite itself can communicate itself and fill the desire of the human heart. This movement, this opening of the self to God, does not remain empty and unfulfilled. It is not a condition of eternal return, a permanent situation of Prometheus and Sisyphus. The Infinite gives itself to human beings and, while preserving the otherness of creator-creature, forms a reconciling unity of God with the human person.

Christianity saw in Jesus of Nazareth the realization of this longing in human nature. Consequently it called him the Word incarnate, God made human, and God with us. In this, nothing miraculous or strange is being affirmed, nothing foreign to the possibilities offered by human nature. What is declared is the maximum realization of the human person itself in God. Thus Jesus Christ, God and man, is not a myth but the eschatological realization of the fundamental possibility that God placed in human nature.

The Cosmic-Evolutionist Interpretation of Jesus

This same line of thought is taken a step further and made more profound in terms of cosmic evolution by

Teilhard de Chardin and his followers.[45] It is not only human nature that leaves itself open to the Transcendental but the whole process of progressive evolution. A movement of growth, of unity, and of consciousness pervades the whole evolutionary process and all its strata. Jesus Christ, believed and preached in the Gospels and the church, represents the Omega point of convergence for all progressive lines of evolution. Through him there occurred the outburst of the mystery of almighty God in all things.

The incarnation of God not only signifies that a man, Jesus of Nazareth, has been assumed. It also signifies that all matter in evolution was touched, because Jesus of Nazareth is not a monad lost within the world but a vital part and result of a whole process of millions and millions of years of convergent evolution. In this way Jesus Christ can be regarded as the greatest gift that creation offered to God and at the same time the greatest gift that God gave to human beings. In him the paths of the world meet with those of God; in him the irreversible zenith, the very goal toward which all the forces of evolution tend, is attained.

*The Interpretation of Jesus with
the Categories of Depth Psychology*

Another current of thought, still in its infancy, makes use of the categories of depth psychology, especially those of C. G. Jung, to comprehend some fundamental facets of the Jesus-phenomenon.[46] Here it is not a question of trying to understand the conscious life of Jesus in a psychological manner; this question has long since been superseded. Rather, an attempt is being made to unravel conditionings of the collective unconscious implied in the action of Jesus and the movement unleashed by him. The unconscious is structured by myths, archetypes, symbols, and images. In psychology, myth does not have the same connotation as for the history of religions, i.e., stories of Gods or fantastic tales of supra-terrestrial beings, their destiny, wars, defeats, and heroic victories. Myth is the form whereby the collective unconscious represents for itself the radical meaning of permanent situations in life such as relations with God, father, mother, woman, man, the king, the priest, animals, evil, sex, etc. The myth possesses a language, a logic, and structures of its own. It is not absurd or arbitrary even though it might appear so to a conscious analytical reason orientating itself in the examination of objects.

In myth, the unconscious speaks, not the conscious. This is the reason why mere "scientific," "objective" research cannot understand myth, because it approaches myth with categories taken from conscious life. Neither does the truth of the myth consist in its "objective" realization in the world of reality. "Scientific" and "critical" research proceeding in this manner disqualified the myth as fable and illusion from the start. The error, however, lies not in the myth but in the scholars who completely falsified their own perspective by operating under the illusion that human beings are solely conscious life and rationality. Consciousness and the world of objects, as Freud said, merely form the tip of the iceberg, the greater part of which (the unconscious) remains hidden under the water.

Demythologization does not signify unmasking the myth by confronting it with objective reality (which would be not to comprehend the myth), but it means to explain the myth as the language of the unconscious, accept it as a legitimate form of logical comprehension, and integrate it in the process of the individualization of personality. To search for the meaning of myth is not to detect its genetic origins (whether it came from the Persians or the Greeks), nor to decifer the traditions that gave it form. The meaning and truth of a myth consist in the interpretative capacity it possesses to explain existence. Thus, in Jesus, the myth of the kingdom of God, expressed in apocalyptic symbols, represents the search for and the promise of the full realization of the meaning of all reality: The breakthrough of the goal of history is imminent. This event signifies a radical crisis for the conscious, which must reorganize its existential arrangements and give rise to an archetype of the unconscious that will transform the horizon of existence.

In the preaching of Jesus there appears in an extreme form the breakthrough of the meaning of existence as communion and participation of all with God. The myth of the kingdom implied a new image of God. He did not reveal himself anymore as the God-law, but as God the Father who indiscriminately called all people, good and bad, just and unjust, to participation in the kingdom. This generated conflict among the Jews and the consequent liquidation of Jesus. Jesus, in turn, suffered the conflict as a form of reconciliation with his own torturers. He preached love. Though dying because of hate he taught forgiveness. Thus he created a new vision of fraternity before the same Father who transcends all limitations. The resurrection confirmed the inauguration of the new being and the radical meaning of life as eternal life no longer threatened by death. Nevertheless, insofar as the myth is not yet realized for all people and for the cosmos it cannot be totally demythologized.

There are precious intuitions in this perspective that clarify obscure and still uncomprehended points in the message of Jesus, such as the announcement of the imminent coming of the kingdom, the conflict with the law, and others. It was the rationalist conception, with its criteria taken from conscious life, that led Albert Schweitzer to affirm that Jesus had miserably misled himself in his preaching concerning the kingdom and that therefore he could not be God. Consequently he abandoned theology, studied medicine, went to Africa, and tried to live with admirable fidelity to the end what was left of the gospel of Christ: his message of love and humanity toward all, especially the weak.

The Secular, Socio–Critical Interpretation of Jesus

This current of Catholic and Protestant theology clearly perceived the quality of privatism that the message of Christ assumed in church tradition and in the more recent transcendental, existential, and personalist orientation in theology.[47] The revolutionary message of Christ had been reduced to a decision of faith made by individuals without relation to the social and historical world, their natural context. The message had been preached with the use of categories taken from the context of intimate, private, I-Thou, interpersonal relationships. Conversion too had taken on a private character and had come to mean a change in the life of an individual, not calling for any involvement in the politico-social world that remained safeguarded against all criticism.

However, the gospel and the message of Christ outlined a large public domain. They bit into the social and political context of the day. The intrigue lying behind the death of Christ was political in nature. Likewise, his message concerning the kingdom, though it did not take sides, undoubtedly possessed a political connotation. The word "kingdom" in classical tradition implied involvement in public life, in the relations of people with the world and with others. The kingdom of God cannot be made private, given only a spiritual dimension such as pardon for sins and reconciliation with God. It implies a transformation of persons, the world of people, and the cosmos. The most forceful preaching of Jesus possessed a critical content, confronting the social and religious traditions of his people and the canons of Old Testament religion. All this was gradually overlooked and spiritualized in the church. And in the end Christianity lost its historic power of contestation and criticism, in the name of the liberty of the children of God, against any manipulation of religion for the purpose of legitimating the interests of religious or ecclesiastical groups.

This theological current emphasizes in Jesus and his message precisely those elements of criticism, contestation, and liberation that, when read into our cultural context, take on a special political and religious relevance. The message of Christ assumes a critical-liberating function against repressive situations, be they religious or political. He did not come to found a new religion but to bring a new humanity. Thus, Jesus Christ and his mission cannot simply be put into the framework of religious canons. He transcends the sacred and the profane, the secular and the religious. Consequently, the church cannot identify itself with Jesus Christ nor with the kingdom of God. The church itself comes under the "eschatological reservation," i.e., it is not the goal and the end in itself but the instrument and the sacrament of the kingdom. Its function is to carry forward the liberating cause of Christ, not only in the personal realm (calling individuals to conversion), but also in the public sphere (calling society to continuous transformation).

Confronted with the definitive situation which has yet to manifest itself, everything in the present is ecclesiastically, dogmatically, and politically relative and susceptible to improvement and criticism. Now this understanding of Jesus and the gospel necessitates a very serious criticism within the church itself and not merely outside of it. For example, far too often Christ was used to justify the immediate interests of the church. Out of this emerged so-called "political Christology" that justified a church triumphant over persecutions and now, by design of God, the inheritor of the Roman Empire.[48] The fathers of the third century, such as St. Cyprian, used to say that the *pax Romana* had been replaced by the *pax Christiana*. In short, the *Holy Roman Empire* had been founded. Jesus was now presented not as the friend of all, in particular the poor and humbled, but as

Emperor, Proclaimer of Laws, Judge, Philosopher, Cosmic Lord and Ruler of all.[49]

We need only look at the images of Christ in the great churches from the third century on. Jesus of Nazareth, weak in power but strong in love, who renounced the sword and violence, was replaced by a political Christ constituted Lord of the earth by the resurrection. His representatives, popes and bishops, govern in his name and use force to destroy all "the enemies of God." Official circles of the post-Constantinian church rapidly forgot the violent criticism launched by Jesus against the form in which power was exercised in the old world: "You know that among the pagans the rulers lord it over them, and their great men make their authority felt. This is not to happen among you. No, anyone who wants to be great among you must be your servant, and anyone who wants to be first among you must be your slave, just as the Son of Man came not to be served but to serve, and to give his life as a ransom for many" (Matt. 20:25–28; Luke 22:25–27; Mark 10:42–45). According to Jesus, *hierarchia* (sacred power) is proper to the pagans and *hierodulia* (sacred service) is proper to Christians.

The church in time succumbed to the temptation of pagan-style power with its domination and honorific titles learned in the Roman and Byzantine courts. The humble life of the poor Christ was reread in terms of the categories of power. Sculpture and painting, up to recently, presented us the birth of Christ as a parousia of a Roman Emperor surrounded by jewels and princely airs. The poor shepherds were transformed into princes, the humble stable into a royal palace, the holy virgin and good Joseph into members of the court. The miracles and preachings of Christ appeared in new clothing as a sumptuous and luxurious halo that startled the poor and humiliated the contrite of heart. But Christ identified himself precisely with these and announced the great joy to them.

The consequences for piety and ecclesiastical praxis

were disastrous. This has been demonstrated by excellent Catholic researchers, people of the caliber of Jungmann and Karl Adam.[50] Instead of a sense of intimacy in the hands of the Father there entered fear; instead of filial immediacy there reigned restraint before the imperial Christ; instead of feeling themselves all as brothers and sisters, people saw themselves caught up in a hierarchical web that interposed itself between Christ and the faithful. In the light of this they began to venerate the saints rather than Christ. The saints were nearer and could act as mediators with Christ. In addition to the saints there emerged innumerable sacramentals, creating a sacred cosmos through which simple people could live their religious experience since they felt themselves alienated by the politicization of the figure of Christ and the structures of the church. And this cosmos is all pervasive in the religious and cultural unconscious of our western Christianity.

As is clear from this short exposition, in former times Christ was politicized to justify concrete situations of the church. Today we are confronting the inverse: The same ideological preoccupation imposes a tendency to present an apolitical, private Christ in order to justify the position of an established church enjoying its historical triumphs. This church is, however, organized in outmoded structures that imperil the very essence and internal life of Christianity in vast regions of the world. A socio-critical vision of Jesus and his message seeks to shed light on ideological interpretations whereby the church can be manipulated. Jesus is an element of continuous internal criticism. He is a source of discomfort. He does not allow himself to be domesticated by a theological system. But he does allow himself to be loved through liberating faith.

The Experience of Christ Among Modern Youth

It is in the above context of reflection that the new experience of Christ among today's youth gains social and religious relevance. Since the sixties we can observe a frenzied agitation in student circles of the western world, especially the capitalist and postindustrial world.[51] There emerged an impressive movement that challenged the traditional and established scheme of values. The utopia of a global consumer society, a society without dire needs, revealed itself as truly illusionary. Technology, instead of liberating, enslaved people in the most subtle form. Urban society and secular empirical technology, instead of creating greater conditions of personal liberty, restricted citizens ever more thoroughly. As an analyst of contemporary North American youth said: "For three hundred years, science and scientific technology enjoyed a merited and unblemished reputation: It was a great adventure, bestowing benefits and liberating the spirit of the errors of superstition and traditional faith. . . . In our generation, however, they came to be seen by many, and especially the youth, as essentially inhuman, abstract, massifying, hand in hand with power, and even diabolical."[52]

The protest exploded inexorably and without compassion: "Oh, middle-aged generations, look at yourselves; you need two shots of strong liquor to find the courage to converse with another human person. Look at yourselves, you need your neighbors' wives to prove to yourselves that your are alive. Look at yourselves, exploring the earth, the sky, and the sea in search of lucre and calling all this the Great Society. Is it you that will tell us how to live? You must be joking."[53] Thus emerged a counterculture, preached and lived especially by the "hippy" youth. Through them, the search for peace and love, for meaning beyond self-interested profit, for spontaneity, for friendship, for universal fraternity, made itself a collective passion.

At first they tried by means of sexual liberation, alcohol, and drugs. Then they tried the transcendental meditation of Maharishi Mahesh Yogi, prophet of the Beatles. Finally they discovered Jesus. He is seen, admired, loved and followed like a superstar, as one who first lived and then preached that which all seek: peace, love, solidarity, and communion with God. He is worth more than an LSD trip. He is a tremendous high. They hail one another with phrases from the New Testament, use shirts stamped with the image of Christ, recite as ejaculations: "Jesus is salvation," "The Messiah is the message," "We return to Jesus," "He is coming," "He will not delay."

Though we should be critical in evaluating such a movement it ought to make the church and society think.[54] Modern secular, antireligious, and rationalist society thought it had answered the fundamental problems of the human person by means of economic affluence. But its effect was to make everything one-dimensional. It made the problem of the meaning of life, God, and Jesus Christ a mere private concern of the individual. God is useless. He has no value as an economic factor. However, the human person is more than economy, more than a mouth that eats. People seek insatiably another bread that can satisfy them to the roots. They seek to decipher the mystery that envelops our existence, the mystery that calls itself God, that manifested itself in our flesh and calls itself Jesus Christ. He is the radical meaning of existence.

The youth movement ought to lead the church to a christological reflection also. Why did the youth not join the church? Because their Jesus is not the Jesus of its preachings and dogmas but of the gospels? To many of them, Jesus Christ had been made a prisoner of the church, of its ecclesiastical interpretations and its dogmatic casuistry. The mystery and fascination of Jesus had been lost. He had been locked within the frame of reference of an ecclesial structure. We must liberate Jesus from the church so that he can speak once again and create community, community that can justifiably be called the church of Christ. It is symptomatic that the song "Jesus Christ, I am here" was sung by millions. Through this song, a shout of faith and hope, a new parousia of Jesus occurred in the lives of many. This song expressed their desire that Christ's mission be fulfilled: to unite all humanity in a single multitude, in a single race, in a single nationality, in search of one ideal only, an encounter with God (one God only, though adored in different ways by the faithful of all religions) on the road of peace and love.[55]

This return to Jesus may be a sign of the times, as asserted by Paulo Evaristo Arns, Archbishop of São Paulo, a sign of a return to the essential that can truly fill human lives and hearts.[56] "Jesus represents love in the world. He is a kind of light. His message of love permits us to discover others and love them for what they are."[57] In him radical humanity shone forth in anticipation, as an eschatological first moment, a humanity madly sought after by the new generation.

How Can We Know Christ?
The Hermeneutic Problem

To inquire, Who art thou, Jesus of Nazareth? is to make an inquiry concerning a Person. To inquire concerning a person is to touch upon an unfathomable mystery. The more a person is known, the more that person becomes open to further knowledge. We cannot inquire concerning a person without becoming a part of that person's atmosphere. Consequently, in defining Christ we are defining ourselves. The more we know ourselves, the more we can know Jesus. In attempting to delineate our position with regard to Jesus within a Latin American context, we insert all our peculiarities, our life and preoccupations into this task. In so doing, we would wish that he prolong his incarnation within our history and reveal a new face especially known and loved by us.

The issues already raised will surely have stimulated in us the following question: But how then can we know Jesus Christ? For most people the answer presents itself clearly: through the writings of the New Testament, especially the Gospels. We need only interpret them correctly (hermeneutics) to enlighten ourselves concerning Jesus. This reply, though it appears self-evident, contains a very intricate problem. It is called the hermeneutic (interpretation) problem, the central theme of modern philosophy and, as was always the case, of theology and exegesis.[1]

THE HERMENEUTICS OF HISTORICAL CRITICISM

In order to know Jesus we must critically confront the literary documents that speak of him, the Gospels. This task presents internal difficulties because these documents were written approximately two thousand years ago, and within a prescientific, mythical, and uncritical mentality, one quite different from our own. The method of historical criticism tries to sift for the original meaning of the text, insofar as this is possible, and to get beyond later interpretations. The element of strangeness between the meaning of the text and our mode of perceiving constitutes an essential element that must be taken into account for the correct understanding of the message of Jesus. The method of historical criticism obliges us to sound out the message of another age, to critically distance ourselves from the present, and to question ourselves from the standpoint of what is being analyzed and brought to the fore in the text itself. This does not have to be an archeological venture but it is an opportunity to widen our very horizons, question our evidence that appears unquestionable, and create interior space for a possible *metanoia* (conversion).

Historical criticism's research has shown that in their present form the Gospels are the final products of a long process: the reflection, preaching, and catechizing about Jesus elaborated by the community of disciples. We can even say that the present Gospels represent a crystalization of primitive church dogma. By means of the method of historical criticism one can distinguish the various layers of a text or evangelical pericope, the interpretations and influences injected by tradition, and under what theological aspect they were finally written. The Gospels contain little of the historical Jesus (what he was like and how he lived) but a great deal concerning the reaction of faith among the first Christians who reflected on the words of Christ and compared them with the vital situations of their milieu.

Critical exegesis developed various methods for the study of evangelical texts, which we shall now consider.

Form Criticism (Formgeschichte)[2]

Form criticism divests the Gospels of the framework in which they come clothed (the preaching of Jesus in Galilee, the journey to Jerusalem, the trial, death, and resurrection in the holy city) and considers the pericopes (forms) in themselves. It studies the living milieu—preaching to the pagans, cult, catechesis—in which they matured. It tries to see whether we are dealing with a saying of Jesus himself or whether a particular saying has been interpreted or even elaborated by the community (a community that felt itself united to the resurrected Christ and full of his spirit) and then placed in the mouth of Jesus. With this method, the study of the Gospels became extremely conscientious and demanding.

One cannot always decide in a convincing manner whether or not a particular saying did or did not come from Jesus, even though in the present elaboration in the Gospels it is uttered by Christ. Form criticism permeates this entire study. At times we have made decisions of a theological nature based on a critical reflection inspired by this method. At other times, we have interpreted a text as not being the actual words of Jesus (especially those concerning his titles) even though common tradition, having no critical preoccupations, has always interpreted it as coming directly from Jesus.

Tradition Criticism (Traditionsgeschichte)[3]

Tradition criticism prolongs and deepens form criticism. It studies the traditions in the texts and takes note of creative activity, be it in the theology or cult of the primitive community. The Gospels are not simply books concerning Jesus. They are primarily books that reflect the traditions and the dogmatic development of the primitive church. Let us take for example the difficult parable of the fraudulent administrator who pardons the debt of his clients in order to recruit friends (Luke 16: 1–3).[4] In this parable we encounter various layers. First there is the layer coming from the historical Jesus (vv. 1–7). Jesus alludes to a fraud noted in the chronicle of that period. He draws a lesson: Just as the dishonest administrator made use of the time given him before the judge intervened and thereby guaranteed his future, so the people ought to make use of their time and guarantee that they will be among the number of those who will inherit the kingdom, since with Jesus the final hour has come. However, the primitive Christian community added to this another interpretation, taken from daily experience: "For the children of this world are more astute in dealing with their own kind than are the children of light" (Luke 16:8b). It is a distressing discovery: Christians will always be in a disadvantageous position in business matters because they cannot employ the illicit methods used by the children of darkness. The parable, on this level of tradition, reflects the resignation of the Christians.

In another milieu, the parable was traditionally interpreted in a different manner, drawing a lesson concerning the use of money: "And so I tell you this: use money, tainted as it is, to win you friends, and thus make sure that when it fails you, they will welcome you into the tents of eternity" (v. 9). Luke, who picked up the parable, also took on this interpretation, especially since he had a clear theological preoccupation in favor of the poor, natural heirs of the kingdom. If the rich also enter, it is because they have divested themselves of their money and made themselves poor.

Thus to the original eschatological lesson drawn by Christ (the kingdom is near, it is urgent that you be speedy in making friends with your enemies to assure entrance into the kingdom) two other interpretations made by the primitive communities were added, one concerning the resignation of Christians in earthly dealings, and the other concerning the correct use of riches. The present version of the parable, however, places all in the mouth of Christ. Nevertheless these studies, having sifted the various traditions compiled in the present texts, help us see distinctly the theological and interpretative work of the primitive community during the thirty or forty years after the death of Christ, the epoch in which the present Gospels were written.

Redaction Criticism (Redaktionsgeschichte)[5]

Form criticism and tradition criticism tended to see the evangelists as collectors of community sayings and interpretations. Redaction criticism sees the evangelists as editors who used the material that had become traditional within some order of composition; their own theological perspectives dictated the selection of sayings and traditions. The evangelists were theologians with their own personal and typical interpretations. This demonstrates that the present gospels are not biographies of Jesus, but *martyria*, that is, witnesses of faith concerning the significance of the life, death, and resurrection of Jesus. This method draws attention to the fact that the pericopes cannot be interpreted in and of themselves, but always within the context created by the last editor, who in a manner of speaking elaborated the final commentary on them. Comparing the three Synoptic Gospels, the editorial work of each evangelist can be clearly seen: in the corrections in style, in the omission of a word or text that might not fit in with his theological perspective, in the addition of another word or of another tradition, in the frequent reference to the texts of the Old Testament (especially in Matthew), in the dramatization of a scene, or in the accentuation of some particular theme (as for example in Luke, the theme of the poor, of women, of pagans, etc.).

To conclude, we may say that the tradition of the primitive community preserved of Jesus only that which represented some function in the life of faith of the respective community. Therefore, a filtering was imposed by life and evolution after his death and resurrection. It could well be that precious elements of the preaching of Jesus were irremediably lost. Moreover, the primitive community took great liberties when confronted with the words of Jesus: It interpreted them, modified them, and created new pericopes, always in an effort to make Christ and his message present within their life.

John can be regarded as the principal example of such Christian liberty toward the words of Jesus; he nevertheless grasped profoundly the spirit of those words. The expression "kingdom of God," which certainly comes from Jesus himself and formed the core of his announcement, is employed by John only twice, and then in passing. He translates this expression, which at the time of the editing of his gospel (A.D. 90–100) had been emptied of all meaning, by corresponding words that spoke to the mentality of his listeners: e.g., "eternal life," "light," "way," "truth," "bread," "living water," etc. All this makes it clear that Jesus' history and message were radically amalgamated with the history of the faith and of the people, so much so that they can never be adequately separated, though they can and ought to be distinguished. Perhaps this represents the form whereby the incarnation of God perpetuates itself in the world.

EXISTENTIAL HERMENEUTICS

The interpretation of Jesus produced by historical criticism has its limitations. It gets at what Matthew, Mark, Luke, John, and Paul thought about Jesus. It is truly objective. It does not presuppose faith in the researcher. It cares little for the reality that hides behind each interpretation. But historical knowledge concerning a person like Jesus and his message cannot be reduced to a scientific understanding that orientates itself by a subject-object scheme. Scientific knowledge is neutral, objective, and objectifying. Comprehension, however, like the word *com-prendere*, suggests a knowledge that is *com* (with) a subject and that shackles itself to that subject.[6] In order to comprehend a person, there must be some vital relationship with that person. If not, then we objectify the person and make the person an object of science. A person is always a subject and at bottom a mystery; the more one knows a person, the more unlimited horizons are opened.

Jesus announces realities that relate to me directly, such as salvation and damnation; he promises me an absolute future and confers on me a radical meaning. It is because of this that all comprehension always involves a subject. Direct access to reality without passing through a subject is impossible because it is the concrete subject, with specific conditionings, possibilities, and limitations, that goes to the object. Comprehending will always and inevitably mean interpreting. Only one who interprets can comprehend. It is because of this that when we comprehend we always go to the object with a precomprehension derived from our milieu, education, and the cultural ambience that we breathe.

Nevertheless, we ought to distinguish very clearly between precomprehension and preconception. Precomprehension goes to the object, taking into account the conditioning factors. But it leaves itself open to listen in to the message sent from the object. It allows itself to be questioned by the object. It seeks an encounter between itself and the newly absorbed comprehension. A preconception goes to the object with its concept already constructed and ready for use. It judges the object and does not let itself be judged by the object. Quite often, it triggers unconscious defense mechanisms that disturb our encounter with reality and undermine understanding between human beings.

The Hermeneutic Circle and Its Meaning

The inevitable incompatibility of subject-object is, since Schleiermacher, normally called the hermeneutic circle.[7] Applied to the problematic of Jesus this means that to really comprehend who Jesus is, one must approach him as one touched by and attached to him. To feel oneself touched by him means to live the attitude of faith. Defining Jesus we are defining ourselves. The more we know ourselves, the more we can know Jesus. We cannot escape our life, our culture, and situation to touch Jesus as he really was. We go to him with all that we are and have. The Gospels represent an exemplary phenomenon: They seek to announce Christ and carry on his cause. However, the evangelists insert their whole lives into this task, so that when we study the Gospels we find there, not only references to the life of Jesus, but also well detailed references concerning the lives of the first Christians.

Concretely it also means that today Jesus is known not only through the study, replete with faith, of the Gospel texts, but principally through the community of faith called church. It is within the church that an atmosphere of faith was created, that the Gospels were written, and that the common coordinates by which we confront and situate ourselves before Christ were established. It means, moreover, that Jesus entered the unconscious of our western culture. There he is always present and can at any given moment be evoked and revived as an experience of faith. Even if the world were to become wholly atheistic, even then it would always be possible to believe in and attach ourselves to Christ, because he entered the substratum of our culture for all time and profoundly marked it.

Within the framework of this discussion we can understand somewhat the new experience of Christ occurring among today's youth. This experience does not necessarily come mediated by the Christian churches, but rather by the substratum of our very culture, by means of which Christ also prolonged his incarnation. The incarnation of Christ, as we shall see later, is a process that began one day in Nazareth and that has not yet arrived at its final destination because Christ has not yet Christianized all of reality. It is the task of the church and of culture influenced by Christianity not to pollute Christ's channels of access to reality. Historically, however, those who ought to represent Christ and his cause quite often became countersigns of his divine reality and obstacles to living out the gospel in the world.

The Hermeneutics of Political Existence

Awareness of the reality referred to above led to the birth of a hermeneutics of political existence.[8] Ideological mechanisms can enter the church and the culture influenced by Christ, using and abusing the message of Christ and his person so that, consciously and most of the time unconsciously, they legitimate the interests of groups, they close the horizon to continuous growth, they deny themselves the benefits of self-criticism, and they do not allow the gospel to operate as a disturbing ferment among the masses.[9] Christ did not come to bring any cultural model in particular. Nor did he found a Christian culture. Nor did he establish a rigid dogma, nor a morality without heart. But he came to create an atmosphere, a love and reciprocity that ought to be realized in all situations, in all social and political systems and in every articulation of religion or morality.

Throughout the history of the West, the church has frequently been made synonymous with Christ; a theology made by human beings, with the message from Christ; a morality of laws and commandments, with the Sermon on the Mount. Though these elements always come together, as we saw above when discussing the hermeneutical circle, no attempt is being made to legitimate and justify everything. It is necessary that we know how to distinguish them so as not to confuse the voice of the people with the voice of God. Socio-political existence is subject to ideological machinations even within ecclesiastical circles. Hermeneutics cannot be taken to mean simply the art of understanding ancient texts; it also means comprehending all manifestations of life and knowing how to relate them to the evangelical message, especially in matters concerning not only the individual but also the collective universality of people as expressed by such themes as the kingdom of God, of justice, of peace and reconciliation.

THE HERMENEUTICS OF SALVATION HISTORY

The salvation-history hermeneutic method includes all the other dimensions of the hermeneutic problem.[10] Its point of departure is a conception of a history of salvation that is as extensive as the world. This history of salvation is understood as a history of self-communication on the part of God and as a history of the human responses to the divine proposal. Creation itself is the precondition for self-communication on the part of God, and consequently it ought to be initially conceived as a moment of God's own self-communication (grace).

There exists a dialectic between the salvific proposal of God and the human response, between the concrete-

ness of reality and the transcendence of human liberty.[11] The tension between these poles can never be fully
resolved. Consequently, we can never totally grasp the
proposal of God in our historical responses no matter
how sublime they may be. We can never grasp the totality of reality as such, but only by means of historical
models that ought always to be confronted with reality
and enriched, criticized, corrected, and maintained open
to internal growth and built-in obsolescence.

In a model, including a religious model, we never have
more than a specific mediation between God's proposal
and the human response, between nature and liberty,
subjectivity and objectivity, individual and society. The
religions of the world are historical articulations of this
dialectic of proposal-response. The complete synthesis
of both, the global symphony of human beings with their
world and the elimination of all alienation, signifies salvation and full realization of the meaning of the human
person and the world. Since this has not yet occurred,
revelation is always in process; it has to be continuously
translated for new historical and social contexts.

The identity of truth within a diversity of historical
conditions does not reside in a fetishistic maintenance of
verbal forms. As was well seen by structuralism and the
analytical philosophy of linguistics,[12] especially that of
Wittgenstein in his later phase, words possess their own
coordinates and rules within which they have their
meaning; and these coordinates and rules can vary
throughout time. The identity of meaning, however, can
and ought to be preserved when we try to say the same
thing in a different manner and within other coordinates of comprehension. In the light of this, the literal
meaning of texts cannot be absolutized, but merely understood as an exemplary apprehension within a specific model. The text ought to be open to other models
that grasp reality in a different way and thereby enrich
our comprehension of God's revelation in the world.

In Jesus Christ there occurred a qualitative jump

within the history of salvation: For the first time, divine proposal and human response, word and reality, promises and realization, arrived at a perfect accommodation. In him, therefore, salvation was given in an absolute and eschatological form. In him the dynamism and latent possibilities of all creation became concrete and achieved full clarification. In him we catch a glimpse of the future of the world and the radical meaning of the human person and the cosmos. In this way Christ is constituted as the meeting point of religious hermeneutics, of the history of the world and human beings.

TOWARD A CHRISTOLOGY IN LATIN AMERICA

The hermeneutic reflections developed up to this point ought to have made it clear that we cannot simply speak *about* Jesus as we would speak about other objects. We can only speak *with him as starting point,* as people touched by the significance of his reality. We come to him with that which we are and have, inserted into an unavoidable socio-historical context. We see with our eyes the figure of Christ and reread the sacred texts that speak of him and had him as starting point. Consequently, a Christology thought out and vitally tested in Latin America must have characteristics of its own. The attentive reader will perceive them throughout this book. The predominantly foreign literature that we cite ought not to delude anyone. It is with preoccupations that are ours alone, taken from our Latin American context, that we will reread not only the old texts of the New Testament but also the most recent commentaries written in Europe. The facts will be situated within other coordinates and will be projected within an appropriate horizon. Our sky possesses different stars that form different figures of the zodiac by which we orient ourselves in the adventures of faith and of life. Here are a few characteristics of such a Christology.

The Primacy of the Anthropological Element
over the Ecclesiastical

The special focus in Latin America is not so much the church but the human person that it should help, raise up, and humanize. In Latin American theological thought, there reigns an accentuated ecclesiological skepticism: Here the church reproduced models and structures imported from Europe. Very little creativity was allowed the faith that, lived and tested in our milieu, could have expressed itself naturally and with greater liberty within structures having peculiarly Latin American characteristics. The general horizon was one that dogmatically interpreted canon law and juridically interpreted dogma. This basically impeded healthy attempts to create a new incarnation of the church outside of the inherited traditional framework of a Greco-Roman understanding of the world.

The future of the Catholic church, given the diminution of the European population, is undeniably in Latin America. It is in the more anthropological vision, in the new human being being elaborated here, that we can gather elements to nourish a new, renewed Christian reflection. What are the great expectations among the people to which the faith can address itself, announcing the joyful news? We must be aware of the connection between question and answer if we want to offer a reflection that will heal reality where it hurts.

The Primacy of the Utopian Element
over the Factual

The determining element in the Latin American person is not the past (our past is a European past, one of colonization) but the future. Herein lies the activating function of the utopian element. Utopia ought not to be understood as a synonym for illusion and flight from present reality. As recent studies in philosophy and theology have revealed, utopia is born in the springs of hope. It is responsible for models that seek a perfecting of our reality, models that do not allow the social process to stagnate nor society ideologically to absolutize itself, models that maintain society permanently open to ever increasing transformation.[13] Faith promises and demonstrates as realized in Christ a utopia that consists in a world totally reconciled, a world that is the fulfilment of what we are creating here on earth with feeling and love. Our work in the construction of a more fraternal and humanized world is theologically relevant: It builds and slowly anticipates the definitive world promised and demonstrated as possible by Jesus Christ.

The Primacy of the Critical Element over the Dogmatic

The general tendency of people, and in particular of institutions, is to stagnate in an existential arrangement that was successful during a specific period. Then there emerge the mechanisms of self-defense and the dogmatic mentality that fears and represses every kind of criticism that looks to the proper functioning of all institutions and to that continuous opening to the future that a society ought always protect at the risk of losing the rhythm of history. This explains the primacy of the critical element in Latin American theological reflection. Many ecclesiastical traditions and ecclesial institutions were functional at one time but today have become obsolete. They are centers of a conservatism that locks the door to a dialogue between faith and the world, the church and society. Criticism refines and purifies the core of the Christian experience so that it can be made incarnate within the historical experience we are living.

The Primacy of the Social over the Personal

Latin American society is most afflicted by the problem of the marginalization of immense portions of the population. The question cannot be posed merely within the dimensions of a personal conversion. There are structural evils that transcend individual ones. The church is, whether it likes it or not, involved in a context that transcends it. What will be its function? Shall it be oil or sand within the social mechanism? On the other hand, it ought not to create its own little world within the great world. It ought to participate, *critically*, in the global upsurge of liberation that Latin American society is undergoing. Like Jesus, it ought to give special attention to the nobodies and those without a voice. It ought to accentuate particularly the secular and liberating dimensions contained in the message of Christ. It should emphasize the future that he promises for this world, a world in which the future kingdom is growing between the wheat and the cockle, not for a few privileged people, but for all.

The Primacy of Orthopraxis over Orthodoxy

The weakness in the classical Christology of the manuals resides precisely in that wherein it considers itself to be strong: its theological-philosophical systematization. It did not lead to an ethic and a comportment that was typically Christian. The fundamental theme of the Synoptic Gospels, on following Christ, has been poorly thematized and translated into concrete attitudes. Orthodoxy, that is, correct thinking about Christ, occupied primacy over orthopraxis, correct acting in the light of Christ.

It was also for this reason that, although the church preached Christ the liberator, it generally was not the church that liberated or supported liberation movements. Not rarely the church has left active, participating Christians as complete orphans. This has resulted in recent years in the continuous exodus from the church of the best minds and most active forces. We know nevertheless that for Christ and for the primitive church the essential did not consist in the reduction of the message of Christ to systematic categories of intellectual comprehension but in creating new habits of acting and living in the world. This praxiological moment of the message of Christ is especially perceptible in Latin American theological reflection.

CONCLUSION: BEGINNING WITH JESUS CHRIST, TO SPEAK IN SILENCE

In our christological study we will try to reflect with Jesus Christ as the starting point and within the wide horizon opened up in the above pages. We can no longer be scientifically ingenuous and acritical. Whether we wish it or not, we are inheritors of the christological discussions of the last decades, though the questions will be framed within our Latin American horizons. What we say here with words about Christ and his message is nothing compared with that which faith discerns and gratefully embraces. "Be quiet, recollect yourself, because it is the Absolute," said Kirkegaard, and Bonhoeffer repeated it as he began his treatise on Jesus Christ.[14]

"Concerning things that we cannot speak of," commanded Wittgenstein, "we ought to be silent."[15] Nevertheless, we ought to speak of Jesus Christ, not with a view to defining him but rather ourselves, not the mystery but our position when confronted with the mystery. Every scholar of Jesus Christ has the experience witnessed by the ardent mystic St. John of the Cross: "There is much concerning Christ that can be made more profound, since he is such an abundant mine with many caverns full of rich veins, and no matter how much we tunnel we never arrive at the end, nor does it ever run out; on the contrary, we go on finding in each cavern new veins and new riches, here and there, as St. Paul witnessed when he said of the same Christ: 'In Christ all the jewels of wisdom and knowledge are hidden' "(Col. 2:3).[16]

3

What Did Jesus Christ
Really Want?

Initially, Jesus preached neither himself nor the church, but the kingdom of God. The kingdom of God is the realization of a fundamental utopia of the human heart, the total transfiguration of this world, free from all that alienates human beings, free from pain, sin, divisions, and death. He came and announced: "The time has come, the kingdom of God is close at hand!" He not only promised this new reality but already began to realize it, showing that it is possible in the world. He therefore did not come to alienate human beings and carry them off to another world. He came to confirm the good news: This sinister world has a final destiny that is good, human, and divine.

In the midst of the general confusion of today's ideas, in the dialogue between the various Christian confessions, and in the encounter with other religions, we are brought to ask with all simplicity the following question: What does Christianity really want? What did Jesus Christ really want to bring, and what did he actually bring to us? What are we doing when we profess the Christian faith and try to live out the message of Jesus, imitating and following his life? We must know what it is we want in order to justify to ourselves and to legitimate to others the reasons for our hope (cf. 1 Peter 3:15). If we wish to define the widest possible horizon that is to be our starting point from which Jesus Christ and his message can be understood, then we can briefly say this: Jesus Christ wants to be in his own person God's answer to the human condition.

TO COMPREHEND THE ANSWERS
WE MUST UNDERSTAND THE QUESTIONS

If Jesus Christ wants to be God's answer to the human condition, then we should know for what questions of the human condition he wants to be an answer.[1] Which questions are those? Here are some fundamental ones that have stigmatized all our known existence past and present: Why do people not succeed in being happy? Why can they not love? Why are human beings divided among themselves, tormented by ultimate questions? All the animals have their habitat in the world, and human beings are still looking for their true place. Why is there separation, pain, and death? Why has there been no success in establishing fraternal relations among people, instead of which we find legalism and slavery? Why do people make war in order to achieve peace? Why do people arm themselves and prepare for war in order to avoid war? Of the 3,400 years of human history, 3,166 were years of war. The remaining 234 years were not years of peace but years of preparation for war. Alienation pervades all human, individual, social, and cosmic reality. Who will bring peace? Salvation? Reconciliation of all with all?

In humankind there is a principle of hope[2] that generates great happiness and utopian visions. This is attested to by all cultures and civilizations, even the most primitive, ranging from the Epic of Gilgamesh among Babylonian peoples or our own Tupi-Guarani Indians down to the modern utopias of a wonderful new world or of a world completely tamed and full of love. This same principle is also attested to in the book of Revelation, where it says: "He will wipe away all tears from their eyes; there will be no more death, and no more mourning or sadness. The world of the past has gone. . . . Now I am making the whole of creation new" (Rev. 21:4–5). All religions and ideologies know of these questions and each in its own way gives an answer. But the human person, still desolate, continues to say with Paul: "What a wretched man I am! Who will rescue me from this body doomed to death?" (Rom. 7:24).

In the meantime, a man appeared in Nazareth. A man rose up in Galilee, later revealed himself as God in human condition, and announced God's answer to all this: "The time has come and the kingdom of God is close at hand. Repent and believe the Good News" (Luke 4:18ff.).

JESUS PREACHES AN ABSOLUTE MEANING
FOR OUR WORLD

Christ did not begin by preaching himself. Nor did he announce himself as Son of God, Messiah, and God. The titles of Jesus that the Gospels attribute to him are in most cases expressions of faith on the part of the primitive community.[3] The resurrection of Jesus constituted a great turning point for that community: Only now did they profoundly understand who Jesus was and what he signified for the whole history of salvation. In the atmosphere of this understanding they went about deciphering the ultimate secret of the preacher and wonder-worker of Nazareth (cf. Acts 2:22–23) attributing to him titles of superiority ranging from the Holy One, the Just One (Acts 3:14), and the Servant of God (Acts 4:27) to Son of God, Messiah, and finally God himself. What was implicit and latent in the words, signs, and attitudes of the historical Jesus became patent and explicit after the resurrection. The titles that faith attributed to him express precisely who Jesus was, from his birth to his cross: the one awaited by all nations, the savior of the world, the Son of God, God himself made human.

Christ did not begin by preaching himself but the kingdom of God.[4] What does "the kingdom of God," which indisputably constitutes the center of his message, signify? To Jesus' own listeners it signified something quite different than it does to the ears of a modern disciple. "Kingdom of God," which occurs 122 times in the Gospels and 90 times on the lips of Jesus, signified for Jesus' listeners the realization of hope at the end of the world, when all human alienation and all evil, be it physical or moral, would be overcome, when the consequence of sin—hate, divisions, pain, and death—would be destroyed. The kingdom of God would mean the manifestation of the sovereignty and lordship of God over this world dominated by satanic forces in a struggle with the forces of good. The term signified that God is the ultimate meaning of this world; God will intervene shortly and restore the foundations of all creation, establishing a new heaven and a new earth.

This utopia, the longing of all peoples, is the object of the preaching of Jesus. He promises that it will no longer be utopia but a reality introduced by God. Thus, preaching for the first time in a synagogue of Galilee he read from Isaiah 61:1ff.: "The spirit of the Lord has been given to me, for he has anointed me. He has sent me to bring the Good News to the poor, to proclaim liberty to captives and to the blind new sight, to set the downtrodden free, to proclaim the Lord's year of favor." And he adds, "This text is being fulfilled today even as you listen" (Luke 4:18–19, 21). To the question of the imprisoned John the Baptist: "Are you the one who is to come or have we got to wait for someone else?" Jesus responds, "The blind see again, and the lame walk, lepers are cleansed, and the deaf hear, and the dead are raised to life and the Good News is proclaimed to the poor" (Matt. 11:3,5).

Here is a sign of a total about-face: Whosoever succeeds in introducing such realities, he will be the liberator of humanity. Christ understands himself as Liberator because he preaches, presides over, and is already inaugurating the kingdom of God. The kingdom of God is a total, global and structural transfiguration and revolution of the reality of human beings; it is the cosmos purified of all evils and full of the reality of God. The kingdom of God is not to be in another world but is the old world transformed into a new one. If Matthew speaks of the kingdom of heaven instead of the kingdom of God, it is because as a good Jewish Christian he seeks to avoid the name of God and in its place uses "heaven." The kingdom of God does not simply signify the annihilation of sin but the annihilation of all that sin means for human beings, society, and the cosmos. In the kingdom of God, pain, blindness, hunger, tempests, sin, and death will not have their turn.

Luke spoke well when he announced that in Jesus came "the Lord's year of favor" (4:19). Behind this expression there hides one of the great utopias of the Old Testament.[5] Exodus refers to the fact that every seven years a sabbatical ought to be celebrated (Exod. 23: 10–12; 21:2–6). In that year, all ought to feel as children of God and because of this should consider one another as brothers and sisters. Slaves should be liberated. Debts should be pardoned and land distributed equally. No employer ought to forget that in God's eyes each person is free (Deut. 15:12–15). Leviticus (28:8–16) reveals this social idea prescribing that every fifty years a jubilee year be celebrated. It will be the Lord's year of favor. All will be free. All will return to their land, which will be given back to them and their families. However, this social idea was never fulfilled. Egoism and concrete interests were always stronger. For this reason it gradually became a promise to be realized in messianic times (cf. Isa. 61:1f). God himself will install the sabbatical year of favor, social reconciliation, and forgiveness of debts. Jesus rises up in Galilee and proclaims that he will bring the Lord's year of favor! He will realize the old utopia of the people! Egoism will be overcome by a new order of things in this world.

AN OLD UTOPIA IS BEING REALIZED

The miracles of Christ, more than revealing his divinity, seek to demonstrate that the kingdom is already present and fermenting within the old world. A utopia as old as the human race is being achieved: total liberation. "But if it is through the finger of God that I cast out devils, then know that the kingdom of God has overtaken you" (Luke 11:20). "But no one can make his way into a strong man's house and burgle his property unless he has tied up the strong man first. Only then can he burgle his house" (Mark 3:27). He is the stronger one that conquers the strong. He is eschatology realized. With his coming the nuptials of the time of salvation are being celebrated. He is the new wine and the new mantle (cf. Mark 2:18–22) of a new cosmos.[6]

His presence transforms the world and all people; ailments are cured (Matt. 8:16–17), struggle is transformed into joy (Luke 7:11–17; Mark 5:41–43), the elements obey him (Matt. 8:27), death has been transformed into mere sleep (Mark 5:39), sins are forgiven (Mark 2:5), and impure demons give way to the spirit of God (Matt. 12:28). It is a time of joy and not of fasting. Therefore he cries out: "How happy are you who are poor: yours is the kingdom of God. Happy you who are hungry now: you shall be satisfied. Happy you who weep now: you shall laugh" (Luke 6:20–21). With Christ is announced "the Lord's year of favor" (Luke 14:19) that will never again know sunset.

THE KINGDOM OF GOD IS NOT A TERRITORY
BUT A NEW ORDER

The kingdom of God that Christ announces is not a liberation from this or that evil, from the political oppression of the Romans, from the economic difficulties of the people, or from sin alone. The kingdom of God cannot be narrowed down to any particular aspect. It embraces all: the world, the human person, and society; the totality of reality is to be transformed by God. Hence the phrase of Jesus: "The kingdom of God is among you" (Luke 17:21). This difficult expression "the kingdom of God is among you" signifies, according to most recent exegesis: "The new order introduced by God is at your disposition. Do not ask when it may be established in the future. Don't run here and there as if the kingdom of God were attached to some place. But opt for him, enlist in his ranks. God wants to be your Lord. Open yourselves to his will. God awaits you especially at this time. Prepare yourselves and accept this final offer of God."[7]

The kingdom of God, as is evident, implies a dynamism; it notifies us of an event and expresses the intervention of God already initiated but not yet fully completed. Because of this, Christ, as he preached and made present the kingdom, taught us to pray: "Your kingdom come" (Luke 11:2; Matt. 6:10). The preaching of the kingdom is realized in two moments of time, the present and the future. The present we have seen above. Its future remains to be seen: The time of the sinful will have passed (Matt. 19:28; Luke 17:26–30), sufferings will disappear (Matt. 11:5), there will be no more mourning (Mark 2:19), death will be no more (Luke 20:36), and the dead will rise up (Luke 11:5). The foundations of the old order will crumble: "Many who are first will be last, and the last first" (Mark 10:31), the one who makes himself little shall be great (Matt. 18:4), the humble shall be masters (Matt. 5:5), and the oppressed shall be freed

(Luke 4:18). The situation of the human person before God will be totally transformed because sins will be forgiven (Matt. 6:14) and glory will be returned to human beings (the heavenly clothing of the angels) (Mark 12:25), the dispersed elect will be reunited (Luke 13:27), and the sons of God will meet in the father's house (Luke 15:19), where all hunger and thirst will be satiated and the joyful laughter of the time of liberty will overflow (Luke 6:21).

THE KINGDOM OF GOD IS NOT MERELY SPIRITUAL

One fact is clearly deducible from the above discussion: The kingdom of God, contrary to what many Christians think, does not signify something that is purely spiritual or outside this world. It is the totality of this material world, spiritual and human, that is now introduced into God's order. If this were not so, how could Christ have enthused the masses? Some of the ancient texts still conserve this original tone: "I tell you solemnly, I shall not drink any more wine until the day I drink the new wine in the kingdom of God" (Mark 14:25). At other times he promises to whoever abandons all for love of the kingdom a hundredfold in houses and lands (Mark 10:30). To the disciples he says: "And now I confer a kingdom on you; . . . you will eat and drink at my table in my kingdom and you will sit on thrones to judge the twelve tribes of Israel (Luke 22:29–30; cf. Matt. 19:28). The breakthrough of this new order is imminent: "I tell you solemnly, before this generation has passed away all these things will have taken place" (Mark 13:30). On one occasion he makes it still more concrete and affirms: "I tell you solemnly, there are some standing here who will not taste death before they see the kingdom of God come with power" (Mark 9:1). He assures the disciples: "I tell you solemnly, you will not have gone the round of the towns of Israel before the Son of man comes" (Matt. 10:23).

Christ is aware of the fact that the end of the old world has begun with him. He himself already belongs to the kingdom. Adhesion to the person and message of Jesus is a condition of participation in the new order. Such preaching is characteristic of the apocalyptic atmosphere (the expectation of the end of the world), typical in the time of the New Testament. Jesus as a man of his times also breathes this atmosphere, but he distinguishes himself profoundly from it. In spite of this, the following question is valid: Why did Christ adopt the idea of the kingdom of God, of messianism, and of the end of the world as the vehicles of his message? Why does he refer to the imminent breakthrough of the kingdom? Why does he speak of the Son of Man who will come upon the clouds in glory, of a final judgment and of all the symbolism of messianic hope? To answer these questions, we must consider briefly the religious meaning of apocalyptic language.[8]

A FEELING OF EXPECTATION
HAS GROWN AMONG THE PEOPLE

Flavius Josephus in his *Antiquities* tells us that the principal preoccupation of the Jews between the years 100 B.C. and A.D. 100 was "to be liberated from all kinds of domination by others, so that God alone might be served" (*Ant.* 17,11,2). Since the exile (587 B.C.) the Jews had lived practically without liberty. From the successors of Alexander the Great, they passed under the yoke of the Romans. The possibilities for liberation had been exhausted. Only an intervention of God could restore independence. Therefore in the abundant apocalyptic literature, especially at the time of the Maccabees, beginning with the book of Daniel, the goal was to inspire confidence in the people and open up the possibility of a way out. This was done through descriptions of a future kingdom, the restoration of Davidic sovereignty, and the enthronement of the absolute lordship of God.

The theme of the kingdom of God is central in the post-exilic biblical literature and the time between the two Testaments. "Kingdom of God" undoubtedly possessed a political connotation for the Jews for whom politics was a part of religion and "kingdom of God" concretely designated liberation from all oppressing forces. God's lordship over all had also to be demonstrated politically. The Messiah is he who will install the kingdom of God.

All the people prepared for his coming. The Pharisees thought they could speed up the coming of the transformation of this world by the minute observance of all the laws. The Essenes and monks of the Qumran community retired to the desert so that in absolute purification, legal observance, and an ideal life, they could await and accelerate the breakthrough of the new order. The Zealots (the fervent ones) were of the opinion that they ought to provoke the salvific intervention of God by means of guerrilla tactics and violence. Their motto was: "Only Yahweh is King and Him only will we serve."[9] They thus contested the Caesars, the census, the taxes, and especially the head tax, which at that time was the equivalent of recognizing the emperor as lord and god. The coming of the Messiah would transform all and would also realize the end of this world by beginning the eternal reign of God. The apocalyptic writers studied and tried especially to decipher the signs of messianic times; they made calculations of the weeks and years in an attempt to determine, in terms of space and time, the occasion of salvific events.

In spite of the catastrophic elements, the Jewish apocalyptic vision reveals an eternal optimism, which is the essence of all true religion. There will be an end to the ambiguous and sorrowful condition of this sinful world. Some day God will have pity on us and free us of all alienating elements. The kingdom of God is a symbolic expression of this truth. To preach and announce the kingdom of God, as the apocalyptic writers as well as

Jesus did, is to witness to the ultimate meaning of the world and its radical perfectability to be realized by God and only by God. Messianism and the apocalyptic categories of expression were, in this sense, the means used by Jesus to communicate adequately a liberating message and reveal who he was: the Son of God, God incarnate and Savior of the world. Only through this language could Jesus make himself understood by his listeners, "a feeling of expectation has grown among the people" (Luke 3:15).[10] He participated in the fundamental longings in the human heart for liberation and a new creation. This hope, expressed in the bizarre apocalyptical language, was the carrier of God's greatest revelation in the world.

In spite of these common elements, Christ's preaching differs from the messianic expectations of the people. Christ never fed the nationalism of the Jews; he never said a word about rebellion against the Romans, nor did he ever allude to the restoration of the Davidic king, though the people acclaimed him as such on the occasion of his entry into Jerusalem (Mark 11:10) and the inscription at the head of the cross read: "King of the Jews" (Luke 15:26). The disciples themselves did not hide their nationalistic tendencies: "Our own hope had been that he would be the one to set Israel free" (Luke 24:21; cf. 19:11), said the resigned youths of Emmaus. And the apostles in their final goodbye to Jesus asked: "Lord, has the time come? Are you going to restore the kingdom to Israel?" (Acts 1:6).

Christ disappointed everyone on this point. The preaching of Christ concerning the kingdom also differed markedly from the astounding speculations of the apocalyptic writers concerning the end of the world and the signs to be found in nature and among peoples. He renounced the showy descriptions of the final judgment and the resurrection of the dead. In answer to the question that most preoccupied the people, "Lord, how much longer?" (cf. Ps. 80:5; 74,10; cf. Dan. 9:4–19), Christ replies: "You too must stand ready because the Son of Man is coming at an hour you do not expect" (Matt. 24:44). What is most emphasized in Jesus is the authority with which the kingdom is announced and is made already present by signs and unspoken gestures.

Nevertheless, political messianism, as the temptations of Jesus narrated in the Synoptics show (Mark 1:12ff.; Matt. 4:1–11; Luke 4:1–13), constitutes for Christ a real temptation. For a long time exegetes have been interpreting the temptations as "a spiritual experience of Jesus, put in symbolic form (*mashal*) for the instruction of the apostles."[11] Christ overcame temptations to political messianism, which at the time manifested itself in three currents: prophetical, in the appearance of the Messiah in the desert; sacerdotal, in the manifestation of the Liberator in the temple; and political, in the revelation of the Messiah on the mountain of God. The three temptations narrated by the Synoptics try to show how Jesus overcame the three types of messianism, of the desert, of the pinnacle of the temple, and of the mountaintop.

He is indeed the Messiah-Christ, but not one of a political nature. His kingdom cannot be particularized and reduced to a part of reality, such as politics. He came to heal all reality in all its dimensions, cosmic, human, social. The great drama of the life of Christ was to try to take the ideological content out of the word "kingdom of God" and make the people and his disciples comprehend that he signified something much more profound, namely, that he demands a conversion of persons and a radical transformation of the human world; that he demands a love of friends and enemies alike and the overcoming of all elements inimical to God and humankind. To those who are scandalized by the paradox of his pretentions and his simple origins in a humble family he gives this assurance: "Rejoice when that day comes and dance for joy, for then your reward will be great in heaven" (Luke 7:23; Matt. 11:6). The kingdom of God is presented as fragile and without grandeur. But it is like a seed thrown upon the land (Mark 4:26ff.), like a mustard seed, the smallest of all the seeds of Palestine (Matt. 13:31ff.) or as the yeast mixed in flour (Matt. 13:33ff.).

The apparent littleness hides and promises a glorious future: A little yeast leavens all the flour; the seed grows and gives wheat in abundance; the mustard seed "once it is sown . . . grows into the biggest shrub of them all and puts out big branches so that the birds of the air can shelter in its shade" (Mark 4:32). From the beginning, the end is already present. With Christ the kingdom has already begun to act in the world. The old order is already moving in the direction of its end. A sun has arisen that knows no setting; the time of liberation has already made its breakthrough. In the next chapter we will analyze the preaching of Jesus concerning the kingdom, which signifies a revolution in our way of thinking and acting and the total transformation of the world.

CONCLUSION: HE TOOK ON OUR DEEPEST LONGINGS

Of all the above we ought to hold on to one thing very securely: The incarnation of Jesus does not simply mean that God made himself man. It means much more. He really participated in our human condition and took on our deepest longings. He used our language, heavily laden with ideological content—as was the idea of the kingdom of God. But he tried to give our language a new meaning of total liberation and absolute hope. He demonstrated this new content with typical signs and actions. The kingdom of God that he preached is no longer an unattainable human utopia, "for nothing is impossible to God" (Luke 1:37); it is a reality already initiated in our world. With Jesus began a "great joy for all" (Luke 2:10) because we already know here and now that all that the apocalypse promises us will be true. The new order introduced by him means the breakthrough of the new heaven and the new earth (Rev. 21:14). With him we can already hear with certainty, though as an echo from afar, those "faithful and true" words: "Now I am making the whole of creation new.... It is already done" (Rev. 21:5).

4

Jesus Christ, Liberator of the Human Condition

In the Jewish religion at the time of Jesus, everything was prescribed and determined, first relations with God and then relations among human beings. Conscience felt itself oppressed by insupportable legal prescriptions. Jesus raises an impressive protest against all such human enslavement in the name of law. In this chapter we shall show the fundamental attitude of Jesus: liberty, yes, before the law; but this liberty is for good, not for libertinism. The law possesses merely a human function: one of order, one of creating the possibilities for harmony and understanding among human beings. Because of this, the norms of the Sermon on the Mount presuppose love, a new person free for greater things.

The theme of Christ's preaching was neither himself nor the church but the kingdom of God. "Kingdom of God" signifies the realization of a utopia cherished in human hearts, total human and cosmic liberation. It is the new situation of an old world, now replete with God and reconciled with itself. In a word, it could be said that the kingdom of God means a total, global, structural revolution of the old order, brought about by God and only by God. Consequently, the kingdom is a kingdom *of God* in a subjective and objective sense. Christ understood himself·not only as a preacher and prophet of this good news (gospel) but as an element of the new transformed situation. He is the new human person, the kingdom already present though veiled in weakness.

Adherence to Christ is an indispensable condition of participation in the new order to be introduced by God (Luke 12:8–9). In order that such a liberation from sin, from its personal and cosmic consequences, and from all other alienation suffered in creation, be realized, Christ makes two fundamental demands: He demands personal conversion and postulates a restructuring of the human world.

THE KINGDOM OF GOD IMPLIES A REVOLUTION IN OUR THINKING AND ACTING

In the first place the kingdom of God concerns persons. It demands their conversion.[1] Conversion means changing one's mode of thinking and acting to suit God, and therefore undergoing an interior revolution. Because of this Jesus begins by preaching: "Be converted, for the kingdom of heaven is close at hand" (Matt. 3:2;4:17). Being converted does not consist in pious exercises, but rather in a new mode of existing before God and in the light of the tidings announced by Jesus. Conversion always implies a rupture: "Do you suppose that I am here to bring peace on earth? No, I tell you, but rather division. For from now on a household of five will be divided: three against two and two against three . . . " (Luke 12:51,52). Nevertheless this reversal in one's mode of thinking and acting is to be life-giving, it is to lead a person to a crisis and to deciding for the new order that is already in our midst, that is Jesus Christ himself (Luke 17:21).

Jesus is not so much interested in whether a person before all else observed all the laws, paid tithes on all things, observed all the legal prescriptions of religion and society. He is primarily interested in whether a person is disposed to sell all properties to acquire the field with hidden treasure; whether one is ready to sell all to buy the precious pearl (Matt. 13:4–46); whether, in order to enter the new order, one has the courage to abandon family and fortune (Matt. 10:37), risk one's life (Luke 17:33), tear out an eye and cut off a hand (Mark 9:43 and Matt. 5:29). This *no* to the established order does not signify asceticism but an attitude of readiness to comply with the exigencies of Jesus.

Now, therefore, it is urgent that one open oneself to God. This demand goes so far that Jesus threatens us with the following harsh words: "If you do not change your way of thinking and acting, you will all perish" (Luke 13:3,5). The flood is imminent and it is the final hour (Matt. 24:37–39; 7:24–27). The ax has been put to the root of the tree; if it will not bear fruit, it will be cut down (Luke 13:9). The owner of the house will close the door and those that are late will hear these sad words: "I do not know where you come from" (Luke 13:25b); it is already too late (Matt. 25:11). For this reason, those are called prudent who understood this situation of radical crisis (Matt. 7:24; 24:45; 25:2,4,8,9; Luke 12:42) and opted in favor of a kingdom, making a choice capable of supporting and conquering all temptations (cf. Matt. 7:24–25). The invitation is given to all. Most, however, find themselves to be so busy with their affairs that they reject the invitation to the nuptial feast (Luke 14:16–24). Chiefly the rich are so installed (Mark 10:25; cf. Matt. 23:24). The gate is narrow and not all make sufficient effort or work hard in order to pass through it (cf. Luke 13:24). The necessity for conversion at times demands a rupture from the most rudimentary ties of love for dead relatives that are about to be interred (Luke 9:59f.;

Matt. 8:21f.).[2] A person who has opted for the tidings of Jesus looks only ahead. The past is past (cf. Luke 9:62).

There is a certain quality of intimidation in Jesus' invitation. An "agraphon" transmitted by the apocryphal St. Thomas and regarded by good exegetes as authentically of Jesus states preemptively: "Whoever is near me, is near the fire; whoever is far from me is far from the kingdom."[3] The option for Jesus cannot remain at some half-way point like the constructor of a tower who laid the foundation but ceased work when it was half finished, or like a king who leaves for war with triumphal airs but when confronted with the force of the enemy has to retreat and make peace (Luke 14:28–32). It is urgent that one reflect before accepting the invitation. To say, "Lord, Lord," is easy, but one must also wish to do what the Lord says (Luke 6:46). Otherwise, one's last state is worse than the first (Matt. 12:43–45b; Luke 11:24–26). Conversion itself is like a nuptial gown, like an oiled head and a washed face (cf. Matt. 6:17), like music and dance (Luke 15:25), like the joy of the son who returns to the father's house (Luke 15:32; 15:7), like the satisfaction one has on finding lost money (Luke 15:8–10).

And all this begins to emerge from the moment one becomes as a child (Matt. 18:3). The phrase "unless you change and become like little children you will never enter the kingdom of heaven" (Matt. 18:3; cf. Mark 10:15; Luke 18:17) does not seek to exalt the natural innocence of children. Christ is not a sentimental romantic. The point of comparison is elsewhere: Just as a child depends completely on the help of its parents and can do nothing on its own, so it is with the human person in the face of the demands of the kingdom.[4] John allows Jesus to say clearly: "Unless a man is born from above, he cannot see the kingdom of God" (John 3:3). A new mode of thinking and acting is demanded. This becomes even clearer if one considers the attitude of Jesus before the law.

Jesus Christ, the Liberator of Oppressed Conscienciousness

In the Jewish religion at the time of Christ everything was sanctioned as the will of God expressed in the sacred books of the law. The law became so absolutized that for some theological circles God busied himself in its study for hours every day in heaven. Consciences were oppressed by the insupportable regimentation of legal prescriptions (cf. Matt 23:4). Jesus protests this enslavement of the human person in the name of the law.[5] "The sabbath was made for man, not man for the sabbath" (Mark 2:27). It had been clearly stated, "You must add nothing to what I command you, and take nothing from it, but keep the commandments that Yahweh the God of your fathers is giving you" (Deut. 4:42). Nonetheless Jesus takes the liberty of modifying various prescriptions of the Mosaic law: the death penalty for adulterers caught in the act (John 8:11), polygamy (Mark 10:9), the law on the observance of the sabbath (Mark 2:27) regarded as a symbol of the chosen people (Ezek. 20:12), the prescriptions concerning legal purity (Mark 7:15), and others.

Jesus comports himself as one higher than the laws. If the laws help the human person, increase love, or make love possible, he accepts them. If, on the contrary, they legitimate enslavement, he repudiates them and demands that they be broken.[6] It is not the law that saves, but love: In this we have a summary of the ethical preaching of Jesus. He de-theologizes the conception of law: The will of God is not to be found only in the legal prescriptions and sacred books; it manifests itself principally in the signs of the times (cf. Luke 12:54–57). The love he preaches must be unconditional, both for friends and enemies (Matt. 5:44).

Nevertheless if Christ liberates the human person from the laws, he does not hand people over to libertinism or irresponsibility. Rather he creates even stronger bonds and ties than those of the law. Love must bind all people among themselves. The following story, which clearly reveals the attitude of Jesus before the law, is told in place of Luke 6:5 in Codex D: On the sabbath Jesus meets a man working in a field and says: "Man, if you know what it is you are doing, you are blessed. If however you do not know, you are damned and a transgressor of the law." What does Jesus want to say? Does Jesus want to definitively abolish holy days and the sabbath? Jesus' liberty and nonconformity are apparent ("You have learnt how it was said to our ancestors. . . . But I say to you": Matt. 5:21ff.). Jesus' point is this: "Man if you know why it is you work on a sabbath day as I who cured the man with the withered hand on a forbidden day (Mark 3:1), and the woman that was bent double (Luke 13:10) and the man with dropsy (Luke 14:1), if you know how to work on a sabbath day to help someone, and if you know that for the children of God the law of love is above all laws—then you are blessed. If however, you do not know and because of frivolity, caprice, or to indulge your pleasure you profane the sabbath, you are damned and a transgressor of the law."[7]

Here we see the fundamental attitude of Jesus: freedom, before the law, but only for good and not for libertinism. Christ is not *against* anything. He is in favor of love, spontaneity, and liberty. It is in the name of this positiveness that at times he has to be against something. Paraphrasing Rom. 14:23, we can reasonably say: All that does not come from love is sin. On another occasion we witnessed the same preoccupation in Jesus to free people from conventions and social prejudices. In the time and country of Jesus, a man had the privilege of possessing various women and power to get rid of them. The law of Moses said: "Supposing a man has taken a wife and consummated the marriage; but she has not pleased him and he has found some impropriety of which to accuse her; so he has made out a writ of divorce for her and handed it to her and then dismissed her from his house" (Deut. 24:1). In the jurisprudence of the epoch the following reasons for a woman not pleasing a man were regarded as valid: not being pretty, not knowing how to cook well, not having children, etc. Against this, Jesus rises up and definitively states: "What God has united, man must not divide" (Mark 10:9). These words reveal Jesus' noble opposition to legalized anarchy.

In the kingdom of God there ought to reign liberty and fraternal equality, which Jesus won. Paul, who at an early date had profoundly understood this tiding of Jesus, writes to the Galatians: "When Christ freed us, he meant us to remain free. Stand firm therefore, and do not submit again to the yoke of slavery, . . . but be careful or this liberty will provide an opening for self-indulgence. Serve one another, rather, in works of love. Since the whole of the law is summarized in a single command: Love your neighbor as yourself" (Gal. 5:1,13–14).

The Comportment of the New Person

The conversion sought by Jesus and the liberation he won for us are related to a love that knows no discrimination. To make love one's norm of life and moral conduct is to impose something very difficult on oneself. It is easier to live within laws and prescriptions that foresee and determine everything. It is difficult to create a norm inspired by love for each moment. Love knows no limits. It calls for creative imagination. It exists only in giving oneself to, and putting oneself at the service of, others. And it is only in giving that one has. This is the "law" of Christ: that we love one another as God has loved us. This is the only comportment for the new person, free and liberated by Christ, invited to participate in the new order. This love expresses itself in radical formulas, as for example in the Sermon on the Mount: Not only one who murders but also one who is angry with a brother or sister will answer for it before the judgment (Matt. 5:22); if a man looks at a woman lustfully, he has already committed adultery with her in his heart (Matt. 5:28); do not swear at all; say yes if you mean yes and no if you mean no (Matt. 5:34,37); offer the wicked person no resistance; if anyone hits you on the right cheek, offer the other as well; if a man takes you to law and would have your tunic, let him have your cloak as well (Matt. 5:39–40).

Is it possible to organize life and society with these norms? Julian the Apostate already saw here an argument for rejecting Christianity *in toto:* it is simply impracticable for the individual, family, and society. Some think that these demands of the Sermon on the Mount wish to show how it is impossible for the human person to do good, that they seek to carry the desperate and those who are convinced of their sin to Christ, who fulfilled all the precepts for us and thereby redeemed us. Others say that the Sermon on the Mount merely preaches a morality of good intentions. God does not look especially to *what* we do but *how* we do it: with alacrity, obedience, and upright interior intention. A third group believes that the demands of Jesus ought to be understood within a historical situation. Jesus preaches the proximate breakthrough of the kingdom of God. Time is short. It is the final hour of option, the twenty-fourth hour. During this short interval of time before the breakthrough of the new order, we should risk all and prepare ourselves. Jesus' laws are ones of exception. His is an interim morality, one of between-times, before the final catastrophe when at last the new heaven and new earth will appear.

All three solutions contain some truth. But they do not hit upon the essential, because their starting point is the presupposition that the Sermon on the Mount is a law. Christ did not come to bring a more radical and severe law, nor did he preach a more perfect pharisaism. He preached a gospel, which signifies good news: It is not the law that saves but love. Law merely possesses a human function, one of order, of creating the possibility of harmony and comprehension among peoples. The love that saves is superior to all laws and reduces all norms to absurdity. The love demanded by Christ is superior by far to justice. Justice, in the classical definition, consists in giving to each his own. Evidently, this "his own" presupposes a given social system. In slave society, giving to each his own consists in giving to the slaves what is theirs and to the masters what is theirs; in bourgeois society it means giving to the owners what is theirs and the workers what is theirs; in neocapitalist systems it means giving to the magnates what is theirs and to the proletariat what is theirs.

In the Sermon on the Mount Christ breaks this circle. He does not preach any such system of justice that signifies the consecration and legitimation of a social status quo that has as its starting point discrimination between people. He announces a fundamental equality: All are worthy of love. Who is my neighbor? This question is fallacious and ought not to be asked. All are neighbors to each person. All are children of the same Father and because of this all are brothers and sisters. Consequently, the preaching of a universal love represents permanent crisis for all social and ecclesiastical systems. Christ announces a principle that checkmates all fetishistic and inhuman subordination to a system, be it social or religious. The norms of the Sermon on the Mount presuppose love, a new human person and one liberated for greater things: "If your virtue goes no deeper than that of the Scribes and Pharisees, you will never get into the kingdom of heaven" (cf. Matt. 5:20).

Originally the Sermon on the Mount did have an eschatological character; Christ preached an imminent end. Thus he demanded a total, loving conversion. In Matthew's redaction, however, the words of Jesus are situated within the context of a church for which the end of the world means some undetermined future date. But even within this new situation the essential preaching of Jesus has been preserved. His message is not one concerning law but the gospel and love. The Sermon on the Mount, in its current formulation, is a catechism of comportment for a disciple of Jesus, for one who has already embraced the good news and is seeking to construct norms that conform to the tidings brought by Christ: divine sonship.[8]

THE KINGDOM OF GOD IMPLIES A REVOLUTION OF THE HUMAN WORLD

The preaching of Jesus about the kingdom of God concerns not only persons, demanding conversion of them. It also affects the world of persons in terms of a liberation from legalism, from conventions without foundation, from authoritarianism and the forces and powers that subject people. Let us see how Christ reacted when confronted with the mentors of the established order of his day.[9] Concretely, for the simple people the mentors of the religious and social order were not so much the Romans in Caesarea by the sea or in Jerusalem, nor the high priest in the temple, nor the immediate governors set up by the Roman occupation forces such as Herod, Philip, Archelaus, or Pontius Pilate.

Those who distributed justice, resolved cases, and catered to the public order were the scribes and Pharisees in particular. The scribes were rabbis, theologians who carefully studied the Scriptures and mosaic law, principally the religious traditions of the people. The Pharisees constituted a congregation of especially fervent and pious laity.[10] They observed the letter of the law and made sure that the people too observed all strictly. They were spread throughout all Israel, ruled in the synagogues, possessed enormous influence over the people, and for each case they had a solution drawn from the religious traditions of the past and the commentaries on mosaic law *(halacha)*. They did all this in function of the established order "to be seen by men" (Matt.

23:5). They were not evil. Rather, on the contrary, they paid all their taxes (Matt 23:6); they took the first places in the synagogue (Matt. 23:6); they were so zealous for their system that they would travel the world in search of a follower (Matt. 23:15); they were not like the rest of men who could be grasping, unjust, adulterers, and tax evaders (Luke 18:11); they observed fasts and paid tithes on all they got (Luke 18:12); they so appreciated religion that they built holy monuments (Matt. 23:29).

Though "perfect," they nevertheless possessed a basic defect denounced by Jesus: "You have neglected the weightier matters of the law—justice, mercy, good faith!" (Matt. 23:23). "These you should have practiced," he comments, "without neglecting the others" (Matt. 23:24). They do not practice what they preach. They tie up heavy burdens of precepts and laws and lay them on the shoulders of others. They themselves will not lift a finger to move them (Matt. 23:3–4). To enter the kingdom it is not sufficient to do what the law ordains. The present order of things cannot save people from their fundamental alienation. It is order in the midst of disorder. A change of life is required, a complete turnabout of the old situation.

It is because of this that the marginalized of the present order are nearer the kingdom of God than all others. To these, Jesus feels himself especially called (Matt. 9:13). He breaks the social conventions of the period. We know how class distinctions were strictly observed between rich and poor, neighbors and strangers, priests of the temple and levites of the small villas, Pharisees, Sadducees, and tax officials. Those who practiced despised professions were avoided and condemned: for example, shepherds, doctors, tailors, barbers, butchers, and principally the publicans (tax collectors) who were considered Roman collaborators.[11]

How does Jesus react when confronted with this social stratification? He disdains it. He does not comply with religious conventions such as washing one's hands before eating or before entering a house. He does not respect the division of classes. He speaks with all. He seeks contact with the marginalized, the poor, and the despised. To those who are scandalized he cries out: "I did not come to call the just but sinners. The healthy do not need a doctor" (Matt. 11:19). He converses with a prostitute and welcomes Gentiles (Mark 7:24–30); he eats with a great thief, Zaccheus, and accepts in his company a greedy man who later betrayed him, Judas Iscariot; three ex-guerrillas become his disciples; and he allows women to accompany him on trips, something unheard of for a rabbi of his time. The pietistic ones comment: "Look, a glutton and a drunkard, a friend of tax collectors and sinners" (Matt. 11:19).

Jesus secularizes the principle of authority. Established authorities are not entirely the representatives of God: "Give back to Caesar what belongs to Caesar —and to God what belongs to God" (Matt. 22:21). He says of King Herod, who expelled him from Galilee: "You may go and give that fox this message: Learn that today and tomorrow I cast out devils and on the third day attain my end" (Luke 13:32).[12] Authority is a mere function of service: "You know that among the pagans, rulers lord it over them, and their great men make their authority felt. This is not to happen among you. No, anyone who wants to be great among you must be your servant, and anyone who wants to be first among you must be your slave" (Matt. 20:25).

Do not concern yourself with social conventions: "Men who are first will be last and the last first" (Mark 10:31) and "tax collectors and prostitutes are making their way into the kingdom of God before you" (Matt 21:31). Why? Because of their marginalized situation within the socio-religious Jewish system, they are quicker to listen to and follow the message of Jesus. They have nothing to lose because they have nothing and are nothing socially. They have only to wait. This is not so for the Pharisees. They are structured into the system that they created for themselves. They are rich, well known, have religion, and are confident that God is at their side. Sad illusion. The parable of the proud Pharisee who fulfilled the law and the humble repentant publican teaches us something quite different (Luke 18:9–14). The Pharisees do not wish to listen to Jesus because his message is disquieting, obliging them to de-establish themselves; it demands a conversion away from the safe and solid ground of the law and to the norm of a universal love that is superior to all laws (Matt. 5:43–48).

It is not surprising that the Pharisees murmur (Luke 15:2) and make a mockery of Jesus (Luke 16:14), calumniate him as possessed by the devil (Matt 12:24; John 8:48,52), plot cunning interviews for him (Matt. 22:15–22; John 7:38–8:11), try to trap him (Matt. 21:45f.; John 7:30,32,44) and even kill him (Mark 3:6; John 5:18; 8:59; 10:31), collect material with which to accuse him (Matt. 12:10; 21:23–27). And finally it is among them that we find those who will condemn him to death. But Jesus is not intimidated. He goes on preaching individual and social conversion because the ultimate end is nigh: "The time has come and the new order to be introduced by God is close at hand" (Mark 1:15; Matt. 4:17).

CONCLUSION: THE THEOLOGICAL RELEVANCE OF THE ATTITUDES OF THE HISTORICAL JESUS

The figure of Jesus that emerges from these incisive *logia* and brief stories is of a man free from preconceived ideas, whose eyes are open to essentials, who gives himself to others, especially those that are abandoned physically and morally. By doing this he shows us that the established order cannot redeem fundamental human alienation. This world, as it is , cannot be the location of the kingdom of God (cf. 1 Cor. 15:50). It must suffer a restructuring of its very foundations. It is love that saves, the disinterested acceptance of others and the complete opening of self to God. There are no more friends or enemies, neighbors or strangers. There are only brothers and sisters. Christ, with all his energies, tried to create the conditions for a breakthrough of the kingdom of God and a total transfiguration of human and cosmic existence.

Independent of his success or lack of success (success is not a criterion for Christianity), the comportment of Jesus of Nazareth possesses great significance for our Christian existence.[13] It is true that it is not the historical Jesus who lives among us but the resurrected Christ who is beyond history. Nevertheless, it is valid that we make such a reflection because the resurrected Christ is the same as the historical Jesus of Nazareth, only totally transfigured, raised to the right hand of God, at the end of history, and now present among us as Spirit (cf. 2 Cor. 3:17).[14] He brought a new situation. In the words of Carlos Mesters:

It is not for us to judge others, defining them as good or bad, faithful or unfaithful, since the distinction between good and evil people disappears if you are good to others. If evil people exist, then examine your conscience: You have closed your heart and have not helped others to grow. The misery of this world is neither an excuse nor a motive for flight, but an accusation against yourself. It is not you who should judge misery, but misery judges you and your system and makes you see its defects (cf. Matt. 7:1–5).

The distinction between neighbor and stranger no longer exists. It depends entirely on yourself now. If you are neighbor to another, the other will be your neighbor. If the contrary be the case, then the other will not be neighbor to you. It will depend on *your* generosity and openness. The golden rule is: treat others as you would like them to treat you (Matt. 7:12). The distinction between pure and impure no longer exists outside of the human person, but depends on you, on the intentions of your heart, wherein lies the root of your actions. In this regard, the support given by the crutch of law no longer exists. If we have purified ourselves, all around us will be equally pure (cf. Luke 11:41). The distinction between pious and profane works no longer exists, because the manner of practicing works of piety ought not to be distinguished from the manner of practicing other works (Matt. 6:17–18). The true distinction is that which a person establishes in his conscience when confronted with God (Matt. 6:4,6,18).

The clear and juridical vision of the law no longer exists. Jesus offers a clear objective, expressed in the Sermon on the Mount: an objective of total giving that will demand exertion, generosity, responsibility, creativity, and initiative on our part. Jesus permits us to observe traditions insofar as they do not harm but favor the principal objective (Matt. 5:19–20; 23:23). Participation in worship no longer gives us a guarantee that we are good before God. The guarantee lies in the interior attitude that seeks to adore God "in spirit and truth." This attitude is more important than the exterior form and it is this attitude that judges and tests the validity of the exterior forms in worship.[15] The attitudes of Jesus ought to be followed by his disciples. They inaugurate a new type of human being and humanism, one we believe to be the most perfect that has ever emerged; and it has the capacity to assimilate new and different values without betraying its own essence.

According to this new vision, the Christian does not belong to any family, but to the family of the whole world. All peoples are the Christians' brothers and sisters. As the author of the letter to Diognetus (c. A.D. 190) said: "They obey the established laws, but their life surpasses the perfection of law. . . . All foreign lands are a fatherland to them and all fatherlands a foreign land."[16] They are in this world, work in it, help in its construction and also its direction. Nevertheless, they do not place their ultimate hopes in it. People who have dreamt of a kingdom of heaven as Jesus did, are no longer content with this world as they find it. Confronted with this world they feel themselves full of ambiguities, like a "parishioner," in the strong primitive sense that this word had for St. Clement of Rome (d. 97) or for St. Ireneus (d. 202). That is, they feel themselves strangers en route to a more human and happier fatherland. For a little while they must live here, but they know that since Jesus appeared we can dream of a new heaven and a new earth.[17]

By thus overcoming the profound alienations that had encrusted humanity and its history, Jesus gave people back to themselves. In the important questions of life nothing can substitute for the human person: neither law, nor traditions, nor religion. People must decide from within, before God and before others. Because of this they need creativity and liberty. Security does not come from a minute observance of the laws and unreserved adherence to social and religious structures, but from the vigor of one's interior decision and from the responsible autonomy of those who know what they want and why they live.

It is not without reason that Celsus, the eminent pagan philosopher of the third century, considered Christians as people without a fatherland and without roots who challenged the divine institutions of the empire. By their way of living, said the philosopher, the Christians raised a shout of revolt *(fone staseos)*,[18] not because they were against pagans and idolaters, but rather because they were in favor of indiscriminate love, for pagans, Christians, barbarians, Romans, and because they unmasked the imperial ideology that made the Emperor a God and the structures of the vast Empire something divine. As the *Kerygma Petri* said, the Christians formed a *tertium genus*,[19] a third genus of human beings, different from Romans (the first genus) and the barbarians (the second genus) and formed indiscriminately of both. What counts now is not exterior categories and labels that people can adhere to or not.

What matters is what is revealed in the heart that opens itself to God and to others. It is this that determines who is good or bad, divine or diabolic, religious or irreligious. The new comportment of Christians provoked a nonviolent social and cultural revolution in the Roman Empire, a revolution that is at the base of our vastly secularized western civilization today, which has forgotten its beginnings. Jesus affected human beings at their very roots, activating their hope-principle and making them dream of the kingdom, which is not an entirely different world but this world completely new and renewed.

5

Jesus, a Person of Extraordinary Good Sense, Creative Imagination, and Originality

Before giving divine titles to Jesus, the Gospels permit us to speak of him in a very human way. With him, as the New Testament tells us, "appeared the goodness and humanitarian love of God." He does not paint the world as better or worse than it is. Nor does he immediately moralize. With extraordinary good sense, he faces up to reality; he possesses a capacity to see in perspective and place all things in their proper place. Allied to this good sense was the capacity to see human beings as greater and richer than their concrete and cultural surroundings. In him, that which is most divine in humanity and that which is most human in God was revealed.

The message of Jesus is of a radical and total liberation of the human condition from all its alienating elements. He already presents himself as a new man, as of a new creation reconciled with itself and with God. His words and attitudes reveal someone liberated from the complications that people and a history of sin created. He sees clearly the more complex and the simple realities and immediately goes to the essential in things. He knows how to speak of them, briefly, concisely, and with precision. He showed an extraordinary good sense that surprised all about him. Perhaps this fact gave origin to Christology, that is, an attempt on the part of faith to decipher the origin of the originality of Jesus and to answer the question: But who really are you, Jesus of Nazareth?

JESUS, A PERSON OF EXTRAORDINARY GOOD SENSE AND SOUND REASON

To have good sense is the natural endowment of people that are truly great. We say that people have good sense when they immediately discover the core of things, when they have the right word and the necessary comportment for each situation. Good sense is related to concrete knowledge of life; it is knowing how to distinguish the essential from the secondary, the capacity to see things in perspective and place them in their proper place. Good sense is always situated opposite exaggeration. For this reason, the lunatic and the genius, who resemble one another in many ways, are fundamentally distinguished on this point. The genius is one who has radicalized good sense. The lunatic is one who has radicalized an exaggeration.

Jesus, as he is presented by gospel witnesses, gave evidence of being a genius of good sense. A freshness without analogies pervades all that he does and says. God, human beings, society, and nature are immediately present to him. He does not theologize. Nor does he appeal to superior moral principles. Nor does he lose himself in a minute and heartless casuistry. But his words bite into the concrete world until it is forced to

make a decision before God. His determinations are incisive and direct: "Be reconciled with your brother"
(Matt. 5:24b). "Offer the wicked man no resistance. On
the contrary, if anyone hits you on the right cheek, offer
him the other as well" (Matt. 5:39). "Love your enemies,
and pray for those who persecute you" (Matt. 5:44).
"When you give alms, your left hand must not know
what your right hand is doing" (Matt. 6:3).

Jesus Is Prophet and Master: But He Is Different

Jesus' style recalls the great prophets. Certainly he
emerges as a great *prophet* (Mark 8:28; Matt. 21:11,46).
Nevertheless he is not like the prophets of the Old Testament, who needed a divine call and legitimation on the
part of God. Jesus does not claim any vision of celestial
mysteries to which he alone has access. Nor does he
pretend to communicate hidden incomprehensible
truths. He speaks, preaches, discusses, and gathers
disciples around him like any *rabbi* of his day. And
nevertheless the difference between the rabbis and
Jesus is as the heaven is to the earth. A rabbi is an
interpreter of the Sacred Scriptures: He discerns in
them the will of God.

Jesus' doctrine is never a mere explanation of the
sacred texts. He also discerns the will of God outside of
the Scriptures: in creation, history and the concrete
situation. He accepts people into his company that a
rabbi would very clearly reject: sinners, tax officials,
children, and women. He draws his doctrine from the
common experiences that all live and can verify. His
listeners understand immediately. The only presuppo-
sitions demanded of them are good sense and sound
reason. For example, all know that a city built on a
hilltop cannot be hidden (Matt. 5:14); that each day has
enough trouble of its own (Matt. 6:34); that we ought
never to swear, not even by our own head since we
cannot turn a single hair white or black (Matt. 5:36);

that we cannot add one single cubit to our span of life (Matt. 6:27); that the human person is worth much more than the birds in the sky (Matt. 6:26); that the sabbath was made for man, not man for the sabbath (Mark 2:27).

Jesus Does Not Want to Say Something New Merely for Effect and Whatever the Cost

Jesus never appeals to a higher authority, one coming from outside, to reinforce his own authority and doctrine. The things he says possess an internal evidence. He is not interested in saying something esoteric and incomprehensible, something new at any cost. He says rational things that people can understand and live. On close inspection, we see that Christ did not come to bring a new morality, different from the one people already had. He brings to light that which people always knew or ought to have known but because of their alienation were unable to see, comprehend, and formulate.

Consider as an example the golden rule of charity (Matt. 7:12; Luke 6:31): "Always treat others as you would like them to treat you."[1] Thales of Miletus (600 B.C.) relates that on being asked to state the highest rule of good living he answered: "Do not do the evil you find in others."[2] In Pittacus (580 B.C.) we find a similar formula: "Do not yourself do whatsoever you dislike in others." Isocrates (400 B.C.) states the same truth in a positive formula: "Treat others as you would wish them to treat you." Confucius (551–470 B.C.), when asked by a disciple if a norm existed that one could follow throughout one's life, said: "Love of the neighbor. Whatsoever you do not desire for yourself, do not do unto others." In the national epic poem of India, the *Mahabharata* (between 400 B.C. and A.D. 400), one finds the following truth: "Learn the highest point of the law and when you have learnt it, think on it: Whatsoever you hate, do not do unto others." In the Old Testament one reads: "Do to no one what you would not want done to you" (Tob. 4:15).

At the time of King Herod, a pagan appeared before the celebrated Rabbi Hillel, teacher of St. Paul, and said to him: "I will accept Judaism on condition you tell me all the law while I am standing on one foot." To which Hillel answered: "Do not do unto others whatsoever you do not wish them to do unto you. The law consists in this. All the rest is commentary. Go and learn!"

Jesus never read Thales of Miletus, or Pittacus, much less Confucius and the *Mahabharata*. Jesus stated his formulation in the positive form that infinitely surpasses the negative, because it puts no limit to one's openness to, and preoccupation for, the suffering and joy of others. He thus joins the long line of great sages who preoccupied themselves with *humanitas*. "The epiphany of the humanity of God is culminated when Jesus professed the golden rule of human charity."[3] Jesus does not wish to say something new, merely for effect and whatever the cost, but something as old as humankind; not something original, but something that is valid for all; not astonishing things, but things people can comprehend on their own if they have clear vision and a little good sense. St. Augustine had good reason for thinking: "The substance of that which today is called Christianity was already known to ancient peoples, nor was it absent from the beginnings of the human race to the time when Christ came in the flesh. Since that time, the true religion that already existed began to call itself the Christian religion."[4]

Jesus Wants Us to Understand:
He Appeals to Sound Reason

Other examples taken from the many possible will give us evidence of Jesus' good sense and the appeal he makes to sound reason: He commands that we love our enemies. Why? Because all, friends and enemies, are children of the same Father who causes his sun to rise on the wicked as well as the good, and his rain to fall on the honest and dishonest alike (Matt. 5:45). He commands that we do good to all without distinction. Why? Because if we do good to those who do good to us, what thanks can we expect? For even sinners do that much (Luke 6:33). He forbids men to have more than one woman. Why? Because monogamy existed at the beginning of creation. God created one couple, Adam and Eve (Mark 10:6). It is no good simply to say: Do not kill, or do not commit adultery. Anger and covetous looks are already sinful. Why? What use is it to combat the consequences if first one does not heal the cause (Matt. 5:22,28). Human beings were not made for the sabbath, but the sabbath for human beings. Why? If an animal fell down a hole on the sabbath day, would one not go and take it out? A person is far more important than an animal (Matt. 12:11–12).

We ought to have faith in the providence of God. Why? Because God looks after the lilies in the field, birds in the sky, and every hair on our heads. "You are worth more than hundreds of sparrows" (Matt. 10:31). "If, then, you who are evil know how to give your children what is good, how much more will your Father in heaven give good things to those who ask him" (Matt. 7:11). The law says that it is a sin to walk with sinners, because they will make one unclean. Christ is not worried on this score. He uses sound reason and argues: "It is not the healthy who need the doctor, but the sick. I did not come to call the virtuous, but sinners" (Mark 2:17). It is not what enters a person that makes one unclean, but what comes out. Why? "Whatever goes into a man from outside cannot make him unclean, because it does not go into his heart but through his stomach and passes out into the sewer. . . . It is what comes out of a man that makes him unclean. For it is from within, from men's hearts, that evil intentions emerge: fornication, theft, etc." (Mark 7:18–22). This use of sound reason by Jesus is still theologically very relevant for us today, because it shows us that Christ wants us to understand things. He did not demand a blind submission to the law.[5]

Jesus Does Not Paint the World
Better or Worse Than It Is

Jesus' look at the world is penetrating and without preconceptions; he goes immediately to the core of the problem. His parables show that he knows the whole reality
of life, good and bad. He does not paint the world better
or worse than it is. Nor does he immediately moralize.
His first position with regard to the world is not one of
censure but of comprehension. Nature is not celebrated
as numinous, as in Teilhard de Chardin and even St.
Francis of Assisi. Rather nature is seen in its created
naturalness. He speaks of the sun and rain (Matt. 5:45),
of storm clouds and the south wind (Luke 12:54–55), of
lightning that strikes in the east and flashes far into the
west (Matt. 24:27), of birds that neither sow nor reap nor
gather into barns (Matt. 6:26), of the beauty of the flow-
ers growing in the fields and the grass that is there
today and thrown into the furnace tomorrow (Matt.
6:30), of the fig-tree that when its leaves come out you
know that summer is near (Mark 13:28), of the harvest
(Mark 4:3ff., 26ff.; Matt. 13:24ff.), of moths and wood-
worms (Matt. 6:19), of dogs that lick sores (Luke 16:21), of
vultures that eat corpses (Matt 24:28). He speaks of
thorns and thistles; he knows the gestures of the sower
(Luke 12:16–21); he refers to the farm that produces
(Luke 16:21); and he knows how to construct a house
(Matt. 7:24–27).

He knows how a woman makes bread (Matt. 13:33);
with the care of a pastor he goes in search of the lost
sheep (Luke 15ff.). He knows how peasants work (Mark
4:3), rest, and sleep (Mark 4:26ff). He knows how the
master demands an account of his employees (Matt.
25:14ff.) and how they can be whipped (Luke 12:47–48).
He knows that the unemployed sit in the square waiting
for work (Matt. 20:1ff.); that children want to play at
marriage in the public square but their companions are
unwilling to dance; that they want to play at a burial

service but the others do not wish to lament (Matt. 11:16–18). He knows the joy of a mother when a child is born (John 16:21), and that the powerful of the earth enslave others (Matt. 20:25). He knows what the obedience of soldiers is like (Matt. 8:9).

Jesus uses strong examples. He takes life as it really is. He knows how to draw a lesson from the steward of a company who steals and is smart (Luke 16:1–12). He refers with naturalness to the king who goes to war (Luke 14:31–33). He knows the jealousy that people experience between themselves (Luke 15:28), and he compares himself to a robber (Mark 3:27). There is a parable that is considered authentically of Jesus and transmitted in the apocryphal Gospel of St. Thomas that shows clearly the strong and real sensitivity of Christ: "The kingdom of the Father is like a man who wished to kill an important lord. When at home, he took out his sword and pierced the wall. He wanted to know if his hand was sufficiently strong. Afterwards, he killed the important lord."[6] With this he wanted to teach that when God begins some project he always concludes it, just as this assassin.

All this clearly shows that Jesus is a person of extraordinary good sense. Whence did he derive this? To answer this question is to do Christology. We will return again to this theme.

*All That Is Authentically Human Is Seen in
Jesus: Anger and Joy, Goodness and Toughness,
Friendship, Sorrow, and Temptation*

The gospel stories tell us of the absolute normality of Jesus' life. He is a person of profound sentiments. He knows natural affection for the children he embraces (Matt. 9:36); he lays his hands on them and blesses them (Mark 10:13–16). He is impressed by the generosity of the rich young man: "Jesus looked steadily at him and loved him" (Mark 10:31). He rejoices over the faith of a pagan

(Luke 7:9), and the wisdom of a scribe (Mark 12:34). He is surprised at the incredulity of his compatriots from Nazareth (Mark 6:6). On seeing the funeral of a widow's only son, he was moved and "felt sorry for her"; he approached and consoled her, saying: "Do not cry" (Luke 7:13). He took pity on the hungry people, because they lost their way like sheep without a shepherd (Mark 6:34). If he is angered by the lack of faith in people (Mark 9:18), he is so happy with the good will of simple people that he says a prayer of thanks to the Father (Matt. 11:25–26). He feels the ingratitude of the nine blind men that were cured (Luke 7:44–46) and he irately reproaches the cities of Chorazin and Bethsaida and Capernaum because they have not done penance (Matt. 11:20–24). He is grieved by the blindness of the Pharisees and "he looked angrily around at them" (Mark 3:5).

Jesus employs physical violence against those who profane the temple (John 2:15–17). He complains of the disciples because they too do not understand (Mark 7:18). He gives vent to this against Philip and says to him, "Have you been with me all this time, Philip, and you still do not know me" (John 14:19). He also gives vent to his anger toward the Pharisees "with a sigh that came straight from the heart" (Mark 8:12): "Why does this generation demand a sign?" (Mark 8:12). He is agitated by the revengeful spirit of the apostles (Luke 9:55) and with Peter's insinuations: "Go behind me Satan" (Mark 8:33). But he rejoices with them on their return from a mission. He concerns himself to see that they want for nothing: "When I sent you out without purse or haversack or sandals, were you short for anything? No, they said" (Luke 22:35). When with them, he does not want them to call him master but friend (Luke 12:4–7; John 15:13–15). All that is his is also theirs (John 17:22). Friendship is a characteristic theme with Jesus because to be a friend to someone is a form of love.[7] And he loved all even to extremes.

The parables demonstrate how well Jesus knew the

phenomenon of friendship: One gets together with friends to celebrate (Luke 15:6,9,29) and have banquets (Luke 14:12–14); one runs to a friend even though it may be inopportune (Luke 11:5–8); there are inconstant friends who betray others (Luke 21:16); friendship can exist even between two rogues like Pilate and Herod (Luke 23:12). Jesus' comportment with the apostles, his miracles, his action at the wedding in Cana, the multiplication of the loaves, all reveal his friendship. His relationship with Lazarus is one of friendship. "Lord, the man you love is ill. . . ." "Lazarus our friend is resting, I am going to wake him," said Jesus (John 11:11). When Jesus weeps at the death of his friend they all comment: "See how much he loved him" (John 11:37). He felt at home in Bethany with Martha and Mary (Matt. 21:17) and likes to return there (Luke 11:38,42; John 11:17).

For many men friendship with women is tabu. This was even more so at the time of Christ. A woman could not appear in public with her husband, much less with a travelling preacher like Jesus. And nevertheless we know of Jesus' friendship with some women who followed him and fed him and his disciples (Luke 8:3). We know the names of a few: Mary Magdalene; Joanna, the wife of Chuza, a functionary of Herod; Susanna; and others. There is a woman beside the cross. It is they who will bury him and go to cry for the dead Lord at the sepulcher (Mark 16:1–4). It is also women who see the resurrected Jesus. He breaks a social tabu by allowing a woman of ill repute to anoint him (Mark 14:3–9; Luke 7:37ff.), and he converses with a woman heretic (John 4:7ff.).

Aristotle used to say that friendship could not be possible between divinity and human beings because of the differences in nature. The philosopher could not have imagined the emergence of God in warm, receptive human flesh. All that is authentically human appears in Jesus: anger and joy, goodness and toughness, friendship and indignation. He possesses all the human dimensions of vigor, vitality, and spontaneity. He partook of all our feelings and the common conditionings of human life such as hunger (Matt. 4:2; Mark 11:12), thirst (John 4:7; 19:28), tiredness (John 4:6; Mark 4:37ff.), cold and heat, an insecure life without a roof (Luke 9:58; cf. John 11:53–54; 12:36), tears (Luke 19:41; John 11:35), sorrow and fear (Matt. 26:37), and strong temptations (Matt. 4:1–11; Luke 4:1–13; Heb. 4:15; 5:2,7–10). His psyche can plunge to the depths of desperation: "My soul is sorrowful to the point of death" (Matt. 26:38); he lived through the terror and anguish of a violent death (Luke 22:44). For this reason the good shepherd of souls that wrote the epistle to the Hebrews commented that Jesus is capable of "feeling our weaknesses with us, because we have one who has been tempted in every way that we are, though he is without sin" (Heb. 4:15).

JESUS, A PERSON OF EXTRAORDINARY CREATIVE IMAGINATION

It may seem strange to speak of the creative imagination of Jesus.[8] The church and theologians are not accustomed to express themselves in this manner. Nevertheless, we ought to say that, as the New Testament itself shows us, there are many ways of speaking about Jesus. Is it not possible that for us this category "imagination" may not reveal the originality and mystery of Christ? Many understand little about imagination and think that it is synonymous with dreams, a daydreamer's flight from reality, a passing illusion. In truth, however, imagination signifies something much more profound. Imagination is a form of liberty. It is born in confrontation with reality and established order; it emerges from nonconformity in the face of completed and established situations; it is the capacity to see human beings as greater and richer than the cultural and concrete environment that surrounds them; it is having the courage to think and say something new and to take hitherto untreaded paths that are full of meaning for human beings. We can say that imagination, understood in this manner, was one of the fundamental qualities of Jesus. Perhaps in the whole of human history there has not been a single person who had a richer imagination than Jesus.

Jesus, a Person Who Has the Courage to Say: I

We have already seen that Jesus does not accept without question the Judaic traditions, laws, sacred rites, and established order of his day. At the beginning of his Gospel Mark says that Christ taught "a new doctrine" (Mark 1:27). He does not repeat what the Old Testament taught. Consequently he had the courage to rise up and say: "You have heard what was said by our fathers" —and here he was thinking of the law, Moses, and the prophets—"I however say to you." He is a person who boldly proclaims "I" without guaranteeing himself by other authorities from outside himself.

The new tidings he preaches are not completely unknown to humankind. Rather, his message is what good sense commands and what had been lost by the religious, moral, and cultural complications created by the people. Christ came to discover the good tidings of what is most ancient and original in the human person made to the image and likeness of the Father. He does not concern himself with order (which is often order in disorder) but allows creative imagination to reign. In so doing he disconcerts established people who now ask themselves: Who is he? Is he not the carpenter, son of Mary? (Mark 6:3a; Matt. 13:53–58; Luke 4:16–30; John 6:42).

He walks among forbidden people and accepts doubtful persons in his company, such as two or three guerillas (Simon, the Canaanite, Judas Iscariot, Peter bar Jonah);[9] he gives a complete turnabout to the social and religious framework, saying that the last shall be first

(Mark 10:31), the humble shall be masters (Matt. 5:5), and tax officials and prostitutes will find it easier to enter the kingdom of heaven than the pious scribes and Pharisees (Matt. 21:23). He does not discriminate against anyone, neither heretics nor schismatic Samaritans (Luke 10:29–37; John 4:4–42), nor people of ill repute like the prostitute (Luke 7:36–40), nor the marginalized (sick, leprous, and poor),[10] nor the rich whose houses he frequents even while saying to them: "Alas for you who are rich: you are having your consolation now" (Luke 6:24). Nor does he refuse the invitations of his indefatigable opposition, the Pharisees, though seven times he takes the liberty of saying to them: "Alas for you, scribes and Pharisees, you hypocrites and blind guides" (Matt. 23:13–39).

Jesus Never Used the Word "Obedience"

The established order is relativized and human beings liberated from the tentacles that have kept them prisoners. The preaching and demands of Christ do not presuppose an established order. Rather, on the contrary, he frustrates it because of his creative imagination and spontaneity. Insofar as we can judge, the word "obedience" (and its derivatives), while occurring eighty-seven times in the New Testament, was never used by Christ.[11] We do not mean to say by this that Jesus made no harsh demands. Obedience for him is not a question of fulfilling orders, but a firm decision in favor of what God demands within a concrete situation. The will of God is not always manifested in the law. Normally it reveals itself in the concrete situation where conscience is caught unawares by a proposal that demands a response.

The great difficulty encountered by Jesus in his disputes with theologians and masters of his time consisted in precisely this: We cannot resolve the question concerning what God wants from us by merely having recourse to the Scriptures. We must consult the signs of the times and the unforeseen in a situation (cf. Luke 12:54–57). This is a clear appeal to spontaneity, liberty, and the use of our creative imagination. Obedience is a question of having our eyes open to the situation; it consists in deciding for and risking ourselves in the adventure of responding to God who speaks here and now. The Sermon on the Mount, which is not a law, is addressed to everyone, inviting us to have extremely clear consciences and an unlimited capacity for understanding people, sympathizing with them, being tuned into them, and loving them with all their limitations and realizations.

Jesus Does Not Have Prefabricated Notions

Jesus himself is the best example of this way of life, as is summarized in a phrase of the Gospel of John: "Whoever comes to me, I shall not turn him away" (John 6:37). He receives everybody: the sinners with whom he eats (Luke 15:2; Matt. 9:10–11) and the little one (Mark 10:13–16); he pays attention to the crippled woman (Luke 13:10–17), the anonymous blind man by the wayside (Mark 10:46–52), the woman who is ashamed of her bleeding (Mark 5:21–34). He receives the well-known theologian at night (John 3:1ff.). He did not even have time to eat (Mark 3:20; 6:31) and goes into a deep sleep because of fatigue (Mark 4:38). His speech can be harsh when inveighing against those who do things for appearance' sake (Matt. 3:7; 23:1–39; John 9:44), but it can also be full of comprehension and forgiveness (John 8:10–11).

In his way of speaking and acting, in his treatment of various social strata, he never sees people according to prefabricated notions. He respects all persons in their own originality: the Pharisees as Pharisees, the scribes as scribes, the sinners as sinners, the sick as sick. His reaction is always surprising: He has the right word and

corresponding gesture for every person. John properly
said: "He never needed evidence about any man, he
could tell what a man had in him" (John 2:25). Though no
one had told him, he knew of the sin of the paralytic
(Mark 2:5); of the state of Jairus's daughter (Mark 5:39);
of the woman who suffered from a hemorrhage (Mark
5:29ff.); of the man possessed by a demon (Mark 1:23ff.;
5:1ff.); of the intimate thoughts of his opponents (Mark
2:8; 3:5). He is surely a charismatic figure without analogy in history.[12] He demonstrates impressive superiority.[13] He unmasks trick questions (cf. Mark 12:14ff.) and
gives surprising answers. He can make his adversaries
speak, but he can also silence them (Matt. 22:34). The
Gospels often refer to the fact that Christ was silent
himself. Listening to the people and feeling their problems is also one of the ways of loving them.

Was Jesus a Liberal?

Some years ago one of the greatest exegetes of the day
asked this question and answered: "Jesus . . . was a 'liberal.' No qualification whatsoever of this statement is
possible, even though churches and devout people
should declare it blasphemous. He was a 'liberal,' because in the name of God and in the power of the Holy
Spirit he interpreted and appraised Moses, the Scriptures, and dogmatics from the point of view of love, and
thereby allowed devout people to remain human and
even reasonable."[14] To see how true this is, we need only
remember the following episode that marvelously puts
into relief the liberty and open-mindedness of Jesus:
"Master, we saw a man who is not one of us casting out
devils in your name, and because he was not one of us we
tried to stop him." But Jesus said, "You must not stop
him: No one who works a miracle in my name is likely to
speak evil of me. Anyone who is not against us is for us"
(Mark 9:38–40; Luke 9:49–50).
    Christ differs from many of his sectarian disciples

throughout history. Jesus came to be and to live Christ and not to preach Christ or announce himself.[15] Because of this he feels his mission realized wherever he sees people that follow him and—even though there be no explicit reference to his name—do what he wanted and proclaimed. What he wanted is clear: the happiness of human beings that can be found only if we open ourselves to others and to the Great Other (God) (cf. Luke 10:25–37; Mark 12:28–31; Matt. 22:34–40). There is a sin that is radically mortal: the sin against the humanitarian spirit. According to the parable concerning anonymous Christians in Matt. 25:31–46, the eternal Judge will not ask people about the canons of dogma, nor whether they made any explicit reference to the mystery of Christ while they lived. He will ask if we have done anything to help those in need. Here all is decided. "Lord, when did we see you hungry or thirsty, a stranger or naked, sick or in prison, and did not come to your help?" He will answer them: "I tell you solemnly, insofar as you neglected to do this to one of the least of these, you neglected to do it to me" (Matt. 25:44–45). The sacrament of brotherhood is absolutely necessary for salvation. Those who deny this deny the cause of Christ, even when they always have Christ on their lips and officially confess themselves for him.[16]

Imagination postulates creativity, spontaneity, and liberty. It is precisely this that Christ demands when he proposes an ideal like the Sermon on the Mount. Here, one can no longer speak of laws, but of love that surpasses all laws. Christ's invitation: "You must therefore be perfect just as your heavenly Father is perfect" (Matt. 5:48) knocked down all possible barriers to religious imagination, whether they had been raised by religions or by cultures or by existential situations.

THE ORIGINALITY OF JESUS

When speaking of the originality of Jesus we ought first to clear up an equivocation. Original does not refer to someone who says entirely pure and new things. Nor is original synonymous with strange. "Original" comes from "origin." Those who are near the origin and root of things and by their lives, words, and works bring others to the origin and root of their own selves can be properly called original, not because they discover new things, but because they speak of things with absolute immediacy and superiority. All that they say and do is translucent, crystal clear, and evident. People perceive this immediately. All those in contact with Jesus encountered themselves and that which is best in them. All are led to discover their own root. Confrontation with this source generates a crisis: One is constrained to make a decision and either convert or install oneself in that which is derived, secondary, and part of the current situation.

Good sense consists in grasping the original nature of human beings, which we all live and know but find difficult to formulate and translate into images. Christ knew how to verbalize this original core of human nature in a genial manner, as we saw above. Consequently he can resolve conflicts and put an "and" where most put an "or." The author of the letter to the Ephesians tells us the truth: Christ broke down the walls that separated Gentiles from Jews and "has made the two into one" (Eph. 2:24,15).[17] He broke down all barriers, sacred and profane, of conventions and legalism, of divisions between peoples and sexes, of people with God, because now all have access to God and can say "Abba, Father" (Eph. 3:18; cf. Gal 4:6; Rom. 8:15). All are sisters and brothers and children of the same Father. Therefore the originality of Jesus consists in being able to grasp the profundity of the human person, which is a concern of all peoples without exception. Thus, he does not found yet another new school, nor elaborate a new ritual of prayer, nor prescribe a supermorality. But he arrives at a dimension and marks a horizon that obliges all reality to be revolutionized, to be renewed, and to be converted.

Why is it that Christ is so original, superior, and exalted? The Christology of yesterday and today emerge from this question . Before giving divine titles to Jesus the Gospels themselves permit us to speak very humanly about him. Faith tells us that in him "appeared the goodness and humanitarian love of God" (Tim. 3:4). How do we discover this? Is it not perhaps in his extraordinary good sense, in his singularly creative imagination, and in his unequalled originality?

CONCLUSION: THE THEOLOGICAL RELEVANCE
OF THE COMPORTMENT OF JESUS

Interest in the attitudes and comportment of the historical Jesus begins with the presupposition that in him is revealed that which is most divine in persons and most human in God. Therefore, what emerged and was expressed in Jesus ought to emerge and be expressed also in his followers:[18] complete openness to God and others; indiscriminate love without limits; a critical spirit in confronting the current social and religious situation because the situation does not incarnate the will of God in a pure and straightforward manner; a critical spirit that cultivates creative imagination, which in the name of love and the liberty of the children of God challenges cultural structures; and giving primacy to persons over things, which belong to and exist for persons. Christians ought to be free and liberated persons. We do not mean by this that they may be lawless anarchists. Christians understand the law in a different way. As St. Paul says "we are no longer living by law" (Rom. 6:15) but living by "the law of Christ" (1 Cor. 9:21) that permits us—"being totally free" (1 Cor. 9:19)—to live with those who are subjects of the law or again with those who have no law so as to win both (1

Cor. 9:19). The law is relativized and put at the *service* of love. "When Christ freed us, he meant us to remain free. . . . Do not submit again to the yoke of slavery" (Gal. 5:1).

We see all this realized in exemplary fashion by Jesus of Nazareth with a spontaneity that is not paralleled, and never will be, in the history of religions. He detheologizes religion, making people search for the will of God not only in holy books but principally in daily life; he demythologizes religious language, using the expressions of our common experiences; he deritualizes piety, insisting that one is always before God and not only when one goes to the temple to pray; he emancipates the message of God from its connection to one religious community and directs it to all people of good will (cf. Mark 9:30–40, John 10:16); and, finally, he secularizes the means of salvation, making the sacrament of the "other" a determining element for entry into the kingdom of God.

Nevertheless he did not come to make our life more comfortable. Rather, the contrary is true. In the words of Dostoyevski's Grand Inquisitor: "Instead of dominating conscience, you came to make it even more profound; instead of encircling human liberty, you came to make its horizon even wider. . . . Your desire was to liberate people for love. Free, they ought to follow You, feel themselves attracted to You and as Your prisoners. Instead of obeying the harsh laws of the past, people ought to begin as of now to decide in Your presence what is good and what is bad, having Your example before their eyes." To attempt to live such a lifestyle is to follow Christ with the richness that this term—to follow and imitate Christ—has for the New Testament. It means liberation and the experience of a new redeemed and reconciled life. But it can also include, as in the case of Christ, persecution and death.

In conclusion, how beautifully resound the profound words of Dostoyevski on returning from the house of the dead, his prison of forced labor in Siberia:

At times God sends me moments of peace; on these occasions, I love and feel that I am loved; it was in one such moment that I composed for myself a credo in which all is clear and sacred. This credo is very simple. This is it: I believe that there is nothing on earth more beautiful, more profound, more appealing, more virile, or more perfect than Christ; and I say to myself, with jealous love, that greater than he does not and cannot exist. More than this: should anyone prove to me that Christ is beyond the range of truth, and that all this is not to be found in him, I would prefer to retain Christ than to retain the truth.[19]

6

The Meaning of the
Death of Jesus

The whole life of Jesus was a giving, a being-for-others, an attempt to overcome all conflicts in his own existence, and a realization of this goal. In the name of the kingdom of God, he lived his "being-for-others" to the end, even when, sensitive to the depths of despair, he experienced the death (absence) of God on the cross. But right up to the end he was confident and believed that God would accept him as he was. Even the meaningless had for him a secret and ultimate meaning.

A tragedy hovers over the efforts of Jesus to liberate people from themselves, from the complications they create and from that which, in a word, we call sin. His "new doctrine" (Mark 1:27) set all the authorities of his day against him: Pharisees, the religio-political party that was fanatically attached to the traditions and observance of the law to the point where they made life dismal and almost impossible; scribes, the erudite theologians of the Sacred Scriptures; Sadducees, an extremely conservative and opportunistic group of priests and well placed families; the elders, rich laity and high functionaries of the capital, Jerusalem; Herodians of Galilee, the party friendly to Herod, who wanted independence from the Romans; and finally the Romans, the occupation forces themselves. All these held Jesus to be their enemy.

THE PROSECUTION OF JESUS

The Gospels give the following reasons why the liberating task of Jesus was made difficult and why, finally, he was arrested, tortured, and condemned to death.[1]

The Popularity of Jesus

The acceptance that Jesus found among the popular masses worried the authorities and provoked jealousy and bad will among them (Mark 11:18; John 4:1–3; 7:32,46; 12:10,19). It was believed that he preached subversion (Luke 23:2; John 7:12), that he prohibited the payment of the head tax to the Roman Emperor (Luke 23:2), that perhaps he even had serious pretentions of assuming power against the ruling regime (cf. John 19:12; 5:15; Luke 23:2). Indeed his criticisms touch those who had influence over the people, such as the Pharisees (Matt. 23), Herod (Luke 13:32), those who exercise power in general (Matt. 20:25; Luke 2:25), and the rich (Luke 6:24–26; 18:25). Panic-striken they say: "If we let him go on in this way everybody will believe in him and the Romans will come and destroy the Holy Place, and our nation" (John 11:48). In fact all feared for their power positions and privileged status, especially those who exploited the business of the temple by selling sacrificial animals, like the family and house of Annas.

Some of Jesus' sayings sought to stress the urgent need for conversion because of the imminence of the kingdom. When read from another angle of vision, however, they could easily cause political misunderstand-

ings: "It is not peace I have come to bring but the
sword"; "for I have come to set a man against his father,
a daughter against her mother"; "I have come to bring
fire to the earth, and how I wish it were blazing already!" (Luke 12:49). Clearly Christ did not want violence. On the contrary, he commands that we love our
enemies (Matt. 5:44–48). At the very moment when he
could have initiated violence he immediately orders:
"Put your sword back, for all who draw the sword will die
by the sword" (Matt. 26:52).

Jesus, One Who Disconcerts

Jesus teaches without ever falling back on any authority, though he was never ordained rabbi nor did he frequent the schools (Mark 6:2; John 7:15). He places himself above casuistry—regarded as holy as the law
itself—in the interpretation of the law (Mark 3:2–5:17;
John 5:8–13; Luke 13:13–17; 14:1–6). He tolerated in his
company people with whom contact meant legal impurity (Mark 2:16; Matt. 11:19; Luke 7:39; 15:1–2; 19:7). He
spoke with God and of God in words and gestures held to
be blasphemous (Mark 2:7; John 5:18; 7:29; 8:58; 10:30).
He is unrelenting in his fight against all kinds of false-
ness and meaningless formalism (Mark 12:38–40; Matt.
23:1–39; 5:20; Luke 12:1; 16:15; 18:11). These dogmatic-
religious positions exasperated the Pharisees especially, who "began a furious attack on him and tried to
force answers from him on innumerable questions"
(Luke 11:53). Jesus confounds all. And all ask: Who is he?
From where does he derive such power? (John 8:25;
Mark 4:41; Luke 4:36; Matt. 8:27).

Jesus, One Who Provokes a Radical Crisis

Jesus especially worries people when he assumes attitudes that pertain to God alone: He places his author-

ity above that of Moses, which is the equivalent of arrogating divine powers to himself (Mark 7:1–2; Matt. 5:21-48: "You have heard what was said to our fathers"). He forgives sin, a matter that pertains to God alone (Mark 2:7; Luke 7:49). He performs miracles with supreme power. He shows those marginalized by sin or destiny that because of this fact alone they are not rejected by God but now they too have their opportunity and can sit at the same table with him. The God of Jesus Christ is a God of mercy and pardon, who rejoices more over one repentant sinner than over ninety-nine virtuous people who have no need of repentance (Luke 15:7). Jesus' actions provoke a crisis in his listeners. "Crisis" signifies decision and judgment. They ought to decide for or against Christ. This crisis and decision in fact signifies a scission between light and darkness (John 3:19–20), life and death, salvation and damnation (John 5:24; 8:39).

Three times, says John the evangelist, Christ divided the people by his attitudes and words, i.e., he provoked a crisis that brought about a rupturing-decision for or against him (John 7:43; 9:16; 10:19). Christ is the crisis of the world:[2] Either one transcends oneself and thereby is saved or one falls back on oneself, eliminating Jesus from one's milieu, and is lost. Religious fanaticism, the will to power, and the desire to maintain guaranteed privileges were, according to the gospel, the main reasons that brought Jesus' enemies—divided among themselves but united against him—to liquidate the annoying prophet of Nazareth. The thesis that the hatred of the status quo for Jesus is caused by his refusal to lead a rebellion against the Romans or because he had relations with guerrilla Zealots is mere speculation and fantasy without basis in the sources we possess.[3] The Gospels tell us nothing about any of this. And they are the only sources except for a few later citations that speak of Jesus: Flavius Josephus *(Ant.*

Jud. 18,3,3; 20,9,1), Pliny (Ep 10), Tacitus *(Annals* 15,44), and Suetonius *(Claudius* 25).

They Use All Available Means Against Jesus

Jesus became a danger for the established order. Consequently, using every means available, they seek to find a legal statute that would justify his prosecution and imprisonment. First, they demand an oral attestation of good conduct from him (Mark 7:5; 2:16; 18:24; 11:27 and throughout John). Next they seek to isolate him from the people and even incite the people against him. His miracles are defamed as works of the devil (Mark 3:22; John 7:20; 8:48,52; 10:20; Matt. 10:25). They call for a miracle on demand in order to study it more closely (Mark 8:11). They hope to put him in a corner with malicious questions or to make him look ridiculous (Mark 12:18–23). In controversial questions, they oblige him to take sides (Mark 10:2); they even bait him with tricky questions that try to make him an enemy either of the people or of the occupation forces (Mark 12:13–17; Luke 11: 53–54; John 8:5–6). He is expelled from the synagogue, which at that time signified excommunication (John 2:22; 12:42). There are a number of attempts to imprison him (Mark 11:18; John 7:30,32,44–52; 10:39), and two attempts to stone him (John 8:59; 10:31). Finally they decide to liquidate him (Mark 3:6; John 5:18; 11:49–50). However, his popularity is a big obstacle (John 7:46; Mark 12:12).

Jesus knows all this, but he is not intimidated. He continues to speak and to ask disconcerting questions (Mark 12:13–17; Luke 13:17; 14:1–6). He goes ahead with his preaching (John 5:19–47; 7:19,25; 8:12–29,37; 10:33). Nevertheless he has to defend himself: When they try to stone him he hides; when they try to arrest him in the temple, he disappears in the midst of the people (John 8:59; 10:39; cf. Luke 4:30). Once he goes incognito to

Jerusalem (John 7:10) and he avoids enemy territory, going from Judea to Galilee (John 4:1–3). Even there he avoids the Pharisees, who often pestered him as he travelled north to a pagan zone or beyond the lake of Gennesareth (Mark 7:24; 8:13; cf. Matt. 12:15; 14:13). After one very difficult confrontation he retired alone to Bethany (John 10:40). On knowing of the Sanhedrin's decision to kill him (John 11:49,50,53), he goes to Ephraim near the desert with his disciples (John 11:54). On his last stay in Jerusalem, according to John, he remains more or less hidden (John 12:36). At night he goes outside the city to Bethany or the Mount of Olives (Mark 11:11,19; Luke 21:37; John 18:2).

The authorities do not know his whereabouts. A proclamation was published soliciting the assistance of the people in discovering his whereabouts so that they might imprison him (John 11:57). Judas reacted to this declaration of the authorities. For the price of a slave (thirty denarii of silver) he betrayed Jesus (Matt. 26:15). Judas's betrayal, which has suffered the most extraordinary interpretations,[4] consisted—this the Gospels make clear—in indicating to the authorities where Jesus was and where he might be arrested without provoking a sensation and popular tumult. Perhaps he performed this act motivated by a profound deception: he, just as the other disciples (cf. Luke 24:21; 19:11; Acts 1:6), expected that Jesus would liberate Israel, politically expelling the Romans.[5] Christ however understood his liberation in a much more universal manner, as total transfiguration of this world, people and cosmos, calling it the kingdom of God.

Jesus Is Condemned as a "Blasphemer"
and a Guerrilla

Mark's words—the oldest account of the passion of Jesus—concerning the betrayal of Judas—are characterized by a sinister tone, all the more emphasized by their brevity and dryness: "Now the traitor had arranged a signal with them. 'The one I kiss,' he had said, 'he is the man. Take him in charge, and see he is well guarded when you lead him away.' So when the traitor came, he went straight up to Jesus and said, 'Rabbi,' and kissed him." Jesus retained his sovereign composure: He merely says: "Am I a brigand that you had to set out to capture me with swords and clubs. I was among you teaching in the Temple day after day and you never laid hands on me" (Mark 14:44–49).

The historical character of the scenes that follow is highly debated because the accounts were given in the light of the resurrection and of a profession of faith in Jesus as Christ.[6] These scenes fall under a category of a "handing over": by Judas, he is *handed over* to the Sanhedrin (Mark 14:10,42); by the Sanhedrin, he is *handed over* to Pilate (Mark 15:1,10); by Pilate, he is *handed over* to the soldiers (Mark 15:15), who anonymously, in the name of all the powerful of this world, *hand him over* to death (Mark 15:25); finally, God himself *hands him over* to his own fate, allowing him to succumb on the cross (Mark 15:34). But a dual process takes place before this occurs: one *religious*, before the Jewish authorities, and the other *political*, before the Roman authorities. Arrested in the Garden of Olives, he is taken to the palace of the high priest; there he spends the night awaiting the following day when, in accordance with the law, the Sanhedrin can assemble and carry out legal proceedings against him. During this long vigil he is minutely interrogated by Annas, the previous high priest, father-in-law to the officiating high priest, Caiaphas, and by other Jewish leaders, concerning his doctrine, his companions in religion, and his intentions. It is very much disputed whether or not these interrogations before Annas have any official character.[7] Either way, Jesus refuses with dignity to give any more explanations. He is made an object of derision, struck, spat upon in the face, and tortured, scenes described by the Synoptics (and today quite frequent in police circles throughout the world).

The following day, in the southwest corner of the Temple (cf. Luke 22:66), the Sanhedrin assembles with the high priest Caiaphas (which means "Inquisitor"). The session begins with the presentation of the evidence of witnesses. We know nothing concerning the context of the accusation; probably it was a question of the liberal position of Christ concerning the sabbath (Mark 2:23ff.; John 5:9ff.), which constituted a permanent cause for scandal among the Jews, or a question of his being a false prophet and expelling devils in the name of devils (Mark 3:22; Matt. 9:34). The only result of all this was that the witnesses' evidence was conflicting (Mark 14:56). Another grave accusation that at another time led Jeremiah to a death sentence (Jer. 26:1–19) is brought against Jesus: He claimed he would destroy the Temple and raise it up again in three days (Mark 14:58 and John 2:19). But here too the witnesses conflict with one another. Then Caiaphas rises up and enters into action, submitting Jesus to a rigorous interrogation, at the end of which Jesus is declared worthy of death for the crime of blasphemy (Mark 16:64).

In what did this crime of blasphemy consist? According to Mark 14:61–63 it was the fact that when Jesus was asked by the high priest, "Are you the Christ, the Son of the Blessed One," he answered, "I am. And you will see the Son of man seated at the right hand of the Powers and coming with the clouds of heaven." Catholic and Protestant exegetes ask many questions: Is this a historical account or a profession of faith by the primitive community, which in the light of the resurrection interpreted the figure of Jesus as being the Messiah-Christ and the Son of man in Daniel 7?[8] It is difficult to decide this question by exegetical methods. What is certain is that the gospel does not try to be a historical work. It is a profession of faith where history and interpretation of history in the light of faith are amalgamated in a vital unity. In itself, for Jesus to declare himself Messiah-Christ did not constitute blasphemy: Already, before Jesus of Nazareth, various liberators had presented themselves as Messiahs,[9] and they were never condemned to death for this. It would also be problematical were Jesus to express his awareness of himself as preacher and realizer of the kingdom of God by using titles such as Messiah-Christ, Son of man, and others. All seems to indicate, as we shall see in greater detail later, that Christ separated himself from all known and common titles of his time. He was far too original and sovereign to lock himself into the frame of comprehension of a single religious culture.

Based on historical data, however, we can say this: Christ, at least at the end of his life, had a clear awareness of his mission to liberate people from all alienation; he believed that with him the time had come for the breakthrough of the kingdom of God and that with his presence and activity this new order of things had already begun to ferment and manifest itself.[10] This awareness appeared clearly during the solemn interrogation by Caiaphas. To sustain any such pretention is to situate oneself in the sphere of the divine. And this, for a human being, is blasphemy, especially since Jesus provoked an unheard of scandal: On the one hand he arrogated to himself an awareness that partook of the divine and on the other hand he was weak, without adequate means for his mission, and at the mercy of bailiffs. Does not such a figure mock Yahweh's promise of total liberation, especially from political enemies?[11] Confronted with such blasphemy the whole sanhedrin with all its seventy-one members voted: *Lamaweth! Lamaweth!* that is, "Let him be condemned to death!"

A decisive step had been taken. From this moment on

the whole history of the world would be transformed, beginning with Peter, who repents (Mark 14:72), and Judas, who hangs himself (Matt. 27:5; cf. Acts. 1:6–10), and including the possibility of the existence of the church of Christ as bearer of his preaching and life. The political proceedings before the Roman governor, Pontius Pilate, seek to ratify the decision of the sanhedrin. By means of diabolically refined tactics, the accusations in the religious sphere are transformed into defamations of a political nature. Only in this way have they a chance of being heard (see a parallel case with Paul and Gallio in Acts 18:14ff.). They accuse him before Pilate of regarding himself as a political liberator (Messiah), which Jesus never wished to be; they say that he preaches subversion among all the people, beginning with Galilee (Luke 23:25). On hearing the word "Galilee" Pilate is reminded of Herod, who was also in Jerusalem at that time (Luke 23:6–12). As tetrarch of Galilee, scene of the principal activities of Jesus, he was competent to pronounce a decisive word. Christ is brought before Herod and interrogated by him. Jesus' silence irritates him. Herod gives him back to Pilate clothed as a mock king, "and though Herod and Pilate had been enemies before, they were reconciled that same day" (Luke 23:12). By mocking the innocent, even evil people can encounter one another and establish a unifying friendship against an enemy.

Pilate, however, immediately perceives that Jesus is no political revolutionary like the Zealots, nor does he threaten violence against the Romans. Perhaps he may be an ingenuous religious dreamer. Consequently, three times he says: "The man has done nothing that deserves death" (Luke 23:4,15,22). The New Testament, whether for apologetic reasons (the governor ought to testify that Christianity is not a danger to the state) or reflecting on a historical situation, shows three attempts by Pilate to save Jesus when confronted by those who, with ever renewed insistence, shouted, "Crucify him, crucify him" (Luke 23:21): the episode with Herod, the frustrated attempt to exchange Jesus for the guerrilla and bandit Barabbas (Luke 23:17–25), and finally the scene of "Ecce Homo" after the torture (John 19:1–6). On the other hand, we know from other sources of the "corruption, violence, plunder, bad treatment, offenses, continuous executions without trial, and meaningless cruelty" in the personality of Pilate (Philo, *Leg. ad Caium*, 38). He takes pleasure in taunting the Jews, pretending to save the innocent Jesus. Only when confronted with a threat of becoming Caesar's enemy (John 19:12) does he give in to the shouts of the populace and Jewish leaders. John says without pathos: "So in the end Pilate handed him over to them to be crucified" (John 19:16). His *titulus* was yet to be written in three languages: "*Iesus Nazarenus Rex Iudaeorum.*" All is ready. The sacrifice can begin.

According to Roman custom those condemned to death on the cross (generally only slaves and rebels, according to Cicero, *Verrines* 2:5,65,165: "a most barbarous and terrible punishment") were first whipped without mercy.[12] Then they had to carry the crossbar of the cross on their shoulders to the place of execution, where the vertical part was already in the ground. They were stripped, nailed to the crosspiece and raised up on the cross, which normally assumed the form of a T. They remained two or three meters above the ground for hours without end or days, until they approached death by exhaustion, asphyxiation, hemorrhage, a burst heart, or collapse. Jesus remained on the cross from midday until 3 P.M. The Gospels tell us that he spoke seven times, but the historical value of these sayings is very much in dispute. One is in Mark 15:34, the same is in Matt. 27:46, three are in Luke 23:34,43,46, and the other three are in John 19:26,28,30.

One saying, however, leaves no doubt as to its authenticity. This saying constituted the scandal regarding the self-consciousness of Jesus. Mark still preserves its Aramaic formulation: "Eloi, Eloi, lama sabachthani. My God, my God, why have you deserted me?" (Mark 15:34). Christ lived in unparalleled intimacy with his God, calling him "Abba " (You, my beloved daddy); in the name of this God he preached the kingdom of *God* and continuously witnessed to God (Matt. 11:27). The God of love and humanity left Jesus alone, abandoned him. It is Jesus himself who says it. Nevertheless, if God abandoned him, Christ did not abandon God. Consequently, even while declaring his absolute sense of aloneness, he cries out, "*My* God, *my* God . . ."; "he gave a loud cry and breathed his last" (Mark 15:37), thus handing himself over confidently to the one who had abandoned him but who continued to be "*my* God." God's silence on Good Friday, however, will be interrupted on resurrection Sunday.

"HAVING LOVED, . . . HE LOVED . . . TO THE END"

Death was not a catastrophe that came abruptly into the life of Christ. His message, life, and death form a radical unity. Violent death is in one way or another implied in the demands of his preaching. In a celebrated text from Plato's *Republic*, we read: "The just will be whipped, stripped of their skin, tied and blinded with fire. When they have suffered all these pains, they will be nailed to a cross" (2,5,361 E). Jesus never read Plato. Nevertheless, better than this great philosopher, he knows what people and their religious and social security system are capable of doing. He knows that whoever tries to change the human situation for the better and free people for God, for others, and for themselves must pay with death. He knows that all the prophets died a violent death (Luke 11:47–51; 13:34; Mark 12:2). He also knows of the tragic end of the last and greatest of all the prophets, John the Baptist (Mark 9:13).

Jesus makes the following sovereign claim in his

preaching, one that until then had never been validated: God and his kingdom are coming; God is present for all who are converted and have hope, especially for those who judge themselves to be excluded from salvation and mercy; the poor are not sinners because they are poor, nor are people blind because of their own sin or that of their parents (John 9:3). By preaching this, Christ necessarily clashed with the established religious order.[13] Good and evil, he teaches, as determined by the religious or social system, are not necessarily good or bad in themselves. The world of his day said: "The rabble knows nothing about the Law; they are damned" (John 7:49). Jesus preaches especially to this rabble. People who do not wash their hands before eating are impure, according to the law. Christ cannot see how this can be called an impurity. Impurity comes from inside (Mark 7:19–22). It was said that to hate one's enemies is not a sin (Mark 5:43). Christ says: This is a sin and deserving of eternal fire (Matt. 5:22).

Christ came basically to announce that God as well as human persons cannot be imprisoned within preestablished structures, whether social or religious. People must remain continuously open to the unexpected interventions of God. And the world can use and abuse religion to tie people down in the name of God. Consequently, since Jesus comes in the name of God and announces a total liberation, he is regarded by the system as a blasphemer (Mark 2:7), a madman (Mark 3:24), an imposter (Matt. 27:63), possessed (Mark 3:22; John 7:20), and a heretic (John 8:48). True religion can liberate the human person but it can also enslave human beings. It can do great good, but it can also, when abused, do great evil. And should prophets continue to preach their message, they must count on the violence of the established order. With Christ, all is shaken. With him, the old world is finished. And a new one appears, where people have the opportunity to be judged not by what the moral, religious, and cultural conventions determine, but by what—through good sense, love, and total openness to God and others—is discovered as the concrete will of God.

The Faith and Hope of Jesus

Christ never allowed himself to be determined by the world around him. Sovereign, he entered upon no compromises, but firmly lived out what he judged to be the will of God, the source of happiness and liberation. Faith for the Old and New Testaments is the power to say Yes and Amen to God as God is discovered through life by existing with and basing oneself on God as the absolute meaning of all things; it is a continuous returning to and grasping on to God. According to this definition, Jesus was an extraordinary believer and had faith.[14] Faith was Jesus' way of life.[15] He always allowed himself to be determined by God and the other and never simply took the religious norms and social conventions of the day to be his point of departure. He suffered the contradictions, risks, and temptations that the adventure of faith implies.

The Epistle to the Hebrews rightly presents Christ as an example of someone who believed and could therefore endure the cross, "disregarding the shamefulness of it" (Heb. 12:2). Thus, his faith and hope were especially tried as he perceived the uncompromising opposition that his message and person encountered in the various social strata of his day. At a certain moment, during the so-called Galilean crisis (Mark 9:27ff.; Luke 9:37), Jesus took into account the real possibility of his violent death. Luke 9:51 says that he "hardened his face," that is, he resolutely decided to go to Jerusalem: "Jesus was walking on ahead of them, they were in a daze and those who followed were apprehensive" (Mark 10:32). He went to announce and await the kingdom of

God there. He never withdrew his step. He believed in his liberating mission and hoped against all hope.

Did Jesus Expect a Violent Death?

From the moment we consider the self-consciousness of Jesus, this question is legitimate: He understood himself as the proclaimer of the new order soon to be introduced by God. He himself is the kingdom already present; belonging to the kingdom depends on one's acceptance or rejection of his person. The kingdom of God signifies the total liberation of all reality from all the elements that alienate it, ranging from pain, death, hate, and legalism to sin against God. This being the case, could Jesus expect his violent death? The Gospels, as we know them today, make it clear that Jesus knew of his fatal destiny. Three times he prophesied his sufferings (Mark 8:31; 9:31; 10:32–34) and took each death upon himself as a sacrifice for the redemption of many (all) (Mark 10:45; Luke 22:19f.; Matt. 26:26,28). Nevertheless since the beginning of this century serious exegesis has asked: Are these authentic texts of Christ or a theological interpretation elaborated by the primitive community in the light of faith and the originality of the resurrection?[16] The prophecies are literarily late and presuppose a detailed knowledge of the passion and resurrection. It really appears as though they are *vaticinia ex eventu,* formulated after the fact with a view to making sense of the theological problem contained in the question: If God by the resurrection showed himself to be with Christ, why did he not show this beforehand?

The prophecies would resolve this real problem for the primitive community. The saying, "The Son of man himself did not come to be served but to serve and to give his life as a ransom for many" (Mark 10:45), is one of the most debated in the New Testament. It appears as though in its present formulation it was put on the lips of Christ by the community because its parallel in Luke does not have a soteriological character: "Here am I among you as one who serves."[17] The debate is even sharper concerning the historical content of the eucharistic texts that are sacrificial in nature (cf. 1 Cor. 11:23–26; Mark 14:22–25; Luke 22:15–20; Matt. 26:26–29); these, it seems, presuppose an existing theology and eucharistic praxis on the part of the primitive church.[18] Since Luke's text (22:15–19a,29) "describes a happening that has no organic connection with the life of the church, but only with Christ himself,"[19] all seems to indicate that this is an authentic text. The text is as follows:

"I have longed to eat this passover with you before I suffer; because I tell you, I shall not eat it again until it is fulfilled in the kingdom of God." Then taking a cup, he gave thanks and said, "Take this and share it among you, because from now on, I tell you, I shall not drink wine until the kingdom of God comes! . . . And now I confer a kingdom on you, just as my Father conferred one on me: you will eat and drink at my table in my kingdom, and you will sit on thrones to judge the twelve tribes of Israel."

The Last Supper, according to Luke's text, has an eschatological character. It was an anticipation of the kingdom of God that Christ wished to celebrate with his friends and more intimate acquaintances before the breakthrough of the new order.[20]

From this the question follows: Did Christ expect a violent death? To answer this question it is necessary to remember the following: Christ was conscious of being a determining instrument in the total coming of the kingdom. All the Gospels show the nature of his intimacy with God: he did his will in all things as it manifested itself concretely in his life as preacher and miracle worker, in interactions with the people, in the disputes with the religious authorities of the time. Jesus lived in faith, in the sense explained above, and went about discovering the will of God little by little and ever more clearly. He could even be tempted (Mark 1:12–13; Luke 4:1–13; Matt. 4:1–11; cf. Luke 22:28; Heb. 2:18; 5:15), and not know exactly what future awaited him.

In the apocalyptic atmosphere in which Jesus lived, it was believed that the breakthrough of the kingdom would take place after a great battle between the forces of good and evil. At the end of his public life, when he felt more and more isolated and opposed, his words became solemn (cf. Mark 8:27ff.). Jesus took into account the fact that it is through suffering that one enters the kingdom. Luke preserves one of his sayings that is certainly authentic: "There is a baptism I must still receive and how great is my distress until it is over!" (12:50). Whether this baptism signifies that violent death or some other great plight is about to befall him is certainly not clear to Christ himself. But he remains faithful and never flinches. He knows himself to be in the hands of the Father. He is confident and hopes that God, in the midst of the great difficulties through which he may have to pass, will intervene to save him. The important thing, however, is not to do his own will but that of the Father. And right to the end he does not know exactly whether this implies merely great difficulties or death itself.

Jesus' final great temptation in Gethsemane shows anguish and uncertainty but also his fundamental resolution to always do the will of God: " 'Abba (Father)! ' he said. 'Everything is possible for you. Take this cup away from me. But let it be as you, not I, would have it' "(Mark 14:36).[21] Jesus perceived the possibility of death, but he was not absolutely sure of it. The final cry from the height of the cross, "My God, my God, why have you deserted me?" (Mark 15:34) presupposes unshakeable faith and the hope that God would not let him die but would finally save him. Now, however, on the cross, he knows with full certainty: God wants him to be faithful to his end in death. John marvelously expresses the fidelity of Jesus when on introducing the passion he says: "He had always loved those who were his care in the world, but now he showed how perfect his love was" (John 13:1). Christ accepts the unjust death inflicted by people's hatred as the final will of the Father. Hence, the evangelists express well Jesus' state of mind when they have him say: "It is accomplished" (John 19:30), "Father, into your hands I commit my spirit" (Luke 23:46). It is a final expression of acceptance of his tragic end.

THE MEANINGLESS HAS A SECRET MEANING

What is the meaning of the death of Christ? The apostles were taken by surprise. They fled (Mark 14:27; Matt. 26:31). The imprisonment of Jesus had already provoked the dissolution and dispersal of their community (Mark 14:27; Matt. 26:31). The oldest texts concerning the apparitions of the resurrected tell us that these occurred first in Galilee (Mark 14:28; 16:7; Matt. 26:32; 28:7,16–20). This makes us assume that after the failure of Christ, the apostles returned to Galilee. The youths from Emmaus testify to the frustration of the apostles: "Our own hope had been that he would be the one to set Israel free" (Luke 24:21). Moreover, Jesus died on the cross. Death on the cross, this terrible method of punishment, originated with the Persians. (Herodotus 3,15,9, tells us that in 519 B.C. three thousand rebels were crucified in Babylonia.) Crucifixion was taken over by the Romans. For the Jews, it signified the visible sign of God's damnation (Deut. 21:23; Gal. 3:13) and the ultimate essence in shame and ignominy (Heb. 12:2). According to the Jewish mentality Jesus was actually abandoned by God by the very fact of being crucified.

Everything seems to indicate that in the beginning

the apostles did not see any salvific significance in the death of Christ.[22] Peter's discourses in Acts allow us to perceive this fact. There he says in antithetical form: "You took him and had him crucified by men outside the Law. God however ... raised him from the dead" (Acts 2:23,36; 3:14–15; 4:10; 5:30). Only after the resurrection did they decipher with growing clarity the meaning of death and resurrection as two scenes of the same salvific act. The death of Christ is then seen as pardon for our sins (1 Cor. 15:3). In this light the evangelical sayings were elaborated and placed by faith in the mouth of Jesus: that he would be handed over and die (Mark 8:31; 9:31; 10:32–34), that he would drink of the chalice of suffering (Mark 10:30), that he would be baptized with the baptism of blood (Mark 10:38; cf. Luke 12:50), that he would give his life for the redemption of many (Mark 10:45), etc.

We will analyze later this theological meaning acquired after and in the light of the resurrection. Notwithstanding this interpretation of the community as divine revelation brought by the resurrection, it is worth asking: Has the death of Christ, considered in itself, theological relevance for us today? Yes it has, and very great meaning indeed, for the following reasons: The whole life of Christ was a giving, a being-for-others, an attempt to overcome all conflicts in his own existence, and a realization of this goal. Jesus lived the human archetype just as God wanted, when he made him to his own image and likeness; Jesus always judged and spoke with God as his reference and starting point. Jesus thereby revealed a life of extraordinary authenticity and originality. By his preaching of the kingdom of God he lived his being-for-others to the end, experiencing the depths of despair of the death (absence) of God on the cross. In spite of the total disaster and debacle he did not despair. He was confident and believed up to the end that God would accept him as he was. The meaningless still had for him a secret and ultimate meaning.

The universal meaning of the life and death of Christ, therefore, is that he sustained the fundamental conflict of human existence to the end: He wanted to realize the absolute meaning of this world before God, in spite of hate, incomprehension, betrayal, and condemnation to death.[23] For Jesus, evil does not exist in order to be comprehended, but to be taken over and conquered by love. This comportment of Jesus opened up a new possibility for human existence, i.e., an existence of faith with absolute meaning, even when confronted with the absurd, as was his own death—caused by hate for one who only loved and only sought to do good among people. Hence, Bonhoeffer can say that a Christian today is called to live this weakness of God in the world. "Jesus does not call us to a new religion. Jesus calls us to life.What sort of life? To participate in the weakness of God in the world."[24] This kind of life is a new life and triumphs where all ideologies and human speculations fail, i.e., in despair, in unmerited suffering, in injustice, in violent death.

Is there meaning in all this? Yes. But only when taken on before God, in love and hope that goes beyond death. To believe in this manner is to believe with Jesus who believed. To follow him is to realize the same comportment within our own conditions of life that are no longer his. The resurrection reveals in all its profundity that to believe and persevere in the absurd and meaningless is not without meaning.

In a celebrated poem Bonhoeffer expressed well the profound meaning of the passion for the life of a Christian:

Men go to God when they are sore bestead,
Pray to him for succour, for his peace, for bread,
For mercy for them sick, sinning, or dead;
All men do so, Christian and unbelieving.

Men go to God when he is sore bestead,
Find him poor and scorned, without shelter or bread.
Whelmed under weight of the wicked, the weak, the dead;
Christians stand by God in his hour of grieving.

God goes to everyman when sore bestead,
Feeds body and spirit with his bread;
For Christians, pagans alike he hangs dead,
And both alike forgiving.[25]

Resurrection: The Realization
of a Human Utopia

*Because he rose from the dead, Jesus possesses a decisive
significance for us. In this lies the central nucleus of
Christian faith. Because of the fact of resurrection we
know that life and meaningless death now have meaning.
A door was opened for us to an absolute future and an
ineradicable hope penetrated the human heart. If he, in
truth, arose, then we will follow him and "all men will be
brought to life in Christ" (1 Cor. 15:20,22).*

Jesus announced an absolute meaning to the world as
a total liberation from all alienations that stigmatize
human existence: from pain, from hatred, from sin, and
finally from death as well. His presence made real such a
structural revolution of the foundations of the old
world; he called it, in the language of the time, "the
kingdom of God." Nevertheless, contrary to what one
would expect of him (cf. Luke 24:21), he died on the cross
with the following protest on his lips: "My God, my God,
why have you deserted me?" (Mark 15:34). His death not
only seemed to have buried all hopes for liberation but

also destroyed the first faith of the disciples. The flight of the apostles (Mark 15:50), the frustration of the youths from Emmaus (Luke 24:21), and fear of the Jews (John 20:19) suggest this with sufficient clarity.[1] Had death been stronger than so great a love? Would death and not life be the last word that God pronounced concerning the destiny of Jesus of Nazareth and all human beings?

THE GRASS DID NOT GROW ON THE SEPULCHER OF JESUS

A few days after Jesus' death an unheard of event, unique in the history of humankind, occurred: God raised him up (Acts 2:23; 3:15; 4:10; 10:39–40) and revealed him to his intimate disciples—not as one who returns to the biological life that he had before, such as Lazarus or the youth from Naim, but as one who while conserving his identity as Jesus of Nazareth manifested himself as totally transfigured and fully realized in his human and divine possibilities. What occurred was not the revitalization of a cadaver but a radical transformation and transfiguration of the earthly reality of Jesus, that is, resurrection.

Now all was revealed: God had not abandoned Jesus of Nazareth. He was by his side, at the side of him who, according to the law, was damned (Deut. 21:23; Gal. 3:13; cf. Heb. 4:15). He did not allow the grass to grow on Jesus' sepulcher. God broke all the fetters and Jesus emerged to a life no longer threatened by death but marked for eternity. *Now* the truthfulness of Jesus' preaching was demonstrated: The resurrection is the realization of his announcement of total liberation, especially from the reign of death. The resurrection signifies a concretization of the kingdom of God in the life of Jesus. If humanity's rejection prevented the cosmic realization of the kingdom, God, who is victorious in failure and makes life victorious in death, nevertheless realized it in the existence of Jesus of Nazareth. *Now* we know: Life and meaningless death have their meaning assured in the resurrection of Jesus. Paul, thinking of this, was triumphant and could playfully say: "Death is swallowed up in victory. Death, where is your victory? Death, where is your sting?" (1 Cor. 15:55).

Because he arose, Jesus possesses a decisive significance for us. If he had not arisen, then "your believing is useless" and "we are the most unfortunate of people" (1 Cor. 15:14–19). Instead of joining those that say, "Let us eat and drink today, tomorrow we shall be dead" (1 Cor. 15:32), we would be running away from reality to a myth of survival and resurrection and we would also be leading others astray. However, if Jesus, in truth, did arise, then we will follow him and "all men will be brought to life in Christ" (1 Cor. 20:22). A door was opened for us to an absolute future and an ineradicable hope penetrated the human heart. In this lies the central nucleus of Christian faith. The faith cannot be sustained without this.

At this point, historians are of little use to us. The resurrection is not an ordinary historical fact capable of being grasped by historians. It is a fact grasped only by faith. No one saw the resurrection. The apocryphal Gospel of St. Peter (*c.* A.D. 150), which in imaginative language narrates *how* Christ arose, was rejected by the church, more than likely because Christian consciousness at an early date perceived that one cannot speak of the resurrection of the Lord in such a detailed manner. What we possess are the apparitions and an empty sepulcher. On the basis of these experiences, the apostles, radiant with joy, came to the following true interpretation that touched upon the reality of the new life of Jesus: "The Lord has risen and has appeared to Simon" (Luke 24:34). To secure the reality of faith in the resurrection, questioned by so many today,[2] and to "have your answer ready for people who ask you the reason for the hope that you all have" (1 Pet. 3:15), we ought to reflect briefly on the basic biblical data.[3]

WHAT DOES MODERN EXEGESIS SAY ABOUT
THE RESURRECTION OF JESUS?

As we said, there are two decisive facts in the accounts concerning the resurrection of Jesus: the empty sepulcher and the apparitions to the disciples. According to serious Catholic and Protestant studies[4] concerning the traditions that, collected or edited, gave origin to the present Gospels, the following is established: At first the two accounts were circulated autonomously among the first Christians and without reference to one another. Later, as one can see in Mark 16:1–8, when the Gospels were composed, the two traditions were woven together, though not without internal tensions. The accounts that spoke only of the empty sepulcher now assimilated the accounts concerning the apparitions. The old tradition in Mark 16:5a,8 said this: The women went to the sepulcher; they found it empty; they fled; they told no one because of fear. The apparition of the angel (Mark 16:5b–7) and, in John, of the resurrected Jesus himself (John 20:11ff.) would be an addition from the other tradition, which knows only about the apparitions and not about the empty sepulcher.

The Empty Sepulcher Did Not Give
Rise to Faith in the Resurrection

When we look closely, we see that the fact of the empty sepulcher is not adduced as proof of the resurrection by any evangelist. Instead of provoking faith, it gave rise to fear, fright, and palpitation, so much that "the women fled from the sepulcher" (Mark 16:8; Matt. 28:8; Luke 24:4). The fact was interpreted by Mary Magdalene as a "stealing of the body of the Lord" (John 20:2,13,15). For the apostles, the fact is no more than women's talk (Luke 24:11,22–24,34). As is apparent the empty sepulcher, taken by itself, is an ambiguous sign, subject to various interpretations, one of which might be the resurrection. But there is no intrinsic necessity that obliges such a conclusion. It is only with the apparitions that its ambiguity is cleared up and it can be read by faith as a sign of the resurrection of Jesus. As such, the empty sepulcher is a sign that makes people think and brings them to reflect on the possibility of the resurrection. It is an invitation to faith. It is not yet faith.

Faith that the Lord arose—and here lies the reason for the empty sepulcher—is expressed in the language of the time. The explanation is placed on the lips of an angel: "Jesus of Nazareth has risen, he is not here. See, here is the place where they laid him" (Mark 16:6c). Without wanting to question the existence of angels, we need not admit, according to the biblical criteria themselves, that an angel appeared beside the sepulcher. The angel, especially in post-exilic Judaism, substituted for Yahweh-God in his transcendence as manifesting himself to men (cf. Gen. 22:11–14; Exod. 3:2–6; Matt. 1:20). The women who saw the empty sepulcher knew of the Lord's apparitions to the apostles in Galilee. They immediately guessed the right meaning: The sepulcher is empty, not because someone stole Jesus' body, but because he has risen. This interpretation of the women is held to be a revelation of God. It is expressed in the common language of the time as being a message from an angel (God).[5]

The Apparitions of Christ:
The Origin of Faith in the Resurrection

What really took away all ambiguity concerning the empty sepulcher and gave origin to the exclamation of faith among the apostles—He has really arisen!—were the apparitions. The oldest formulations in 1 Cor. 15:3b–5 and in Acts 2–5, clearly show us, because of their rigid formulation and lack of pathos, that these apparitions were not subjective visions, products of the faith of the community, but really trans-subjective apparitions, a witness to an impact that imposed itself from outside.[6] All exegetes today, both Catholic and Protestant, even the most radical, agree on this.[7] How many apparitions there were, their precise location, and who were the people favored is difficult to determine historically. The current evangelical texts reflect a number of tendencies—apologetic, theological, cultic—that colored primitive traditions in a palpable manner. The oldest text (1 Cor. 15:5–8, from the years between 54 and 57) contains five apparitions of the living Lord. Mark 16:1–8 has none, but clearly states that the resurrected Jesus will be seen in Galilee (7b). The end of Mark 16:9–20 condenses the apparitions related in the other Gospels and for good reasons can be regarded as a later addition. Matt. 28:16–20 knows of only one apparition to the Eleven. The other apparition to the women at the entrance to the sepulcher (28:8–9) is seen by exegetes as a later elaboration on the text in Mark 16:7: The words of the resurrected Jesus are noticeably like those of the angel. Luke 24:13–53 refers to two apparitions: one to the youths from Emmaus and the other to the Eleven and his disciples in Jerusalem. John relates three manifestations of the Lord, all in Jerusalem.[8]

These accounts reveal two fundamental tendencies: Mark and Matthew are interested in Galilee; Luke and John concentrate on Jerusalem and emphasize the corporal reality of Jesus and the identity of the resurrected Christ with Jesus of Nazareth. The work of serious exegetes allows us to affirm that the appearances in Galilee are historically certain. Those in Jerusalem would be the same as those of Galilee, transferred however for theological reasons to Jerusalem.[9] For the Bible, Jerusalem possesses a salvation-history meaning of the first order: "Salvation comes from Zion (Jerusalem)" (Pss. 13:7; 109:2; Isa. 2:3; cf. Rom. 11:26). Jesus' death, Easter, and Pentecost, which are theologically exploited by Luke and John, occurred there.

The Gospels transmit to us the following facts concerning the manner of these apparitions: They are described as a real and bodily presence of Jesus. He eats, walks with his friends, allows himself to be touched, listens to and converses with them. His presence is so real that he can be confused with a traveller, a gardener, and a fisherman. Side by side with this there are strange phenomena: He appears and disappears. He goes through walls. Close observation shows that in the older texts (such as 1 Cor. 15:5–8; Acts 3:15; 9:3; 26:16; Gal. 1:15; and Matt. 28); there is a surprising spiritualized representation of the resurrection. But more recent texts, such as Luke and John, denote an ever increasing materialization, culminating in the apocryphal Gospels of Peter to the Hebrews and in the "Epistle of the Apostles." This is explained when we consider that the Pasch of Christ in the oldest interpretation, witnessed in Acts 2–5, in Luke 24:26, and in Phil. 2:6–11, was not yet conceived in terms of resurrection, but of the *elevation* and *glorification* of a just sufferer. This interpretation is in the apocalyptic vein.

In time, however, owing to the polemics, especially with the Hellenic converts, it was questioned whether the glorification of Christ and his enthronement at the side of God also implied a corporal life. It was asked: Is the Jesus of glory the same as Jesus of Nazareth? Then the primitive community, especially with Luke and John, interpreted the apparitions and empty sepulcher within another horizon of comprehension more adapted to the questions posed, namely, the eschatological horizon, and began to use the terminology of *resurrection*. Christ, in his terrestrial and corporal reality was totally transfigured by the resurrection: He is not a "spirit" (Luke 24:39), nor an "angel" (Acts 23:8–9). The one who died and was buried is the one who arose (1 Cor. 15: 3b–5).[10] Hence the preoccupation with accentuating the wounds (Luke 24:39; John 20:20,25–29), the fact that he ate and drank with his disciples (Acts 10:41), or that he ate before them (Luke 24:43). The accounts concerning the experiences of the resurrected Jesus by individual people—such as Mary Magdalene (John 20:14–18; cf. Matt. 28:9–10) or the two youths from Emmaus (Luke 24:13–35)—are surrounded by theological and apologetic motifs, within the literary schema of legends, so as to make clear to the readers the reality of the living Lord present in the community. The account of the two youths from Emmaus seeks to assure the later community, who no longer had apparitions of the Lord, that it too has access to the resurrected Jesus by means of the words of Scripture and by the sacrament of the breaking of bread, just as the two youths on the way to their city.[11]

A few things are made very clear by all this: The resurrection is not the theological creation of some enthusiastic follower of the person from Nazareth. Faith in the resurrection is the fruit of the impact on the apostles of the apparitions of the living Lord. They were startled and overcome by this impact that was beyond their capacities of representation. Without this, they would never have preached the crucified Jesus as Lord. Without this "something" that happened in Jesus, there would never have been a church, worship, nor glory given to the name of this prophet from Nazareth. Much less would there have been the greatest witness to this truth: the martyrdom of so many in the early church.

However, in asserting belief in the resurrection one not only affirms the *magnalia Dei* that occurred in the life of Jesus. One also gives witness to the possibility of a transfiguration and a total realization of the possibilities of this present world; one affirms that eternal life comes to transform human life and that God can realize his kingdom in the human person. A scandal to many (cf. 1 Cor. 1:23; Acts 17:32), the resurrection is hope and certainty of eternal life for all and for the world (cf. 1 Pet. 1:3; 1 Cor. 15:50ff.). Consequently the early church, faced with the resurrection of Christ, proclaimed its significance *for us* as hope (1 Pet. 1:3) of a future life, as total liberation from our fundamental schizophrenia called sin (1 Cor. 15:3,17; Rom. 4:25; Luke 24:37; Acts 10:43). "But Christ in fact has been raised from the dead, the first fruits of all who have fallen asleep" (1 Cor. 15:20; Col. 1:18). He is "the eldest of many brothers" (Rom. 8:29). What is present for him right now will be the proximate future for us all.

THE RESURRECTION ELUCIDATES ALL

The resurrection brought about a complete reversal in the apostles.[12] They acquired a new horizon and new eyes; in a completely new way they could read the human reality of the past, present, and future. It is appropriate that we develop a few aspects of the significance of the resurrection for the primitive community.

The Resurrection Rehabilitated Jesus Before the World

In the eyes of the world Christ's death on the cross made him a person abandoned by God (Gal. 3:13). The faith that the apostles placed in him, evidenced by the fact that they followed him, preached the good news of the kingdom, and persevered in the time of Jesus' temptations, was now broken. The word of Christ was realized in them: "You will all lose faith" (Mark 14:27; Matt. 26:31). They simply fled and returned to Galilee (Mark 14:50; Matt. 25:26). Now all is revolutionized: They return to a belief in him, not as a messiah and nationalist liberator (note the request of the sons of Zebedee: Mark 10:37; Matt. 20:21; cf. Luke 19:11; 22:38; 24:21; Acts 1:6), but as the Son of Man of Dan. 7: "elevated" and "made to sit at the right hand of God" and "enthroned as the Son of God in power" (cf. Rom. 1:4; Acts 13:33; Matt. 28:18). With all courage, they profess their faith before the Jews: "You had him crucified by men outside the Law. You killed him, but God raised him to life" (Acts 2:23f.; 3:15; 4:10; 5:30; 10:39f.). This faith, as we shall see, will be articulated in ever greater and more penetrating depth until they come to decipher the mystery of Jesus as being God himself, who visited human beings in mortal flesh.

With the Resurrection, the End of the World Has Already Begun

The solid faith of the primitive church held that the resurrection inaugurated the end of the world. Matthew insinuates this conviction even in the literary form he uses to relate the resurrection of Jesus (28:1–5): the descent of the angel, the earthquake, the removal of the rock, the confusion of the guards, as well as the phenomena that occurred at the time of Christ's death, namely, "the bodies of the holy men rose from the dead" (Matt. 27:51–53); all these events reveal clear apocalyptical traces. With the emergence of Christ from the sepulcher the new heaven and the new earth already began to ferment in the heart of the old world: The end, with the resurrection of the rest of the human race, especially those who believe, is imminent (cf. Rom. 5:12; 1 Cor. 15:45ff.; 2 Cor. 5:10). Christ is the firstborn from among the dead; others will follow him shortly (1 Cor. 15:20; Rom. 8:29; Col. 1:18). The same Spirit, by which Christ was resurrected, is already living in the faithful (Rom. 8:11) and forming in all a body of glory.

The Resurrection Revealed That Jesus Died for Our Sins

Fundamentally the resurrection came to reveal that Christ was not a bandit, one abandoned by God, nor was he a false prophet or a false messiah. By means of the resurrection God rehabilitated him before the human race. "It was the stone rejected by the builders that became the keystone" (Mark 12:10). Wickedness, legalism, and hatred had dragged him to the cross, though they may have done so in the name of the holy Law and the current regime. After the resurrection the primitive community began to ask: Why did Christ have to die, if God afterward resurrected him? If God showed by the resurrection that he is on the side of Christ, why did he not show this during his public life? The youths from Emmaus show how much this question interested the early church. They consulted the Scriptures, did theological work, and reflected in the light of the resurrection in order to decipher this profound mystery.

The disciples of Jesus, as portrayed in the evangelical texts called Q,[13] did not yet attribute a salvific character to the death of Christ. For them, Jesus participated in the common destiny of all prophets, violent death (cf. Luke 11:49ff. and parallel passages); Luke 13:34 and par.; 1 Thess. 2:14ff.; Acts 7:51ff.). Nevertheless God exalted him and constituted him Son of Man, about to come in the clouds. This is the image of Christ given us in the Q. Another group in the Palestinian Christian community sought to interpret the tragic death of Christ as a realization of a hidden and preordained plan of God (Acts 2:23; 4:28). It was in this sense they said that Christ "had to die" (Mark 8:31); it was already prophesied in the Scriptures of the Old Testament (Mark 14:49).

In the same line of interpretation the prophecies of Jesus concerning his death and resurrection were conceived, all of which were probably elaborated after the resurrection (Mark 8:31; 9:31; 14:41). His death and resurrection become comprehensible if inserted into the plan of God. Nevertheless this did not explain why the bloody path of Jesus was "necessary" for salvation history. The church sought to decipher its secret meaning. What could be the meaning of the violent death of a just person? Had not the earthly Christ said: "I am among you as one who serves" (Luke 22:27)?

Little by little the Palestinian community began to interpret the death of Christ as an extreme form of service to humanity. It is in this context that it is said: "For the Son of man himself did not come to be served but to serve, and to give his life as a ransom for many" (Mark 10:45). This interpretation was possible because in the milieu of later Judaism and Hellenism the idea was circulated that the death of the martyrs and even of innocent children could assume a representative and redemptive character for sinners (cf. 2 Macc. 7:32,37; cf. 7:18; 2 Macc. 6:28ff.; 17:20–22; 18:4). Isaiah 53 clearly refers to the suffering servant: "and yet ours were the sufferings he bore, ours the sorrows he carried" (v. 4). Though innocent, "Yahweh burdened him with the sins of all of us" (v. 6). However this punishment saved us and "through his wounds we are healed" (v. 5). With such an interpretation the community wanted to express what had already emerged in the life and words of Jesus of Nazareth: After his unjustly inflicted death, God turned to the lost and sinners and invited them to communion with him. A step forward was taken when they interpreted his death as sacrificial expiation for the sins of the world, as appears in Rom. 3:25 and the epistle to the Hebrews. This thought is already contained in the words of the last supper, when he speaks of the blood that will be shed for us (Mark 14:24; Luke 22:20; Matt. 26:8: "for the remission of sins").

Another explanation of the death of Christ is articulated by Paul: the cross signifies the end of the Law— "For our sake God made the sinless one into sin, so that in him we might become the goodness of God" (2 Cor. 5:21). By means of the cross Jesus, the sinless one, took on himself the whole curse of the Law (cf. Deut. 21:23: "for one who has been hanged is accursed of God") and so fulfilled all his demands. By doing this, he abolished the law (Gal. 3:13; 2:13f.; Eph. 2:14–16).

All these interpretations of the early church are attempts, using the representative material and their own way of looking at reality, to give meaning to the death of Christ.[14] The resurrection projected an illuminating light on the meaninglessness of his martyrdom. All, in spite of the diversity in the modes of representation, are unanimous in this: Christ did not die because of his sins and guilt (2 Cor. 5:21; 1 Pet. 2:21ff.; 3:18), but because of the wickedness of human beings. As we have seen, the interpretation of the death of Christ as sacrifice is one among many. The New Testament texts themselves do not allow this interpretation to be absolutized as it has been in the history of the faith within the Latin church.

Nevertheless we ought to say that Christ's death was a consequence of the atmosphere of ill-will, hatred, and selfishness in which the Jews and all humanity lived and still live today. Jesus did not allow himself to be determined by this situation, but loved us to the end. He took on himself this perverted condition; he was in solidarity with us. He died alone so that no one else in the world would die alone; he is with each person so that all might partake of the life that manifested itself in the resurrection: eternal life in communion with God, with others, and with the cosmos.

Jesus' Death and Resurrection Give Origin to the Church

Because of the rejection of the Jews, the kingdom of God, which in the preaching of Jesus had a cosmic dimension, can be realized only in a single person, that is, in Jesus of Nazareth. As Origen said, Christ is the *autobasileia tou Theou:* God realized his kingdom only in his Envoy. Consequently a path was opened up for a church with the same mission and message as Christ: little by little to announce and bring about the kingdom of God among human beings.[15] The good news ought to be announced, not only to the Jews but to all, that the final destiny of humankind and all reality is good and this destiny is corporal and eternal life. The church carries the cause of Christ forward in the world, at the same time giving witness to and realizing it under the veils of faith, love, hope, and mystery. This mission emerged from the conviction that the resurrected Jesus, now in heaven and carried up in power, is the Lord of all.[16] We are urged to announce and bring to all, Jews and pagans, adhesion to whatsoever this signifies in terms of pardon for sin, reconciliation, a certainty of the total openness and accessibility of God the Father, and finally a certainty of liberation from forces that arrogate divine powers to themselves in this world and seek to be venerated as divine.

THE ANTHROPOLOGICAL RELEVANCE OF THE RESURRECTION OF JESUS

Because of the resurrection of Jesus, Christianity is not a nostalgic religion that commemorates the past. It is a religion of the present that celebrates the certainty of a living and personal presence. Christianity thus came to answer the most poignant problem of the human heart: What is to become of humankind?

For the Christian, There Is No Longer Utopia but Only Topia

The human person is essentially a being on the road to itself. People seek to realize themselves on all levels: in body, soul, and spirit; in biological, spiritual, and cultural life. But this desire is continuously obstructed by frustration, suffering, the absence of love, and the lack of unity with self and others. The hope-principle that is part of human nature leads people continuously to elaborate utopias: Plato's Republic, Campanella's City of Sun, Kant's City of Eternal Peace, Marx's Proletarian Paradise, Hegel's Absolute State, Teilhard de Chardin's Total Amorization, or, if we wish, the utopias of our Tupi-Guarani and Apapocuva-Guarani Indians where there are neither tears, nor hunger and thirst.[17] We all sigh with Paul: "Who will rescue me from this body

doomed to death?" (Rom. 7:24) And with the author of
Revelation we long for the situation where "there will
be no death, and no more mourning or sadness. The
world of the past has gone" (Rev. 21:4).

The resurrection of Jesus seeks to be this utopia
realized within the world, because resurrection signifies an eschatologization of human reality, an introduction of the human person, body and soul, into the
kingdom of God, a total realization of the capacities God
placed within human existence. With this, all the
alienating elements that lacerated life have been an-
nihilated, such as death, pain, hatred, and sin. For the
Christian, as of the moment of the resurrection there is
no more *utopia* (in Greek: that which does not exist
anywhere) but only *topia* (that which exists some-
where). Human hope was realized in Jesus resurrected
and is already being realized in each person. To the
question: What is to become of humankind? Christian
faith joyfully answers: resurrection, as total transfiguration of the human reality, both corporal and spiritual.

God Did Not Substitute a New World
for the Old One: He Makes the Old New

One question interests us all: How are we going to be
resurrected? Paul answers: The dead will rise up imperishable, glorious and powerful, in a human reality
full of the spirit of God (cf. 1 Cor. 15:42–44). He even
speaks of an embodied spirit (44a,b). However, we should
clarify this point: To the Pauline and Semitic mentality,
"body" does not signify body as a component of the
human being distinct from soul. "Body" refers to the
whole human being (body and soul) as person, in relationship with others.[18] "Body" refers to human beings in
their capacity for communication.

Now in the present situation, the human being as
body possesses a terrestrial and perceivable life. In the

resurrection, the human being as body receives from God an immortal life and is free from all threat of corruption. The human being as body is transformed from carnal to spiritual (that is, God-filled) existence. Paul insists: "because our present perishable nature [human being] must put on imperishability and this mortal nature [human being as body] must put on immortality" (1 Cor. 15:53). The human being as body, as it is now (flesh and blood), "cannot inherit the kingdom of God" (resurrection: 1 Cor. 15:50a). It must be changed (52b): "to have what must die taken up into life" (2 Cor. 5:4c). Do not think that the resurrected body is completely new; rather God makes the old new. "Body" also does not signify cadaver, nor the physical-chemical conglomerate of our living cells. Body is something more profound: It is the consciousness of human matter or the spirit manifesting and realizing itself within the world. Every so often the matter of our body changes and is modified, yet we always maintain our corporal identity. When we say "I," we express our corporal-spiritual identity. The resurrection transforms our corporal-spiritual "I" into the image of the resurrected Jesus.

The Goal of God's Path: The Human Being as Body

If the human being as body is the whole human person in its capacity to communicate, then the resurrection concretizes and potentializes this to the maximum degree. Already, in its terrestrial situation, the human being-body is communion and presence, a giving and an opening of oneself to others, because it is the body that makes us present to the world and to others. However, at the same time that it communicates, it impedes communication. We cannot be in two places at the same time. We are prisoners of space and time. Communication takes place by means of codes and symbols that are generally ambiguous. All these impediments are destroyed by the resurrection: Total communion reigns;

there is absolute communication with persons and things; the human being, now spiritual body, has a cosmic presence. As we see, the goal of God's path is the human being as body, totally transfigured and made total openness and communication.[19]

Resurrection in Death?

The forces of the coming age are already acting within the heart of the old world (Heb. 6:5). By faith and hope, by following Christ, and by the sacraments, the seed of the resurrection (Jesus himself) is deposited within the reality of the human being as body. It will not be lost in death: "One who believes in the Son has eternal life" (John 3:36; 3:15–16; 11:26; 5:24). All who are clothed with Christ are new creatures (Gal. 3:27; and 2 Cor. 5:17). The being-in-Christ is the beginning of resurrected living and death is a form of being-in-Christ (Phil. 1:23; 2 Cor. 5:8; 1 Thess. 5:10). We will be transformed into the likeness of Christ (Phil. 3:21). Now all that is seed in human beings will receive in death its full reality and definitive character. Just as death is a passage to eternity where there is no such thing as time, so too eschatology will be realized with the resurrection of the dead.[20]

The parousia will reveal what had already been verified at the end of our personal world. At the time of death the human being, the unity of body-soul, will enter into a total and definitive realization of that which was sown on earth: resurrection for life or death. The cadaver can stay behind and be handed over to corruption; our true body, personalized by "I" (which is more than physical-chemical matter) will participate in eternal life. Vatican II teaches us with Christian optimism:

We do not know the time for the consummation of the earth and of humanity. Nor do we know how all things will be transformed. As deformed by sin, the shape of this world will pass away. But we are taught that God is preparing a new dwelling place and a new earth. . . . The expectation of a new earth must

not weaken but rather stimulate our concern for cultivating
this one. For here grows the body of a new human family, a
body which even now is able to give some kind of foreshadow-
ing of the new age. . . . On this earth that kingdom is already
present in mystery. When the Lord returns, it will be brought
into full flower [*Gaudium et Spes*, no. 39].

8

Who Really Was
Jesus of Nazareth?

Each cultural group—Palestinian Christians, Judeo-Christians of the diaspora, Gentile Christians—used the most noble and honorable titles they had in their cultures to express the profundity that lay hidden behind the authority, good sense, and creative imagination of Jesus. In this chapter we analyze how the christological process tried yesterday and today—and as it will always try—to situate Jesus within the totality of human life as it is lived and understood by people within history.

The resurrection of Jesus and his glorification and elevation at the side of God posed a fundamental question: Who really is Jesus of Nazareth? What was and what is his function within the history of the human race? To a great extent the whole New Testament is an attempt adequately to answer this question, posed in a radical manner by the resurrection. The primitive community used more than fifty names, titles, or qualifications to define who Jesus is: The title "Christ" is employed approximately 500 times: "Lord" occurs 350 times; "Son of man," 80 times; "Son of God," 75 times; "Son of David," 20 times; and so on.[1] Jesus is called by names that range from the most human, such as "master," "prophet," "the just one," "good," "saint," to the most sublime, such as "Son of God" and "Savior"; finally he is qualified as God himself. During the thirty years after his death, he attracted to himself all human titles of honor and divinity that existed and could be imagined at the time of imperial Rome.

This process of deciphering the meaning and reality of Jesus of Nazareth we call Christology. Christology, yesterday and today, is an uninterrupted attempt to respond to the question, "Who is Jesus and what does he signify for human existence?" Properly speaking, the christological process did not begin with the resurrection. Already before Jesus' death and glorification, the apostles and Jews asked themselves who he might be and what finally he sought to accomplish. After the resurrection, however, an explicit Christology emerges. There is therefore a continuity in this Christology, just as there is also a continuity between the historical Jesus and the Christ of faith, because he who died and was buried is the same as the one who resurrected. What was latent and implicit at the time of the historical Jesus became patent and explicit with the resurrection.[2] If the christological process, the attempt to decipher who Jesus is, already began during his earthly activity, what data and phenomena launched such reflection concerning Jesus?

THE SOVEREIGNTY OF JESUS:
INDIRECT CHRISTOLOGY

We have already reflected on Jesus' extraordinary good sense, his especially creative imagination, and his originality. When confronted with the religious traditions of his people and the social situation of the day, Jesus comported himself with extreme sovereignty. He spoke with God and of God in a manner regarded as blasphemous by his contemporaries (Mark 2:7; John 5:18; 10:30). He does things that pertain only to God, such as forgiving sins and changing the law of Moses (Mark 2:7; Luke 7:49; Mark 7:1–2; Matt. 5:21–48). He preaches the kingdom of God as a total liberation of human beings from sin, suffering, and death. He feels so identified with the kingdom that he makes possession of the kingdom dependent upon adhesion to his person (Luke 12:8–9). He calls the disciples to follow him to announce the kingdom with him and prepare the people (Mark 1:17; 3:14–15; 6:7–13; Luke 9:16; 10:1–20). He makes harsh demands: the cutting of all human ties (cf. Luke 14:26; 9:59–62); the sacrifice of one's very life (Luke 14:27; Matt. 10:38; Mark 8:34), and the renunciation of all earthly goods (Luke 14:33; Mark 6:8–10). The call to follow him implies a developed faith both in the person and intentions of Jesus. The specific intention of Jesus to act in the name and place of God is quite clear.[3] In his presence the structures of the old world are modified: sicknesses are cured (Matt. 8:16–17), death is conquered (Luke 7:11–17; Mark 5:41–43), and impure devils give way to the spirit of God (Matt. 12:28). In his presence all are astounded and ask: Who is this? (Matt. 21:10).

Astonishment: The Beginnings of
Philosophy and Christology

Greek philosophical tradition always insisted that the origin and basic passion of philosophy consists in the capacity for astonishment. To be astounded by something or someone is to capture the light as it shines and is resplendent in that thing or person. It is to allow oneself to be absorbed in the object without immediately framing it within ready-made schema. Something can provoke astonishment in us precisely because that something does not fit into pre-existent categories but emerges having its own birth and originality.

Jesus was a person who caused enormous astonishment because he disrupted all given schema of interpretation. Already as a boy of twelve, "all those who heard him were astounded at his intelligence and his replies" (Luke 2:47). The first time he appeared in public in the synagogue of Nazareth "they were astonished and said 'where did the man get this wisdom and these miraculous powers? This is the carpenter's son, surely? . . . So where did the man get it all?' " (Matt. 13:54–56; Mark 6:23; Luke 4:22–23; John 6:42). Likewise when he preaches in the synagogue of Capernaum: "And his teaching made a deep impression on them because, unlike the scribes, he taught them with authority" (Mark 1:22; Luke 4:31). When he ended the Sermon on the Mount "the multitude was astonished at his teaching" (Matt. 7:28). The miracles provoke a similar reaction among the people: "Astonishment seized them and they were all saying to one another, "What teaching! He gives orders to unclean spirits with authority and power and they come out' " (Luke 4:36). Others exclaim: "We have never seen anything like this!" (Mark 2:12). "We have seen strange things today!" (Luke 5:26). "Nothing like this has ever been seen in Israel!" (Matt. 9:34). When he calmed the storm that broke over the lake the disciples were astounded and exclaimed, "Whatever kind of man is this? Even the winds and the sea obey him?" (Matt. 8:27; Mark 4:41; Luke 8:25). His fame spread to all places (Luke 4:37) and even reached foreign lands such as Syria (Matt. 4:24). From Idumea, Tyre, and Sidon people came to hear and see what he was doing (Mark 3:7–8; Luke 4:17–18a). This astonishment even reaches a climax that is called fright (Luke 8:37; Mark 5:43b; Matt. 9:8; Mark 4:41).

Who is this? The astonishment provoked by the words and comportment of Jesus already contains a latent Christology. Jesus is aware that with him the kingdom of God is already being realized. It is open to all: to public sinners such as the tax collectors with whom he eats; to guerrilla Zealots of whom three belonged to the group of Twelve; to observers of the law such as the Pharisees; to women, to foreigners, and to children. Thus Jesus shows that God loves all and invites all to the eschatological banquet (Matt. 11:19 and Luke 14).[4] "Provocative to both the right and the left, nearer to God than the priests, freer before the world than the ascetics, more moral than the moralists, and more revolutionary than the revolutionaries, he understands the will of God as the immediate norm of action. And what does the will of God seek? This is clear to Jesus: the happiness of all people."[5] In the name of God, with whom he is united, he speaks with great sovereignty, as one who has power: "I tell you solemnly, . . . For I tell you, . . ." According to faith and the Jewish tradition these formulations have already penetrated the sphere of God.[6]

Negative Christology

Many people are astounded by the sovereignty of Jesus, but, as the Gospels frequently tell us, he scandalized them: "They would not accept him" (Matt. 13:57). They say: He is only a carpenter, the son of Mary, the brother of James, Joseph, Judas, and Simon (Mark 6:3). How can he be so arrogant as to do things that pertain only to God? (Mark 2:7; 14:64). Moreover, he does things that the law prohibits, such as walking on the sabbath day, plucking corn and curing people (Mark 2:24). He and his disciples are not penitent like John's followers (Mark 2:18). He eats with sinners and is a friend of the tax collectors, who were considered allies of the Roman occupation forces and therefore hated by the people (Mark 2:16). He is a drunkard and a glutton (Matt. 1:19). He is a blasphemer (Mark 2:7), possessed by devils (Mark 3:22), a subversive; he prohibits payment of the tax to Caesar and calls himself a political revolutionary leader (messiah-king: Luke 23:2). Relatives run out to take him away because, they say, he is outside himself (Mark

3:20); he is an imposter (Matt. 27:63) and, what is worse, a heretic (Samaritan: John 8:48) and possessed by the devil (Luke 12:24–32; Luke 11:15–22). This negative Christology was elaborated by the adversaries of Jesus who were scandalized because of his liberating, profoundly human, and noble attitudes. Jesus created a permanent conflict with the religious and social status quo, which was closed in upon itself and defamed anything new.

Positive Christology

Nevertheless there were many others who were astonished and grasped the originality of Jesus. How should they qualify him? What name should they give him? They begin by calling him a doctor (Acts 2:22; Luke 5:17; Matt. 8:17); later they call him *rabbi* (a rabbi, master: Mark 9:5; 11:21; Matt. 26:49). However, Jesus, unlike the other rabbis, is not a biblical expert who seeks theological evidence in a biblical text to substantiate his every affirmation: "He taught them with authority and not like their own scribes" (Matt. 7:29).[7] Who among the rabbis of the day spoke with such sovereignty that they dispensed with all exegesis and interpretation of the law and would simply retort: "You have learnt how it was said to our ancestors.... But I say to you ... (Matt. 5:21f.)? And who also further radicalized the prohibition against killing (Matt. 5:21–26), against adultery (Matt. 5:27–30), and against swearing (Matt. 5:33–37), or simply abolished the legal determinations concerning divorce (Matt. 5:31–37), revenge (Matt. 5:38–42), and hatred of enemies (Matt. 5:43–48)?

His way of speaking reminds them of a *prophet*,[8] and in fact he was repeatedly called prophet: "Who is this?"—the people of Jerusalem asked—"and the crowds answered, 'This is the prophet from Nazareth in Galilee' " (Matt. 21:11; Luke 24:19; Matt. 21:46; Mark 6:15; 8:28; 14:65). Jesus sees himself as part of the prophetic line (Mark 6:4; Luke 13:33), but he is aware of being more than this: "There is something greater than Jonah here" (Matt. 12:41) because "it was towards John that all the prophecies of the prophets and the law were leading" (Luke 16:16; Matt. 11:12). Jesus never legitimates his prophetical vocation as the prophets before did (cf. Amos 6:14; Isa. 1:24); he never appeals to visions or voices that come from above. His words sustain themselves and he acts as if he himself were the final word.

Who is Jesus? What title can adequately express his authority, sovereignty, and good sense? Perhaps *Son of David* (Matt. 9:27; 15:22; 20:30; 12:23; 21:9)? Jesus pertained to the lineage of David, according to the witness of the primitive church (Rom. 1:3; Matt. 1:2–17; Luke 3:23–38).[9] But he never gave any importance to this fact. The expectations of the people had imagined a Son of David to be a political liberator-king. Jesus rejects such a political messianism and retorts, "David himself calls him Lord, in what way then can he be his son?" (Mark 12:37). Who is Jesus? Can human beings answer this question? Perhaps Jesus himself ?

JESUSOLOGY: HOW DID JESUS UNDERSTAND HIMSELF?

How did Jesus understand himself?[10] What titles did he use to define himself? Here we ought to distinguish clearly between the awareness that Jesus had of himself and his mission and the forms used to express this. Undoubtedly, and this was made clear in the preceding chapters, Jesus, at least toward the end of his life, possessed a clear awareness of being a decisive factor in the breakthrough of the kingdom and of having a unique relationship with God. Anyone who calls God Abba-Father feels himself to be and is God's son. However the Jesus of the Synoptics never uses the expression "Son of God" directly. Only the devils (Mark 3:11; 5:7), the heavenly voices at his baptism and transfiguration (Mark 1:11; 9:7), and Peter in his confession (considered

to be a revelation of God; Matt. 16:16f.) affirm that Jesus
is Son of God. The mocking crowd at the foot of the cross
place the following affirmation in the mouth of Jesus: "I
am the Son of God" (Matt. 27:43). But this is clearly an
addition of Matthew.

Nevertheless, the absolute expression "Son" is used
by Jesus himself in two instances (Mark 13:32 and Matt.
11:27): "But as for the day and the hour, nobody knows
it, neither the angels in heaven, nor the Son; no one but
the Father"; "everything has been entrusted to me by
my Father; and no one knows the Son except the Father,
just as no one knows the Father except the Son and
those to whom the Son chooses to reveal him." This title
expresses on the one hand the sovereignty of the Son
and on the other his obedience and submission to the
Father, as is made clear in the prayer of thanksgiving
(Matt. 11:25). Although this title "Son" possesses no
messianic significance in Jewish tradition, in this expression the self-consciousness of Jesus emerges.[11] John
adopts it and makes it his theme, showing how the
Jewish opposition was founded precisely on this intimate relation of the Son with the Father (John 5:18;
10:30f.; 19:7).

But this is already Christology and not Jesusology. It
is reflection concerning Jesus made in the light of the
resurrection and not so much an expression of his self-
consciousness. We believe that his profound experience
of the Father, as well as the corresponding sonship,
constitute the basis of Jesus' awareness of being the
messenger and the inaugurator of the kingdom of God.
Jesus did not use the title "Son of God" to express this
religious experience. But his sonship was the basis for
the primitive community to call him the only-begotten
Son of God.[12] Intimacy with the Father gives him authority to speak and act in the place of God.

It appears that Jesus did not use any of the common
eschatological-messianic representations of Judaism or
of the people's expectations for liberation in order to

express his awareness.[13] Jesus was far too simple,
sovereign, original, and attached to the lowly classes
and the socially disqualified to give himself titles of
honor and excellence and even divine titles. Jesus did
not come to preach the Messiah, the Christ, the Son of
God, but to live in words and actions the Son of God, the
Christ, the Messiah. Here lies the meaning of the so-
called messianic secret of the Gospel of Mark. It was the
theological and christological task of the primitive
church, illuminated by the splendor of the resurrection,
to discover in the life of Christ the hidden God and Messiah. It is not because the community calls Jesus the Son
of God and Christ that Jesus is made Christ and Son of
God.[14] It could call him that because he was so in fact.

These reflections are also valid for the title "Son of
man," which in the Synoptics appears almost exclusively on the lips of Christ.[15] There are three patterns in
which this title is used. In the first group, Jesus speaks
of the Son of man in the sense of apocalyptic expectations: He will come upon the clouds.There is always a
distinction between the "I" of Jesus and the Son of man
(Mark 8:38; 13:26; 14:62; Matt. 24:27,37,39,44). The Son of
man is someone different from Jesus. In the second
group of passages, Jesus speaks of the Son of man, not in
the context of the parousia on the clouds but of suffering, death, and resurrection (Mark 8:31; 9:31 10:33f.). We
have already referred to this above. These passages and
prophecies concerning death and resurrection appear
not to have been said by Jesus, because their very details presuppose the passion and crucifixion. This would
have been the christological work of the community of
faith seeking to explain the redemptive meaning of the
death of Christ. There is still a third group that speaks
neither of the sufferings nor of the parousia of the Son of
man, but of his power to forgive sins (Mark 2:10), of his
sovereignty with regard to the sabbath (Mark 2:28), of
his freedom to make friends with his associates and
sinners (Matt. 11:19), and to be without a homeland, or a

place to lay his head (Matt. 8:20). As serious exegetes have observed, in this third group we have the christological work of the primitive church, which had already identified the Son of man in power of Dan. 7 with the historical Jesus. The power of the historical Jesus and his freedom before the social and religious status quo is due to the fact that he is already the Son of man exalted at the right hand of God, though this appears in a hidden and humble form.[16]

It is also very improbable that Jesus would have claimed for himself the title "Son of man coming in power upon the clouds." There is no affirmation of Jesus that establishes a relationship between his earthly existence and his figure as universal Judge. Jesus might indeed have spoken of the future of the Son of man in the third person. However, as Mark 8:38 and Luke 12:8–9 well testify, he interpreted his relationship with the Son of man as a very close one: "I tell you, if anyone openly declares himself for me in the presence of men, the Son of man will declare himself for him in the presence of God's angels." After the resurrection, the primitive community rightly identified Jesus with the Son of man, so that in many passages "the Son of man" substitutes for the pronoun "I" (Matt. 16:13; Mark 8:27) or viceversa (Matt. 10:32f.; Luke 12:8f.; Mark 8:38). After the resurrection the words of the historical Jesus concerning the Son of man could be understood as words concerning Jesus himself. Hence, a bridge was established between Jesusology and Christology: The title "Son of man in power," now reinterpreted, can show the continuity between the historical Jesus and the Christ of faith, between the Son of man who in his terrestrial life remained hidden and the Son of man who, by his resurrection and exaltation to the side of God, revealed himself in a clear manner.[17]

The same is true of the title "Messiah" or "Christ."[18] Critical analysis of the texts does not permit us to say that Jesus claimed any of the three fundamental representations of that time: The Christ (anointed, savior) as a political liberator-king, or as a high priest of the house of Aaron, or as the Son of man coming on the clouds in power. Because of his very origins, the Messiah, or Christ, is not a supernatural figure but simply an earthly liberator. Jesus separates himself from such representations. He does possess an awareness of being a liberator of the *condition humaine* but avoids using titles that objectify him only as a political liberator, a competitor of the Roman Emperor. The confession of Jesus before the Sanhedrin (Mark 14:61) expresses the faith of the primitive community in Jesus as Christ and as the only and true awaited liberator.[19] Peter's confession "You are the Christ" (Mark 8:29) appears not to have been historical. Peter, in the name of the ecclesial community formed after the resurrection, the community of which he is the head, expresses the common faith: You are the Christ. This title afterward simply becomes a name, so that "Jesus Christ" expresses at one and the same time the reality both of the historical Jesus and the Christ of faith. The name already expresses the continuity between Jesusology and Christology.

The important thing is to comprehend that the titles of magnificence and divinity attributed to Jesus are not intended to demonstrate the authority and sovereignty shown in the earthly life of Jesus. On the contrary, they seek to decipher and explain this authority. Why did he act thus? Whence comes such power? Why is he a prophet, Son of David, Son of man, Messiah? None of these titles succeeded in expressing the depths of Jesus' good sense, creative imagination, and sovereignty. It is not the titles that create his authority; rather his authority gave origin to the titles. Nevertheless, none of them succeeds in exhausting the richness of the figure of Jesus before whom all, even the devils, are astounded. Who really are you, Jesus of Nazareth?

THE RESURRECTION OF JESUS:
DIRECT CHRISTOLOGY

The resurrection marked a profound and complete turnabout that eliminated the ambiguities surrounding the life and words of Jesus; it also made negative Christology look ridiculous. The direct christological process that is still with us today was now initiated. The resurrection radicalized still further both the question and astonishment of the disciples: Who is Jesus? How should the mystery of his person be qualified? How should we understand his salvific mission? The primitive church took on the titles and images of its cultural world. First, the Palestinian Jewish-Christian community understood the resurrected Jesus within the eschatological and apocalyptic categories proper to the Judaism of that period. Next, the Jewish-Christian community of the diaspora, already under the influence of Greek culture, widened the horizon of comprehension and gave Jesus other titles. Finally, when Gentile communities were formed in the Hellenistic world, the mystery of Jesus was deciphered within the cultural categories proper to that world.[20]

The christological process will always seek to situate Jesus within the totality of human life as it is lived and understood by human beings within history. In each horizon of comprehension, be it Jewish, Greek, or our own world of the second half of the twentieth century, the faith will say of Christ that he is "all in all" (Col. 3:11).

To the Palestinian Christian Community
Jesus Is the Christ, the Son of Man, etc.

The resurrection of Jesus was first seen by the primitive community as an elevation and a glorification of the just one at the side of God (Acts 2:24,33; 5:30,31; cf. 3:13–15).

Hence the first titles attributed to the resurrected Jesus are those of "Holy and Just One" (Acts 3:14) and "Servant of God" (Acts 4:27).[21]

He took on himself our iniquities and, innocent himself, he died at the hands of evil men (Acts 2:22; 3:14). He was really the suffering servant that Isaiah spoke of (52:13–53:12), the holy one who leads us to life (Acts 3:14). Exalted (Acts 2:33; 5:31) and glorified (Acts 3:13), he is now the Son of Man hidden in heaven and about to come as the eschatological judge (Acts 3:20f.). All power in heaven and on earth has been given to him (Matt. 28:18). He is the Messiah, awaited by the ancients and by all peoples, who in order to bring salvation and liberation first passed through suffering and death (Luke 24:26). However, by the resurrection he has been enthroned as the Messiah-Christ (Acts 2:36), as was predicted by the ancient prophecies (Pss. 2:7; 110:1). This conception of the Messiah-Christ directly contradicts the popular expectations of a glorious political liberator. If he is Messiah, then he must also be Son of David and the eschatological prophet foretold in Deuteronomy (18:15, 18f.; Acts 3:22f.). As Christ he is also Lord of all things (Acts 2:36); with him the restoration of all things has already begun (Acts 3:21). The primitive community expected his definitive manifestation, crying out in Aramaic: *Maranatha*, Come, Lord (Acts 22:20; 1 Cor. 16:22).

In the Palestinian community the resurrected Jesus is even called Son of God. In the Old Testament "Son of God" means primarily Israel (Exod. 4:22); then, the king (Ps. 2:2); and later, the holy one could also be considered Son of God. Nevertheless to the primitive understanding "Son of God" possessed a juridical character, not a physical one, as it had afterward in the elaborations of Paul and Luke.[22] Jesus, Son of David, realizes the prophecy of 2 Sam. 7:14: "I will be a father to him and he a son to me." As Luke says: "The Lord God will give him the throne of his ancestor David, he will rule over the

House of Jacob forever and his reign will have no end" (Luke 1:32). Before the resurrection Jesus was a descendant of David; now he is introduced as a universal king and called juridically "Son of God" (cf. Rom. 1:3). One can deduce, therefore, that all these titles were proper to Jewish culture. Within that culture, Jesus Christ was deciphered and qualified, using all the existing titles that bestowed honor and glory.

To the Jewish Christians of the Diaspora, Jesus Is the New Adam and Lord

The Jewish Christians living in the diaspora were under the influence of Greek culture. They tried to decipher the richness of the mystery of Jesus by employing concepts taken from the Jewish tradition and enriched with new representations coming from the world surrounding them. Thus the title "Lord" was attributed to Jesus.[23] "Lord," initially, as it is today, was a title of nobility, and Jesus was so called by pagans (Matt. 8:8; Mark 7:28) and also by Jews (Matt. 8:21; 18:21). After the resurrection the Palestinian community began to call the resurrected Jesus "Lord," in the eschatological sense: He will come and bring the consummation of the world. In the Hellenic world, the Jewish Christians invoked Jesus as Lord to praise and celebrate him present as the resurrected one in the communities. These Christians even defined themselves as those who "call on the name of the Lord" (1 Cor. 1:2; Rom. 10:13).

This usage comes from the Greek translation of the Old Testament (Joel 2:32; cf. Acts 2:21). The Christians, differentiating themselves from the Jews, did not come together merely in the name of Yahweh-God but in the name of the Lord Jesus. "Lord," in the Hellenic world, signified king. Christ is Lord, but not a political lord. He performs divine functions: He rules over the whole cosmos and over all peoples. "Lord" does not yet signify equality with God; it means merely that God gave Jesus power until the parousia to realize his task of liberation from all forces inimical to God and human beings. Consequently he is presented as the only mediator, and the community acclaims him. With the resurrection, the new human being is manifested. Whoever is in Christ is already a new creature (2 Cor. 5:17). Therefore Christ is seen by the community as a new humanity and a new Adam (Rom. 5:12–21; 1 Cor. 15:15). He is the immaculate high priest, mediator of the new and eternal alliance (Heb. 2:14–18; 4:14).

To the Gentile Christians, Jesus Is the Savior, the Head of the Cosmos, the Only Begotten of God, and God Himself

Gentile Christians, living in the atmosphere of the Hellenistic cultural world, interpreted the meaning of the sovereignty of Jesus in their own categories. Since they were not Jews, the titles of "Messiah," "Son of man," etc., signified practically nothing. "Savior," however, was the title for which they showed an especial sensibility.[24] The emperor was regarded as a savior; in the mystic rites the divinity was invoked as the savior from death and matter. In the New Testament Jesus is venerated as a Savior, especially in his epiphany, which is like the arrival of an emperor in a city (Luke 2:11; 2 Tim. 1:10; Tit. 2:13). This epiphany liberates us from death and sin (2 Tim. 1:10). John calls Jesus the "savior of the world" (4:42; 1 John 4:14), not only in the sense of being liberator of human beings and of the world, but also implying that, in contrast to the emperors, only Jesus is the Savior.

The Gentiles also knew many sons of gods *(theios aner)* born of virgins: e.g., emperors (Alexander the Great), wonder-workers (Apollonius of Tyana), and philosophers (Plato). The Son of God pertains to the divine sphere. The Gentiles began to understand the biblical title attributed to Christ, "Son of God," no longer in its juridical but in its physical meaning.[25] Christ is in fact the Only-Begotten of God sent into the world (Rom. 8:3).

If then he is the Son of God, the next step was to reflect on him as being at the side of God. The celebrated hymn in the Epistle to the Philippians describes the trajectory of the Son of God: First his state was divine, then he assumed the condition of a slave, so as to be finally exalted as the absolute and cosmic Lord (2:6–11). He is the first born, born before all things (Col. 1:15) and hence the image of the invisible God (Col. 1:15); in him, through him, and for him, all things possess their existence and consistence (Col. 1:16–17). He is the head of the cosmos (Eph. 1:10; Col. 2:9) and through him all things come to be (1 Cor. 8:6). The work of redemption is not the only thing that depends on him. Being pre-existent, he also possesses a participation in the creative act of God as the supreme example in which and for which everything has its origin and meaning. Christ is thus in some form the cosmic Christ: "everything, and he is in everything" (Col. 3:11).[26]

A step forward was taken by John when he called Christ "the Logos." The Logos was God (John 1:1b) and became flesh and lived among us (1:14). No matter how much we debate the origin of this title "Logos" (Word)[27] it is certain that, for John, Jesus is the Word even when on earth. For John, the Word cannot be separated from the person and transmitted independently as mere knowledge-content. The Word is a person, so much so that only those who adhere to the person, that is, believe in him, possess salvation. What does it signify then to believe in Jesus-Word? For John it is to accept Jesus as the one who reveals the Father and is one with the Father (John 10:30). If the Word was made flesh, then all reality was also transfigured. Hence Christ can say: I am the light, the true bread, the living water, the way, the truth, the life.

Saying that Christ is the Word and the Word was God (John 1:1b) marks the highest point in the christological process. The sovereignty and the authority of Jesus, confirmed by the resurrection, receives here its most exhaustive interpretation. He is God, and this title clearly occurs at least three times in the New Testament (Heb. 1:8; John 1:1b; 20:28; and more than likely in John 1:18; Tit. 2:13; 1 John 5:20; Rom. 9:5; and 2 Pet. 1:1).[28] This interpretation occurred in about A.D. 90, outside Palestine, and was certainly a great contribution of Hellenist Christians to the christological process. Now the radicalness of the mystery of Jesus had been achieved: He is God incarnate, simultaneously God and man.

The greatest depths of Jesus' authority, good sense, and creative imagination, till then hidden, were uncovered in this final title, "God." Only by using divine names and attributing divinity itself to Jesus can an adequate answer be given to the question: "And you, who do you say that I am?" (Matt. 16:15).

But a long process of interpretation had to occur before arriving at such a formulation. Everything important and essential to human life and history was attributed to Christ, including the most sublime reality that can possibly exist, God. We saw a few of the names given to Jesus. But there are still others, also significant, which can show us how Christ was inserted concretely into life. He is called the foundation of the house (1 Cor. 3:11), the cornerstone that sustains all (Eph. 2:20), the door (John 10:7), the head of all things (Eph. 4:15; 1:10); the beginning and end of everything (Rev. 22:13), God's Yes and Amen to human beings (2 Cor. 1:19–20; Rev. 3:14), the light (John 6:45), water (cf. John 4:10), the good shepherd (John 10:11), the true vine (John 15:1), peace (Eph. 2:14).

He is called the wisdom of God (1 Cor. 1:24), the glory of God (John 1:14), the visible image of the invisible God (2 Cor. 4:4; Col. 1:15), a figure of divine substance (Heb. 1:3), the splendor of the glory of the Father (Heb. 1:31), the Pasch (1 Cor. 5:7), the immaculate lamb (Rev. 5:12; 1 Pet. 1:19), who takes away the sins of the world (John 1:29), the stone from which springs forth water for the Jews to drink (1 Cor. 10:4), the water that kills thirst in the desert (John 7:37–39; 4:13–14), the true manna (John 6:32–34), the new temple (John 2:21), God with us (Matt. 1:23). These and many other names reveal how Christ is essential to human life.

CONCLUSION: IT IS NOT ENOUGH TO GIVE TITLES TO JESUS AND CALL HIM, LORD, LORD!

The titles referred to above always have the same intent, namely, to decipher the figure of Jesus that the apostles knew: "What we have heard, and we have seen with our own eyes, what we have watched and touched with our own hands" (1 John 1:1). To this end, each group—Palestinians, Jewish Christians of the diaspora, Hellenist Christians—used the most noble and honorable titles they had in their cultures. Each collaborated in deciphering the historical Jesus whom they knew in Palestine and who died and rose again in Jerusalem. Let it be emphasized that the titles and names, even the most divine, do not wish to eliminate the man-Jesus. Rather they seek to stress this human aspect of Christ. They do not seek to demonstrate the sovereignty and authority of Jesus, but to express it and bring it into prominence. After a long process of meditation on the mystery that lay hidden in Jesus they say: A human being such as Jesus of Nazareth was in his life, death, and resurrection can only be God himself. And then they called him God. Thus they broke down all human conceptions. A mystery is defined by another mystery. There is, however, one advantage: We can grasp something of the mystery of the human being, because if we live our own humanity with authenticity we are confronted with that mystery at every moment. The human mystery evokes the mystery of God.

What does it mean when we say that a man is God? How can Jesus of Nazareth be the Word incarnate? A mystery is hidden here that faith professes and theology is called upon to ponder more deeply. The name "Jesus Christ" already suggests an answer: There is a unity; Jesus is at the same time Christ. Man and God are distinct, but in Jesus Christ they come to form a unity without confusion and without change. In a later chapter we will try to articulate our faith concerning this christological fact. However in all theological reflection we must not forget that Christology is not primary, nor does it substitute for faith. Life is more important than reflection. In a polemic with the gnostic theologians who had forgotten this basic fact, John clearly stressed that all Christology ought to be united to ethics: "He who says he abides in him ought to walk in the same way in which he walked" (1 John 2:6). "It is not those who say to me, 'Lord, Lord,' who will enter the kingdom of heaven, but the person who does the will of my Father in heaven" (Matt. 7:21–23). Christ continues to call all people and invite all to follow him. We may thus attain the goal that has been pointed out to us, our task to be continuously accomplished, the goal that was fully realized in him.

9

The Christological Process Continues: The Accounts of Jesus' Infancy— Theology or History?

The more one meditates on Jesus, the more one discovers the mystery hidden behind his humble life and the more one returns in search of his origins. When Luke and Matthew edited their Gospels (circa A.D. 75–85) the reflections made by the various communities were collected. It was clear to all that Jesus had been constituted by God as the Messiah, Savior, Son of God, and God himself in a human form. Having this faith as their point of departure, they interpreted the facts surrounding the birth and infancy of Jesus. The very profound and intense theological work performed in an effort to decipher the mystery of Jesus and to announce him to the faithful of that time lies hidden in these accounts. The family scenes of his birth, described by Luke and Matthew, are primarily proclamations of faith in Jesus as Savior rather than neutral accounts of his history.

158

The christological process, as developed by us in the previous chapters, helps us to comprehend how the titles and names attributed to Jesus emerged. Behind each title, be it "Christ," "Son of Man," "Son of God," etc., years of theological reflection lie hidden. This reflection can even achieve the sophisticated level of the most refined rabbinical theology. This is what we will see in the accounts concerning the infancy of Jesus.[1] As far as the feelings of most Christians are concerned, the accounts of the birth of Jesus and the celebration of Christmas are an expression of the heart; they constitute a festival for the heart. Faith becomes sentiment. Faith touches that which is most profound and intimate in the human personality. Life is quickened, made joyful and relished as feeling. The arts and professions, nature, mountains, the waters, the universe of things and human beings: all make peace and are reconciled before the child, surrounded by the donkey and the cow, the virgin and Joseph, the shepherds and the sheep and the star. At least this once on Christmas Day we all become children and allow the little prince that lives in each of us to speak the innocent language of children, who rejoice before the tree, the lighted candles, and crystal balls. The adult seeks out the world of infancy, myth, symbol, and poetry that is life itself. But this life is normally smothered by business and preoccupations with survival that impede us from living as the eternally childlike adult that each one continues to be.

These are values that ought to be defended and nurtured. Nevertheless, to maintain them as Christian values they ought to have a connection with faith. Without this connection the atmosphere and sentiment of Christmas becomes mere sentimentalism to be exploited by the commercial machine of production and consumption. Faith is related to history and the God who is revealed within history. So we ask: What precisely happened at Jesus' birth? Did the angels actually appear on the hillsides of Bethlehem? Did the wise men of the Orient really come? It is hard to imagine a star losing its way and going first to Jerusalem and then to Bethlehem where the child lay. Why did it not go directly to Bethlehem but first shone over Jerusalem, frightening the whole city so that King Herod decreed the death of innocent children?

What is the message that Luke and Matthew sought to transmit in the history of the infancy of Jesus? Is their interest a historical one, or, by means of an edifying and fraudulent exaggeration of a scriptural saying or some real happening, did they seek to communicate a more profound truth concerning the child, who through the resurrection would show himself to be the Liberator of the human condition and the great hope of human and eternal life for all?

The accounts of Jesus' birth are not without problems, both for the historian of the time of Jesus and for one who knows the literary procedures used in the Scriptures. A sophisticated theology, one thought out in every minute detail, lies hidden behind the candid simplicity and the lyricism of the scenes. In fact the nativity accounts were the last to be written. They were elaborated when there had already been a long theological reflection concerning Jesus and the meaning of his death and resurrection; when the accounts of the passion, the parables, the miracles, the principal sayings of Jesus had already been written down and put into an order; when the principal titles such as "Son of David," "Messiah," "Christ," "New Moses," "Son of God," etc., by which they tried to decipher the mystery of the humanity of Jesus, had already been created. It was at the end of all this theological work that the beginning appeared: the infancy of Jesus, thought out and written in the light of a theology and faith created in the context of his life, death, and resurrection. It is precisely here that we find the locus of comprehension for the accounts of his infancy narrated by Matthew and Luke.

FAITH SEEKS TO COMPREHEND

Faith does not exclude nor does it dispense with reason. True faith seeks to comprehend, not to abolish the mystery, but to discern its real dimensions and, in wonder, to praise the gracious logic of God. Faith professed that Jesus is Savior, Messiah, the Meaning of everything (Logos), the predicted prophet (Deut. 18:15–22), the new Moses who would liberate the human race from all the ambiguities of the human condition in a definitive exodus. However, at an early date the apostles became interested in one question: At what point in his life did God institute Jesus as Savior, Messiah and Son of God?[2] The oldest preaching answers: in the death and resurrection (cf. 1 Cor. 15:3–8; Acts 10:34–43). Mark, who wrote his gospel between A.D. 67 and 69, affirms: In the baptism by John, Jesus was anointed by the Holy Spirit and proclaimed Messiah and Liberator. The Gospel of Mark has no account of the infancy of Christ and begins with the preparatory preaching of John the Baptist and the baptism of Jesus.

Matthew, who elaborated his Gospel between A.D. 80 and 85, responds: Jesus, from the very moment of birth, is the long awaited Messiah. Even more, the whole history of salvation since Abraham marched in his direction (see the genealogy of Christ, Matt. 1:1–17). Luke, who wrote his Gospel about the same time, goes one step further and says: Since his birth in the cave at Bethlehem Jesus is the Messiah and Son of God. Moreover, not merely the whole sacred history of Israel since Abraham marched in the direction of his birth in the cave, but the whole history of humanity since Adam (Luke 3:38).

Finally, John (about A.D. 100), inheriting the long and profound meditation concerning Jesus, answers: Jesus was the Son of God even before he was born, in his pre-existence at the side of God, well before the creation of the world, because "in the beginning was the Word, . . . and the Word was made flesh, he lived among us."

As is apparent, the more people meditate about Jesus, the more his mystery is discovered and the more people search for his origins. This whole process is the fruit of love. When one loves someone one seeks to know all there is to be known concerning that person; their life, interests, infancy, family, their ancestors, from what country they came, etc. Love sees a lot further and with greater depth than cold reason. The resurrection revealed the true dimensions of the figure of Jesus: He is of interest not only to the Jews (Abraham), not only to all human beings (Adam), but even to the cosmos, because "not one thing had its being, but through him" (John 1:3). Given the understanding gained in the brightness of the resurrection, the apostles began to reread the whole life of Christ, to reinterpret his words, to retell his miracles; and they began to discover in the facts of his birth, which in themselves are simple, the latent presence of the Messiah and Savior, patently revealed only after the resurrection. With this understanding, many passages of the Old Testament held to be prophetical were seen in a new light and were now amplified and explicated in function of the faith in Jesus, Son of God. Hence, the theological meaning of the accounts of the infancy does not consist in narrating facts concerning the birth of Jesus. Rather through graphic, theological narrations, it is an announcement of Jesus of Nazareth, *who he is* and *what he is*, for the community of faith in about the years A.D. 80–90. Therefore we ought to look less for history and more for the message of faith.

Critical Catholic exegesis lists the following as historical facts contained in the accounts of the birth:[3] (1) engagement of Mary and Joseph (Matt. 1:18; Luke 1:27; 2:5); (2) the Davidic descendency of Jesus (Matt. 1:1; Luke 1:32) by way of the descendency of Joseph

(Matt. 1:16,20; Luke 1:27; 2:4); (3) the name "Jesus" (Matt. 1:21; Luke 1:31); (4) Jesus' birth of the Virgin Mary (Matt. 1:21,23,25; Luke 1:31; 2:6–7); (5) Nazareth as the residence of Jesus (Matt. 2:23; Luke 2:39). We will see below how Matthew and Luke worked with these facts in a literary and theological manner, so that with them and through them they could announce, each in his own way, a message of salvation and joy for human beings: that in this child "wrapped in swaddling clothes and laid in a manger because there was no room for them at the inn" (Luke 2:27), there lay hidden the secret meaning of all history since the creation of the first being and that in him all the prophecies and human hopes for liberation and the fullness of God were realized.

MATTHEW AND LUKE: JESUS IS
THE OMEGA POINT OF HISTORY, THE MESSIAH,
THE AWAITED SON OF DAVID, THE SON OF GOD

The resurrection showed that with Christ history had arrived at its Omega Point: Death had been conquered and humanity had been completely realized and inserted into the divine sphere. Jesus is the Messiah, and if he is the Messiah, then he is of the royal family of David. By giving the genealogies of Jesus, both Matthew (1:1–17) and Luke (3:23–38) want to prove that Jesus and no other truly emerged when history arrived at its Z-point, that he occupies the precise place in Davidic genealogy that corresponds to the Messiah, and finally that by his position in the genealogy he fulfills the prophecy of Isaiah (7:14)—being the son of a virgin— while receiving the name of his adoptive father, Joseph, by which he is inserted into the genealogy.

According to 4 Esdras 14:11–12, the Messiah, the Savior of all human beings since Adam, was expected at the end of the eleventh week of the world. Seventy-seven days are the equivalent of eleven weeks. Luke constructs the genealogy of Jesus from Adam, showing how he appeared in history when the seventy-seven days of the world had been completed, each day having an ancestor of Jesus. Hence the genealogy of Jesus from Adam to Joseph amounts to seventy-seven antecedents. History arrived at its Omega Point when Jesus was born in Bethlehem. We can see that this genealogy is artificially constructed by comparing it with Matthew's. Moreover there are long time intervals between one generation and the next.

Matthew uses a similar procedure to prove that Jesus is the Son of David and hence the awaited Messiah. Substituting the consonants of the name *DaViD* (the vowels do not count in Hebrew) by their respective numbers we get the number 14 (D=4, V=6, D=4:14). Matthew so constructs the genealogy of Jesus that the result, as he expressly points out (1:17), is three times fourteen generations. The number 14 is the double of 7, a number that for the Bible symbolizes the fulness of God's plan or the totality of history. The fourteen generations from Abraham to David show the first high point of Jewish history; the fourteen generations from David up to the Babylonian exile reveal the lowest point in sacred history; and the fourteen generations of the Babylonian captivity up to Christ demonstrate the definitive high point of salvific history, a day that will never know a sundown because the Messiah emerged at that point in time.

Differing from Luke, Matthew also inserts four women into the genealogy of Jesus, all of them women of ill-repute: two prostitutes, Tamar (Gen. 38:1–30) and Rahab (Josh. 2; 6:17, 22ff.); an adulteress, Urias' wife, Bathsheba (2 Sam. 11:3; 1 Chron. 3:5) and the Moabite Ruth, a pagan (Ruth 4:12ff.). With this Matthew wants to teach that Christ assumed the highest and lowest points of history and also that he took human ignominies upon himself. Christ is the final member of this genealogy, the one in whom history arrives at its

Z-point, completing three times fourteen generations. Therefore he alone can be the promised and awaited Messiah.

JOSEPH AND THE VIRGIN'S CONCEPTION IN MATTHEW: A FOOTNOTE TO THE GENEALOGY

In his genealogy of Jesus, Matthew wants to prove that Christ really is a descendant of David. However he does not succeed in doing so because at a decisive moment, instead of saying Jacob was the father of Joseph and Joseph was the father of Jesus, he interrupts and affirms: Jacob was the father of Joseph, the husband of Mary; *of her* was born Jesus, who is called Christ (1:6). In Jewish jurisprudence women do not count in genealogical determinations. Hence, Christ could not be inserted into the house of David through Mary. Nevertheless it is clear to Matthew that Jesus is the son of the Virgin Mary and the Holy Spirit (1:18). Here, therefore, a problem had emerged: How can we insert Jesus into a Davidic genealogy by means of a masculine genealogical tree if he does not have a human father.

To resolve the problem Matthew makes, so to speak, a footnote or a gloss (an explanation of a difficulty) and narrates the conception and origin of Jesus (1:18–25). His intention is not so much to narrate the virginal conception of Jesus, nor to describe, as does Luke, the birth of Jesus. The core of the account consists in this: that Joseph, knowing Mary's state, wants to abandon her at night. The meaning of the account given in Matt. 1:18–25 lies in the fact that he wishes to resolve the problem that had been raised. The clarification comes in verse 25: Joseph gives the boy the name Jesus. By giving him the name of Jesus, Joseph, descendant of David and legally the spouse of Mary, becomes his father in the juridical sense and hence inserts him into the Davidic genealogy. Thus Jesus is a son of David through Joseph and also the Messiah. By means of this footnote Isaiah's

prophecy that the Messiah would be born of a virgin
(Isa. 7:14) is fulfilled and God's plan is fully realized.

DID LUKE WISH TO GIVE AN ACCOUNT OF
THE VIRGINAL CONCEPTION OF JESUS?

The annunciation and birth of Christ are narrated by
the evangelist Luke. Luke is traditionally regarded as a
painter. Truly chapters 1–2 are diptychs. A diptych in
the medieval world (as can be seen in the old churches of
Brazil) was an altar that had two hinged tablets or areas
with matched paintings. Thus Luke 1–2 paints the infancy of John the Baptist in a perfect parallel with the
infancy of Jesus. Matthew will later operate in a similar
manner, tracing parallels between Moses and Jesus.
Nevertheless at each parallel point, Luke shows how
Christ is greater than John the Baptist. Thus there is
perfect correspondence between the annunciation by
the angel Gabriel of the birth of John the Baptist (Luke
1:5–25) and the annunciation of the birth of Jesus
(1:26–56); there are miraculous signs in both cases at the
time of birth, at the circumcision of the child and when
the child is given its name (1:57–66; 2:1–21); the salvific
meaning of John and Jesus is announced in the prophecy
of Zechariah (John) and that of Simeon and the
prophetess Anna (Jesus) (1:67–80; 2:22–40). In both
cases, reference is made to the growth of the two children. However the cycle of Jesus is revealed to be
superior to that of John in all scenes. At the annunciation of the conception of John the angel Gabriel does not
give any salutation (Luke 1:11), whereas he gently sa-
lutes Mary (1:28). The angel says to Zechariah: Your
prayer was heard (1:13), whereas with Mary he rever-
ently observes: You have won God's favor. In the scene
where Mary visits Elizabeth, Mary's salutation makes
the child, now filled with the Holy Spirit, leap in the
maternal womb of Elizabeth. Jesus, on the contrary, is
the bearer of the Holy Spirit from the very beginning,

because he has his origin in the Holy Spirit and the Virgin. John the Baptist appears in the desert (1:80); Christ, however, appears in the temple (2:41–52).

These literary procedures, which emphasize the salvific function of Christ, are used in an even more refined manner at the annunciation of Christ's conception (1:26–38), which occurred in the sixth month after John the Baptist's conception. Six months of thirty days add up to 180 days; nine months from Jesus' conception to his birth give us 270 days; from his birth to the presentation of the child in the temple add up to forty days. The total comes to 490 days or seventy weeks What did seventy weeks signify for the readers of the New Testament? According to Daniel (9:24) the Messiah would come, would liberate the people from sin, and would bring eternal justice after seventy weeks of years. Thus Luke wants to insinuate that the prophecy of Daniel has been fulfilled and Jesus alone is the awaited Messiah.

The words of the annunciation spoken by the angel, the Virgin's reaction, and Gabriel's salutation are all formulated in a strict connection with similar or equivalent words spoken in similar situations in the Old Testament (for Luke 1:42 see Jdt. 13:18; for Luke 1: 28:30–33 see Zeph. 3:14–17; for Luke 1:28 see Gen. 26:3,28; 28.15, Exod. 3:12; 1 Sam. 3:19; 1 Kings 1:37; etc.). The conception of Jesus as an act of the Holy Spirit is not so much an explanation of the biological process of conception (for Luke it is indisputable that Jesus was born of a virgin qua virgin), but rather an attempt to relate Jesus-Savior with other liberating figures of the Old Testament who by the power of the Holy Spirit were instituted in their function (1 Sam. 10:6f.; 16:13f.; 1 Judg. 3:10; 6:34; 11:29; 13:25; 1 Kings 19:19; 2 Chron. 2:8–15, etc.).

Here we can perceive the difference between the perspective of traditional catechesis and that of Luke and Matthew. Traditional catechesis has accentuated Mary's virginity, the fact of her physical and perpetual virginity, "before, during, and after giving birth." For the gospel accounts the personal virginity of Mary is secondary. The virginal conception of Jesus is much more important. As has been well put by Bishop Paulo Eduardo Andrade Ponte:

It was *not* the special preoccupation of the evangelists to emphasize the *virginal* character but the *supernatural, divine* character of this conception. For them, the conception of Jesus was virginal so that it could be supernatural, not supernatural so that it could be virginal. It was virginal so that God could be its cause, not only the first, but the *principal* cause, so that God could be its direct author. . . . On hearing certain sermons and on reading certain spiritual books, one has the impression that the conception of Jesus was supernatural and miraculous in order to preserve the virginity of the mother. Thus she would have been supernatural so as to be virginal and not virginal in order to be supernatural. And this has been inspired by the whole moralizing and Manichean conceptualization of virginity in Christianity.[4]

The perspective of the Gospels is very different: For them Christ is at the center and Mary's virginity is a function of Christ. It is because of this that the New Testament prefers to call Mary "Mother of Jesus" (John 2:1,3,12; 19:25–26; Acts 1:14) instead of "the Virgin," this latter term occurring merely two times in the New Testament texts (Luke 1:27; Matt. 1:23), and then in order to reveal her maternal function itself as a work of the Holy Spirit. The very conception of Jesus is described in a form that expresses how the glory of God is manifested in the tabernacle of the alliance (Exod. 40:32; Luke 1:35). Just as the tabernacle is full of the Spirit of God, so in the same way and much more is the Son of Mary, who truly merits being called "Son of God" (Luke 1:35). By the power of the Holy Spirit there appears a person so impregnated by this same spirit that he gets his existence from the Holy Spirit alone. Christ is the new creation of that same Spirit who created the old world. This is the profound theological meaning that Luke wishes to transmit in his account of the conception of Jesus by the power of the Holy Spirit; his purpose is not so much to describe a miraculous biological phenomenon even though this is presupposed and serves as a reason for theological reflection.

WHERE WAS JESUS BORN: BETHLEHEM OR NAZARETH?

Theological work like that we have seen so far also occurs in the narration of the birth of Jesus at Bethlehem. The birth as such is narrated without any romantic overtones but in its rustic and dry character it gains great profundity: "While they were there the time came for her to have her child, and she gave birth to a son, her first-born. She wrapped him in swaddling clothes and laid him in a manger because there was no room for them at the inn" (Luke 2:6–7). This common event, which could have occurred with any mother, is reread within a theological context after the resurrection. If he is revealed to be the Messiah and is the Son of David on the part of his legal father, Joseph, then the other prophecy ought also be realized in him, namely: in Bethlehem will be born the Messiah, the one who is to rule over Israel (Mic. 5:1; 1 Sam. 16:1ff.), not in Nazareth, the home of Jesus, a place so insignificant that it is never mentioned in the Old Testament.

Luke is not trying to emphasize the geographical location, but is making a theological reflection about Bethlehem and its messianic significance in order to make it clear that Jesus is the Messiah. It is probable that the historical homeland of Jesus was indeed Nazareth, a theologically irrelevant place. To have Jesus born in Bethlehem, Luke creates a situation in which the Holy Family is forced to leave Nazareth and go to Bethlehem. In order to attain this theological goal Luke refers to Caesar Augustus' decree of a census of all the land; this took place in Palestine when Quirinius was governor of

Syria (Palestine belonged to this province). Nevertheless we know this census was only carried out in A.D. 6,
as Luke himself reminds us in Acts (Acts 5:37); the census caused a guerrilla uprising (the Zealots) led by Judas
of Galilee, who protested this measure.

Luke uses this historical fact and projects it into the
past. Thus *on the one hand* he can give a reason for the
journey of Mary and Joseph from Nazareth to Bethlehem (and for theological reasons have Jesus born
there), and *on the other hand* he is able to insinuate that
the Jesus-event is of interest not only to Israel but to all
human beings as "a light to enlighten the pagans"
(Luke 2:32). The references to profane history surrounding the birth of Christ and to the preaching of John do
not so much attempt to give the events a historical situation. Rather they seek to emphasize the strict connection that exists between sacred history and universal
profane history in which God, through Jesus Christ,
realizes salvation.

WHO ARE THE SHEPHERDS
IN THE FIELDS OF BETHLEHEM?

If the simplicity of the account of Christ's birth con-
ceals the ineffable mystery that had taken place within
the history of the world, the narrative of the angels
appearing in the fields of Bethlehem proclaims it with
full clarity. As commonly occurs in the Bible, an angel of
the Lord (here there are legions) proclaims the secret
and profound meaning of the event: "Listen, I bring you
news of great joy, a joy to be shared by the whole people.
Today in the town of David a savior has been born to
you; he is Christ, the Lord" (Luke 2:11). The angels
proclaim the meaning of that night: Heaven and earth
are reconciled to one another because God gives peace
and salvation to all human beings.

In terms of its origin, what is related in Luke 2:8–20 is
not an attempt to bring into tradition an event that
had taken place among the shepherds of Bethlehem.

Theologically speaking, the shepherds are the representatives of the poor, to whom the good news was announced and to whom Jesus was sent (Luke 4:18). Here there is no vestige of pastoral romanticism. The shepherds constitute a despised class and their profession made them impure before the law.[5] They pertained to that class of people who did not know the law, as the Pharisees used to say. Christ—and this Luke allows to appear many times in his Gospel—was sent precisely to the religiously marginalized and the classless. They are the first to hear the joyful message of liberation.

More than likely this message was not transmitted to the shepherds in the fields of Bethlehem, but directed to Luke's listeners in A.D. 80–85 in order to show them that he, in whom they believe, is the true liberator. To those who have eyes of faith, the weakness of the little child wrapped in swaddling clothes hides a mystery that, once unveiled, is a joy to all the people: It is he, the awaited one, the Lord of the cosmos and history (Luke 2:11).

MATTHEW: JESUS IS THE NEW MOSES AND THE DEFINITIVE LIBERATOR

Matthew has four episodes related to the infancy of Christ: the arrival of the Magi following a star from the Orient, the flight of the holy family to Egypt, the killing of the innocents decreed by Herod, and the return of the Holy Family from Egypt to Nazareth (Matt. 2). Are these historical events or are they a theological reflection similar in nature to the midrash (a historization of a passage of the Sacred Scriptures or an amplification that embellishes a fact to emphasize its message), which seeks to express faith in Jesus? This final possibility can be clearly seen in the texts themselves.

What Do the Magi and the Star Mean?

As we have seen, for Matthew, Christ is the Messiah who arrived in the fullness of time and fulfilled all the prophecies spoken concerning him. One of these prophecies refers to the fact that at the end of time kings and nations would come to Jerusalem to adore God and the Messiah and offer him gifts (Isa. 60:6; Ps. 71:10f.). Hence the Magi go to Jerusalem (Matt. 2:1f.) before arriving in Bethlehem. They follow a star from the Orient (Matt. 2:3), called the star of the king of Judah. The star is a motif that was well known at the time of the New Testament. All people had their own star, but this was especially true of the great and powerful such as Alexander, Mithridates, Augustus, the wise men, and philosophers like Plato. Judaism also knows of the star of the messianic liberator in the prophecy of Balaam (Num. 24:17). A star appeared before the births of Abraham, Isaac, Jacob, and Moses. This was the Jewish belief at the time of the New Testament.

A historical fact is also added: Ever since the days of Johannes Kepler, astronomical calculations have shown that in about the year 7 B.C. there indeed occurred a great conjunction of Jupiter and Saturn in the constellation of Pisces. This fact would have hardly passed unnoticed, since at that time belief in the stars was highly cultivated. In Hellenist astrology Jupiter was considered to be the sovereign king of the universe. Saturn was designated the star of the Jews. The constellation of Pisces was related to the end of the world. Given the conjunction of these stars, the wise men of the Orient, Magi who deciphered the course of the stars, naturally gave the following interpretation: In the country of the Jews (Saturn), a sovereign king has been born (Jupiter), one who pertains to the end of time (Pisces).[6] They began their journey and thus the prophecy concerning the Messiah is fulfilled for Matthew. Texts of the Old Testament and astronomical fact motivated the account given by Matthew, which announced the church's faith in Jesus as an eschatological Messiah.

The Last Liberator (Jesus) Is Like the First (Moses)

Just as Luke traces a parallel between the infancy of
Jesus and that of John the Baptist, so Matthew traces a
parallel between the infancy of Jesus and that of Moses.[7]
In New Testament times people believed that the
Messiah-Liberator of the last days would also be a new
Moses, performing signs and miracles just like Moses.
They would even say that the last liberator (the Mes-
siah) is like unto the first (Moses). We know that Mat-
thew in his Gospel presents Jesus as a new Moses, that
like the first liberator Jesus too gave a new law: the
Sermon on the Mount.

Jewish midrash concerning Moses refers to the following (and in this one can see an almost perfect parallel
with Jesus). Pharaoh is notified by Magi of the birth of
the liberator (Moses); Herod is informed by Magi in a
similar manner concerning the final Liberator (Jesus).
Pharaoh and all the people of Egypt are terrified; Herod
and all Jerusalem are perturbed (Matt. 2:3). Both
Pharaoh and Herod decide to kill innocent children.
Both Moses and Jesus escape the slaughter. Moses'
father learns in a dream that his son is to be a future
savior. Joseph, in like manner, learns in a dream that
Jesus will be Savior ("because he is the one who is to
save his people from their sins": Matt. 1:21). The parallel
is forced upon us by the text itself and completed with
another text from Exod. 4:19–23: "After the death of
Pharaoh God said to Moses 'Go back to Egypt, because
those who plotted against your life are dead.' " Moses
takes his wife and child and returns. Matt. 2:2,19–21
says the same thing: "Get up, take the child and his
mother with you and go back to the land of Israel, for
those who wanted to kill the child are dead." Joseph
takes his wife and legal son and returns.

The destiny of the new Moses repeats the destiny of

the first Moses. Just as had occurred in the case of the first liberator so also with the last. The boy-Jesus is really the awaited Messiah-Liberator and the eschatological prophet. The flight into Egypt and the slaughter of innocent children in Bethlehem do not necessarily have to be historical facts.[8] They serve to create a parallel with the destiny of Moses. The sources we have from that epoch, especially Flavius Josephus, who gives us minute details concerning Herod, never mention such a slaughter. Though it cannot be proved historically (nor is such necessary, since in Matthew's account it serves as a theological reflection), it could have occurred. We know that Herod was very cruel; he decimated his own family, so that the fifth-century historian Macrobius (*Saturnalia*, 2,4,11) refers to a saying of Caesar Augustus: I would prefer to be one of Herod's pigs (*hys*) than be his son (*hyos*).

As in a prologue, Matthew 1–2 presents in postpaschal perspective the great themes of the gospel: This Jesus of Nazareth is the one true Messiah, son of Abraham, descendent of the royal messianic house of David, the new Moses, who now, at the apex of history and at its final moment, will take the people of the exodus from Egypt to a definitive homeland.

CONCLUSION: THE BIRTH—THE SAME TRUTH YESTERDAY AND TODAY

A few readers uninformed of today's elementary exegetical procedures may be scandalized by the above discussion. All is mere story? The evangelists led us astray? No, the accounts of the sacred birth are not mere stories nor have we been led astray. It is we who have erred, by approaching the Gospels with a perspective not intended by the authors; we want answers to questions never asked by them. The Gospels, especially the account of the infancy of Jesus, are not historical pamphlets. They are announcement and preaching, where real facts and sayings of the Holy Scriptures or the midrash commentaries of the day were taken on, worked over, and put at the service of the truths of faith the evangelists sought to proclaim. Hence the official magisterium of the church recommends that the scriptural scholar "in order to understand what God wanted to transmit to us, ought to carefully investigate what the sacred authors wanted to have understood and what it pleases God to manifest by means of their words. . . . They ought to take into special account the literary forms" (Vatican II, *Dei Verbum*, no. 12).

At the time the New Testament was composed, the *haggadah midrash* was a widely used literary form; as we have noted, this form takes a scriptural fact or saying and fashions it and embellishes it with the intention of underlining some truth of faith and proclaiming it in an unequivocal form. This is what happens in the infancy accounts. There are real facts in them. But these are clothed in a theological form, in a language that for us today has become almost incomprehensible. But it is within this literary form that the message is hidden, the message we must unravel, retain, and proclaim once again in our present-day language: that this fragile child was not a "nobody," an unimportant person, but God himself in the human condition; that God so loved matter that he assumed it, and so loved human beings that he became one of us in order to liberate us; and that God became human in order to divinize us.

With Jesus the evolutionary psycho-social process attained a zenith, decisive for the remainder of the march to God, because in Jesus the end has already occurred and the goal has already been achieved within time. This is the fundamental message that the infancy accounts of Jesus wish to transmit to us, so that, accepting it, we can have hope and joy: we are no longer on our own in our immense loneliness and search for unity, integration, solidarity, and reconciliation of all with all. He is in the midst of us, Emmanuel, God-with-us; "today a liberator has been born to you, he is Christ the Lord" (Luke 2:11). If we try by every means to safeguard the historicity of every scene in the infancy accounts, we end up losing the message intended by the inspired authors and finally place ourselves outside the evangelical atmosphere created by Luke and Matthew. They did not want to know whether or not the Magi's star appeared, whether or not the angels appeared at Bethlehem; they wanted to discover the religious significance of the Little One who is there to be received by us, not in a cold manger, but in the warmth of our hearts full of faith.

But what will we do with the myths after they have been demythologized? They are continually being represented in the crib and lived in the memory of little and adult children. Have they lost their value? If they have lost their historical factual value, perhaps now they can begin to take on their true religio-anthropological significance. Can we speak of the profound mysteries of God who became flesh, of the unfathomable mystery of the very existence of good and evil, of salvation and damnation without having to resort to stories and the use of myths and symbols? Structuralism has seen (but theology always knew) that myth, symbol, and analogy constitute the core of religious language; we can speak only with great hesitation and must use figurative and representative language when dealing with the most profound realities of life, of good and evil, of joy and sorrow, of human beings and the Absolute.

However, this mode of expression is more involving than cold conceptualization. Because it has no tight and defined limits it is far more suggestive of the ineffable and the transcendent than any other scientific language or historical method. Hence it is good that we continue to speak of the child between the donkey and the cow, of the shepherds and the sheep, of the star and the Magi, of the evil king and good Joseph, of the Virgin-mother and the swaddling clothes that envelop the Little One on dry straw. But at the same time we ought to take into account—and this is necessary if we are not to feed magic and sentimentalism—that all this constitutes an order of symbolism and not of a reality of brute fact. The symbol is, humanly speaking, more real and significant than historically factual cold data. (Guimarães Rosa has said that in the story all is true and certain because all is invented.) Myths and stories, when understood and accepted as such by reason, do not alienate us, nor ensnare us in magic, nor sentimentalize us; rather they make us plunge into the depths of a reality where we begin to perceive the meaning of innocence and reconciliation, to perceive the divine and human transparency in the most banal things as well as the meaning of life. All this can be perceived in the birth of the divine child.

What are we to do with the accounts of the birth and the crib? They should continue to exist. But they should be understood and hence reveal that which they ought to and seek to reveal: that the eternal youth of God penetrated this world never again to leave it, that on the happy night of his birth a sun arose that will never set.

10

Only a God
Could Be So Human!
Jesus, the Man Who Is God

It is not by means of abstract analysis of the nature of God and the human person that we can come to an understanding of Jesus Man-God. But it was by seeing, imitating, deciphering, and living with Jesus that his disciples came to know God and the human person. The God who is revealed in and through Jesus is human. And the human being who emerges in and through Jesus is divine. It was in a human being that the primitive church discovered God. The dogmas do not seek to imprison or to be a substitute for the mystery; rather they establish a doctrinal and communal rule for speaking of the mystery. In this chapter we look at the principal attempts to express the mystery up to the formula of reconciliation of the Council of Chalcedon. Taking into consideration the fact that the words "nature" and "person" have different meanings today, we seek to get nearer the mystery with Jesus himself as our starting point. This profession of faith concerning Jesus and with Jesus as starting point carries with it the demand to imitate his way of being (being-for-others). The Incarnation, therefore, involves a message that refers not only to Jesus Christ but also to nature and the destiny of each person.

The man Jesus of Nazareth revealed such greatness and profundity in his humanity that at the end of a long process of meditation the apostles and those who knew him had to say: Only God himself could be so human. And then they began to call him God. As of that moment, the apostles, who were Jews, left off being Jews in order to become Christians. The Jews held the absolute unity of God as a fundamental doctrine of their faith. The profession of faith that every pious Jew recites twice a day begins: "Listen, Israel: The Lord, our God, is the only God." Nobody can be at God's side, even if he is called Jesus of Nazareth, the resurrected one.

A HUMAN GOD AND A DIVINE HUMAN

Jesus is a Jew of Nazareth; numbered among the despised of Galilee (half of whose population was pagan); juridically the son of the carpenter Joseph and the virgin Mary, whose "sisters" and "brothers" are known, o.g., Jacob, Joseph, Jude, and Simon (Mark 6:3; Matt. 13:56); who was born under the Roman Emperor Augustus in the *immensa romanae pacis maiestas*, raised under Quirinius, governor of the Province of Syria (Luke 2:1), and Pontius Pilate, Roman administrator of Judea (Luke 3:1); and Herod Antipas of Galilee (Luke 3:1), who was crucified under Emperor Tiberius on Friday, the fourteenth (according to John) or the fifteenth (according to the Synoptics) of the month of Nisan, and a few days later rose again. How does one understand that this concrete man, with his individual and datable history, is at one and the same time God? What greatness, sovereignty, and profundity must he not have revealed and lived in order to be called God? What does "God" mean now? What sort of human being is he, that we can make such an assertion about him? What does the unity of the two—God and man—concretely signify in a historical being, one of our brothers, Jesus of Nazareth?

This is one of the central facts of our faith that sets Christianity apart from other religions. Once Christianity affirms that a man is at the same time God, it stands alone in the world. We are obliged to say it: This is a scandal to the Jews and to all the religions and pious peoples of yesterday and today who venerate and adore a transcendent God: one that is totally other, who cannot be objectified, a God beyond this world, infinite, eternal, incomprehensible, and above everything that human beings can be and know. We Christians find that the God of the Jewish, pagan, and world religious experience has become concrete in a man, Jesus of Nazareth, in his life, words, and comportment, in his death and resurrection. We Christians learn the meaning of human persons, their roots and true humanity, by meditating on the human life of Jesus Christ.

However it is not by means of abstract analysis concerning the nature of God and human beings that we come to understand the nature of Jesus Man-God. Rather by seeing, imitating, and deciphering Jesus, by living together with him, we come to know God and human beings. The God who in and through Jesus reveals himself is human. And the human being who emerges in and through Jesus is divine. This is the specific characteristic of the Christian experience of God and human beings, one that is different from that of Judaism and paganism. It was in a man that the primitive church discovered God; and it was in God that we came to know the true nature and destiny of human beings.

Hence when looking at Jesus Christ we can truly say: The mystery of human beings evokes the mystery of God; living out the mystery of God evokes the mystery of human beings. We cannot speak of human beings without having to speak of God and we cannot speak of God without speaking of human beings. The reflections made here concerning Jesus and with him as starting point perhaps allow us to say: The more Jesus presents himself as a human person the more God is manifested; the more divine Jesus is, the more the human person is revealed.

How can such affirmations, which are paradoxical and contain a difficult identity of opposites, be understood? When we speak of Jesus we must always think of God and the human person, both at the same time and in conjunction. The identity of both in Jesus is such that neither God nor the human person loses anything of their essence and reality. The unity of God and human person in Jesus is so profound that it should be possible to discover his humanity in his divinity and his divinity in his humanity. What words can we use to express such a reality? We will briefly discuss various models used by faith in former times and even to this day.[1] We will also develop a line of thought that may, within the framework of our language and the preoccupations of people today, offer us some light to understand the divine and human profundity of Jesus and, on this basis, our own mystery also.

WE CANNOT SPEAK ABOUT JESUS, BUT ONLY WITH JESUS AS OUR STARTING POINT

Faith has always tried to throw some light on the meaning of the phrase: Jesus is true God and true man. Faith that tries to understand is called theology, in this case, Christology. Theology does not seek, nor should it, to control faith. On the contrary, it seeks to help and clarify faith. It seeks to be one among the possible forms of faith: critical, rational, scientific (if possible), always searching for a better analysis of the life of faith, not to violate its intimacy but to detect the rationality and gracious logic of God and thus to love God in a more intense and human way. To speak in a christological manner can never mean to speak *about* Jesus. We do not possess a superior vantage point from which we can speak *about* Jesus in an objective and impartial manner. We can speak *about* things. We can never speak *about* persons, *about* Jesus, *about* God. True theologians can speak only when Jesus Christ is their point of departure, that is, when touched by Jesus' reality lived in faith and love. Only then, after being inserted into his life, can theologians perceive his meaning and begin to see God in the human being and the human being in God.

When we speak and reflect with Jesus Christ as our starting point we use the words, instruments, and models by which we understand others and ourselves and which are taken from the cultural world about us. Our concepts and formulas constitute the exterior and fragile vase that preserves a precious essence. They do not substitute for the mystery but seek to communicate it; though the precious essence be represented in an imperfect manner, it is always expressed within a language that is comprehensible to a particular epoch. Even the dogmas do not seek to imprison and substitute for the mystery; rather, as the great German theologian Karl Rahner says, dogmas establish a doctrinal and communitarian rule for speaking with mystery as one's point of departure.[2] Dogmas are a verbal and doctrinal fixing of the fundamental truths of Christianity for a determined period of time, developed with the help of the instruments of expression offered by that cultural milieu. Hence it is not enough to recite ancient and venerable formulas if we wish to be Christian and orthodox. We are required to live the mystery that the formulas contain and always try to express it anew within our language and for our own times.[3] Only in this manner can the faith cease to be a museum piece and begin to be an inspiration to life focused on God, to the development of human potential continuously overcoming all obstacles.

In the history of faith, there have been many attempts

to explain how Jesus can be simultaneously God and man. Practically every generation confronts this mystery and defines itself anew trying to make responsible use of the language at its disposal. At times it is a happy endeavor and at other times it is less inspired. There have been errors, deviations, and heresies, which are radicalizations of partial truths to a point where the totality of faith is lost or distorted. Nevertheless heresies are witnesses to a passionate interest in Jesus. When confronted with Jesus, God-Man, one can say too much or too little. One can sin by excess or by deficiency. To speak correctly with Jesus Christ as our point of departure consists in this: One neither overstresses the human nor the divine, one neither diminishes the man nor diminishes God.

A DIFFICULT TENSION

In the history of christological reflection we notice the following tendency: At times the God in Jesus is accentuated to the detriment of the man; at times the man prevails in Jesus thus prejudicing God. But it can also happen that the very unity of man and God in Jesus is not maintained in proper balance. There is a tendency to radicalize the union to such an extent that either God absorbs the man or the man absorbs God. The inverse can also occur: The duality of God-Man is so accentuated that it is no longer possible to see how they can both be united in a concrete individual, Jesus of Nazareth. We will try briefly to delineate the great historical moments of the reflection concerning this Christological mystery and to see how orthodoxy held its balance within this powerful dialectical tension. It avoided extremes either on the human or divine side of Jesus up until the Ecumenical Council of Chalcedon (A.D. 451), when orthodoxy formulated with full lucidity the fundamental truth that Jesus is wholly and simultaneously true man and true God.

The first great debate had its origins in biblical

monotheism itself: How could the divinity of Jesus be guaranteed in a comprehensible manner? A first current, already opposed by John the evangelist, affirmed: Yes, Jesus was God, but his humanity was merely apparent. Hence he did not suffer and his death was illusory (Ebionites and Docetists). Another current affirmed the divinity of Jesus but taught that Jesus is the incarnation of the Father: It was the Father who suffered and died (Patripassionism). Others said that Jesus belongs to the divine sphere, but he is subordinate to God (Subordinationism); that he is the Logos and at the side of God, but he was created as the first among all beings (Arianism); and that God is one and unique and his unity cannot be compromised by giving a divine character to Jesus.

Another group affirmed the divine sonship of Jesus, as do many texts of the New Testament, but understood him to be an adopted son (Adoptionism) and not the eternal and only-begotten Son of the Father. Another current struggled vigorously, going so far as arming the monks and divising court intrigues, and affirmed that Jesus was only like unto God but not equal to him nor did he have the same nature (the *omoiousios* of Arius).

At the Council of Nicea they fought fiercely over the letter "i"—*omoousios* (equal) or *omoiousios* (similar) to God—with the full participation of the people in the public squares and the markets. This ecumenical council (A.D. 325) dissolved the polemic, teaching in a solemn and irreformable manner that "Jesus is the Son of God, God of God, light of light, true God of true God, born not created of the same substance as the Father, by whom all things in heaven and earth were made."[4]

As can be seen, faith always opposed any diminution of the divinity of Jesus. He is the true God. Meanwhile another question must be answered: How do these two realities relate to one another—God and man—in a concrete and unique being? On this point there were many disputes between theologians and schools. But in an-

cient times two schools of thought became famous and
their solutions have had repercussions in piety and
theology to this day: the school of Alexandria and the
school of Antioch in Asia Minor.

God Became a Human Being
So That Human Beings Could Become God

In ancient times Alexandria was a cultural and
philosophical center for the most renowned personalities. They had a preference for the various ver-
sions of Plato and cultivated an ardent mysticism of
union with the One and the Absolute. In this school the
Logos is a reference point and key concept for the comprehension of the universe. The Logos pervades the
cosmos, giving it life, order, and unity. In an excellent
way the Logos takes concrete form in the human person,
defined as a rational and logical being. The Logos had its
most perfect incarnation in Jesus Christ. Thus in the
opinion of St. Athanasius, the humanity of Christ is
merely the Logos's organ and instrument of presence
and action in this world.[5] The Logos is present in Christ
in such a profound and radical manner that whoever
stands before Christ stands before God himself. God
made himself a human being so that the human being
could become God: Here we have the preferred formula
of this school, one that expresses the essential unity of
the human being and God in Christ.

However, such affirmations incur the risk of not
sufficiently guarding the dual reality of Jesus. The
Monophysite danger is latent in the Alexandrian school,
i.e., in the effort to accentuate the man-God unity in
Jesus, the divine nature totally absorbs the human nature. There would then be only one nature in Christ, and
this divine, and consequently there would also be only
one person, that of the eternal Word. This position was
first defended by Eutyches. The man Jesus of Nazareth
loses his independence and historical reality, and this

theory once again reduces the mystery of Christ. In fact, such a reduction of the human reality of Jesus in favor of the divine was taught in Alexandria. Apollinaris of Laodicea employed the Aristotelian principle according to which two complete natures cannot form a unity. He argued: In order to have a profound and intimate unity between God and man in Jesus, as is actually the case, one nature must necessarily be incomplete; this evidently is the human nature. Then Apollinaris taught that in the incarnation the Logos substituted for the human spirit. The human being is composed of body, soul, and spirit. In Jesus, the Logos substituted for the spirit.

Against Apollinaris, who thus diminished the man-Jesus, St. Gregory of Nazianzus retorted with a fundamental principle: That which God did not assume he also did not redeem. If the Logos did not assume the human spirit, it was not redeemed.[6] And sin, added another great theologian, Theodore of Mopsuestia, occurs especially in the spirit.[7] Hence, rather than the body it is the spirit that ought to be assumed in order to be redeemed. Prior to this, Arius, working within the same tendency, had affirmed that by the incarnation the Word substituted for the human soul. Once again there is an unorthodox reduction of the humanity of Jesus. Others held that by the fact of incarnation the human intelligence was substituted for by the Word. Others affirmed that it was the human will (Monotheletism). Finally, some taught that the operative principle in Jesus came solely from the Word (Monoenergism); only Jesus-God acts, not Jesus-man.

All these positions were rejected by orthodoxy because they did not succeed in maintaining the difficult tension between the true man and the true God that faith posits in Jesus. The unity in Jesus is profound and intimate; nevertheless it ought not be conceived in such a way that the terms of God and man are eliminated. The erroneous presupposition in all these conceptions consists in understanding the perfection of human nature in a static manner, defining it as closed in on itself and isolated. Later christological discussions will show the exact opposite: The perfection of human beings lies precisely in their total and infinite openness, open to such an extent that they can be full of God.

Monophysitism, the tendency to give too much emphasis to the divine nature of Jesus, is a constant temptation for theology and especially for popular piety.[8] Jesus came to claim that which was his own—humanity. The great temptation of the faithful consists in allowing those sad words of John to be realized: his own did not receive him in the form in which he wished to present himself—as man, brother, participator in our suffering and fragile human condition.

The Entire Human Being Was Assumed by the Eternal Word

Another school was also celebrated in ancient times for its culture and sense of the real and the concrete: the school of Antioch, strongly influenced by Aristotle. This school took a very serious stance on the Aristotelian principle that was also employed at Alexandria: Two complete natures cannot be unified in a single nature. Diodorus of Tarsus (d. 394) deduced from this that the human nature and the divine nature are not united in Jesus of Nazareth, but that they are merely attached one to the other, each remaining perfect in itself. The union in Jesus is not intimate and profound, but accidental. Hence it follows that in Jesus there are not only two natures, but also two distinct persons, one human and the other divine. The Patriarch of Constantinople, the monk Nestorius, brought this comprehension to its logical consequences and began to preach that Mary could not be called the mother of God (*theotokos*) but only the mother of the man Jesus (*anthropotokos*). To be theologically precise, she was the mother of Christ (*christotokos*).

St. Cyril, Patriarch of Alexandria, violently opposed

Nestorius. At the Council of Ephesus (431), called to resolve the misunderstandings, an enormous rift developed between the participants. They mutually excommunicated one another. Finally, though with great difficulty, the expression "Mother of God" (*theotokos*) triumphed as the orthodox expression of Mariology and Christology. The school of Antioch's greatest representatives were St. John Chrysostom, Theodore of Mopsuestia (d. 428), Theodoret of Cyrrhus (d. 466), and John of Antioch. The basic tendency was to emphasize the spontaneity and autonomy of the man-Jesus when confronted with God-Jesus. The eternal Logos united itself to a man, complete and perfect in his intelligence and liberty (*assumptus homo*).

But then the question emerges: Did God and the man pre-exist and become united afterward? If this is the case then Christ is a third being: The man-Jesus is not one with God and he would not exist outside of this unity. If, on the contrary, we say that the man-Jesus began to exist from the moment of the incarnation, then another problem emerges: Did the man-Jesus have his own individuality? If he took on the individuality of the Logos then we ought to say that Jesus was never a man, but, from the beginning, a superman. Once again the Monophysite danger is unfolded—reducing the reality of Christ to only one nature, the divine. A Christology that thinks in terms of a static ontology of the human and divine natures seems unable to escape a basic dilemma: Either one falls into the Monophysite error, giving too much emphasis to the unity with God, or into Nestorianism, exaggerating the independence of the individual concrete man to the point of postulating a duality of persons in Jesus.

Both schools elaborate Christology with the incarnation as their point of departure. However the incarnation should not be one's starting point, but one's destination. If we make it our point of departure, then the whole discussion will be tied down trying to resolve which of Christ's actions ought to be attributed to one or other nature, how they interpenetrate one another in order to constitute the individual and historical being, Jesus of Nazareth, and what ought to be understood in terms of his human nature and what in term of his divine nature. Can we know who God is? Who the human being is? Are we not starting with mysteries in an attempt to explain other mysteries? We do not light up luminous dark spots with less luminous dark spots. As we will show later on, extending the line of christological thought elaborated up to this chapter, the basis of our faith in the divinity of Jesus resides in his profoundly human appearance and radically human way of acting in this world. To conclude this long process of meditation, which seeks to explain the historical Jesus, we can say: He is the incarnation of God himself, his epiphanic and diaphanous appearance within human and historical reality.

CHALCEDON: A FORMULA OF RECONCILIATION BETWEEN DUALITY AND UNITY

The Ecumenical Council of Chalcedon (451) was able to take up the truth in each school, both Alexandrian and Antiochian. There is a unity in Jesus, as the Alexandrian theologians taught, but only in terms of person, not in terms of nature. There is a real duality in Jesus, as was taught by the Antiochian theologians, but solely a duality of natures and not one of persons. A christological formula was then established, under the influence of Pope Leo the Great, which is still the criterion of truth for every interpretation of the mystery of Jesus:

Following the holy Fathers, therefore, we all with one accord teach the profession of faith in the one identical Son, our Lord Jesus Christ. We declare that he is perfect both in his divinity and in his humanity, truly God and truly man composed of body and rational soul; that he is consubstantial with the Father in his divinity, consubstantial with us in his humanity, like us in every respect except for sin (see Heb. 4:15). We declare that in his divinity he was begotten of the Father before time, and in his humanity he was begotten in this last age of Mary the Virgin, the Mother of God, for us and for our salvation. We declare that the one selfsame Christ, only-begotten Son and Lord, must be acknowledged in two natures without any commingling or change or division or separation; that the distinction between the natures is in no way removed by their union but rather that the specific character of each nature is preserved and they are united in one person and one hypostasis. We declare that he is not split or divided into two persons, but that there is one selfsame only-begotten Son, God the Word, the Lord Jesus Christ. This the prophets have taught about him from the beginning; this Jesus Christ himself taught us; this the creed of the Fathers has handed down to us.[9]

This dogmatic formula does not try to explain *how* God and man cooperate to form *one and the same* Jesus, but to settle the criteria that ought to be present in every attempt at explanation, that is, the complete humanity and the true divinity of Jesus ought to be simultaneously maintained without dividing his fundamental unity. The Council's intention is neither metaphysical nor doctrinal but soteriological. Basically the Council wanted to affirm the following, as has been well expressed in a recent study by a Spanish theologian:

a. That if Jesus is not God, then no salvation has come through him. We are still in our sin and have no certainty with regard to the future.

b. That if Jesus is not man, then salvation has not been given to us.

c. That if the humanity is not "God's" (in the same measure that my own being is mine and not merely a linguistic accommodation), then the divinization of humankind has not been fully realized and Jesus is not truly God.

d. That if the humanity coming "from God" is not true humanity or if it does not remain humanity, then it is not humanity that was saved in Jesus the man, but some other being.[10]

The definitive, irreformable, and imperishable character of this christological dogma resides in these four points. To express such a reality, the Council used the Greek model of comprehension, employing the words "nature" and "person." Human and divine *nature* is simply the name for all that perfects the human being and the divine being; it designates that which Jesus has in common with the Father (divinity) and in common with us (humanity). The Council understands the word "nature" in an abstract sense as synonymous with essence or substance. By his divinity, Jesus is of the same essence as the Father and by his humanity, of the same essence as every human being. However, the Person of the Logos is the bearer and the subject of these two natures, conferring unity on one and the same Jesus. This personal unity is so intimate that the qualities of both natures—divine and human—can be attributed to the same Person of the Word. Hence one can say: God was born, God suffered and died, or Jesus Christ is omnipotent, etc. Thus the two *abstract* natures, are *concretely* united in the divine Person of the Eternal Word.

Hence the central thesis of the Council of Chalcedon affirms the unity of the concrete being Jesus. *one and the same* Lord, etc. "Person" (*hypostasis*) in the dogmatic formula only seeks to express the principle of unity in being, that which makes anything one: He who was born of God and the Virgin is one and the same, not two, as the Nestorians thought. The principle of unity in a being is *not a new being.* Hence the absence of a human person in Jesus (in the classical metaphysical sense) does not imply a lack of anything in the humanity of Jesus. Person is not a being or a "thing" in human beings but their way of existing, insofar as they sustain themselves and ontologically affirm their being. The man-Jesus, because of his union with God, is sustained by the same

ontological sustaining force as that of God. The one and
only divine Person is the bearer of the two natures,
divine and human. Nevertheless, how does this unity of
natures by way of Person come about?

This problem was not touched on by the Council of
Chalcedon and remains open to the theological speculation of faith. In the Council, they did not reflect on the
relations between person and nature, nor did they
broach the basic question: How can there be a human
nature without there being a personality also? In the
Council's terms of definition, only the divine person and
not the human one subsists in Jesus. The Council was
certainly not trying to teach that Christ had no conscious center or human "I." It merely happened that the
Council did not regard this as the property of the person,
but of the divine nature. However, it is the property of
the person to be the bearer and sustainer of free acts.
Now in the man-Jesus this was the eternal Person of the
Son. This eternal Person assumed to itself the "human
person" of Jesus; this human person was not annihi-
lated but totally realized, not in itself, but in the divine
Person (in hypostatic union as the patristic tradition
often says).[11] During his concrete existence, the man-
Jesus was never defined with his own self as starting
point but always with God as point of departure. The
basis of his life did not reside in himself, but in the divine
Person. This is the profound meaning expressed by the
Council of Chalcedon through the rigid formulas of nature and person.

This datum could be lost today, because the words
"nature" and "person" have taken on different meanings. "Nature" for us is not a static concept as it was in
the ancient world, but an essentially dynamic one.
Human nature emerges in the development of a long
biological process, and culture, education, and our
milieu have worked together to produce what we are
today. Nature in human beings consists in all that is
physically, psychically, historically, sociologically, and

spiritually given—all that which precedes a free decision and makes it possible. "Person" is this same nature
thus marked, insofar as it is in possession of itself and
realizes itself dynamically and relationally in communion with the totality of surrounding reality.[12] Hence,
person is first *ultima solitudo*,[13] as Duns Scotus said:
Person is possession of self, self-consciousness, and interior autonomy.

Person exists in itself and for itself. Person is an "I."
Nevertheless, in a second instance (not chronological
but logical), person is *essentially* communion, relation,
dialogue. The "I" exists and subsists only if it opens
itself to a "You." The original word is not "I" but
"I-You-We." It is only by means of the "You" that the
"I" discovers itself as an "I." The person is indeed autonomy and freedom though not freedom *from* others
but *for* others. The more one is free for others and especially for the Great Other (God), the more one becomes
person. As can be seen there is no real distinction between nature and person. Person is nature itself insofar
as it takes account of itself, opens itself up, possesses
itself, predisposes itself for relationship, and can, as we
shall see below, identify with the other in that relationship.

Beginning with this reflection, deepened especially by
modern thought, we can see the limits of the Chalcedonian christological model of interpretation.[14] The Chalcedonian formula does not take into account the evolution in Christ that can be seen in the Synoptic Gospels.
Nor does it perceive the transformations that occurred
with the resurrection, where the Logos-flesh (*sarx*) became the Logos-spirit (*pneuma*). The incarnation, as
seen by Chalcedon, makes it difficult to understand the
kenosis of God in Jesus, that is: how God humbles himself and makes himself anonymous. We must respect
and try to understand the anonymity of God in Jesus
and its theological significance. In the Chalcedonian
formula one also notes an absence of a universal, cosmic

perspective. It is a Christology without a Logos.[15] The incarnation not only touches Jesus of Nazareth but all humanity. As *Gaudium et Spes* says: "By his incarnation, the Son of God has united himself in some fashion with every man" (no. 22). By the resurrection, the dimensions of the cosmos are expanded, as the Greek and Latin fathers under the influence of Plato used to accentuate.

Moreover, there is an even more basic limitation. The Council of Chalcedon, when speaking of the two natures of Jesus, one divine and the other human, runs the grave risk of placing God and humanity, the Infinite and the finite, the Creator and the creature, within the same horizon and on the same level. God is not simply a being, like a human being. God is the one who transcends all beings and all our concepts. The unity of two natures in one and the same being does not signify a fusion of two essences and a unification of two dimensions. We will try, using the framework of our current understanding of man-person, to reread the message of Chalcedon with a view to grasping in our language the profound and true meaning of the Council formula: that simultaneously there subsist in Jesus *verus homo* (true man) and the *verus Deus* (true God). We will see that incarnation does not merely signify that God assumed and penetrated the concrete human reality of Jesus of Nazareth, but that Jesus also actively assumes and penetrates the divine reality of the Second Person of the Blessed Trinity. The incarnation is the plenitude of the manifestation of God and the plenitude of the manifestation of the human being.

JESUS: THE HUMAN BEING WHO IS GOD, AND THE GOD WHO IS HUMAN

Most attempts to clarify the divinity and humanity of Jesus start with an analysis either of the human or divine nature, or the meaning of person. We will try the inverse route: we will attempt to understand the human being and God with Jesus himself as our starting point.[16] Humanity in its greatest radicality was revealed in Jesus and this also revealed the human God. Hence it is not by means of an abstract analysis of humanity and divinity that one can clarify the mystery of Jesus of Nazareth, who so fascinated the apostles that they called him God. Anthropology ought to be elaborated with Christology as its point of departure.

The Gospels and our exposition of Jesus' extraordinary good sense, creative imagination, and originality have demonstrated that the existence of Jesus was an existence totally orientated and lived for others and for the great Other (God). He was absolutely open to all, he did not discriminate against anyone, and he embraced all with this unlimited love, especially those socially and religiously marginalized (Mark 2:15–17). He personally lived the love he preached for enemies (Matt. 5:43), forgiving those who crucified him (Luke 23:34–46). He had no prefabricated schema, nor did he immediately moralize, nor did he censure those who came to him: "Whoever comes to me I shall not turn him away" (John 6:37). If he was liberal when confronted with the law, he was rigorous when imposing the demands of love that bind human beings with more liberating ties than those of the law. His death was not merely a consequence of his fidelity to the liberating mission confided to him by the Father; it was also fidelity to human beings whom he loved unto the end (John 13:1).[17]

Jesus was a person who was empty of himself. Hence he could be completely filled by others, whom he received and accepted as they were. They could be women or children, tax-collectors or sinners, prostitutes or theologians, ex-guerrillas (three of whom would become his disciples) or pious people like the Pharisees. Jesus was a man who always understood himself from the point of view of others; his being was continuously a being-for-others. He cultivated a relationship of extreme intimacy with the Great Other, God. He calls God "Abba, Father," in a language suggestive of confidence and childlike trust (Mark 14:36; cf. Rom. 18:15; Gal. 4:6). He feels himself to be God's Son (Matt. 11:27; Mark 12:6; 13:52). His intimate relationship with the Father does not betray any resemblance to an Oedipus complex: It is transparent and diaphonous. He invokes God as a Father, but he is not like a lost son who returns repentant and throws himself into his father's arms.

Jesus never asks for forgiveness or some favor for himself. He does ask to be freed from pain and death (Mark 14:36; Mark 15:34,37; John 11:41–42), but, even then, he wants the Father's will and not his to be realized (Mark 14:36). His final words are ones of serene surrender: "Father into your hands I commit my spirit" (Luke 23:46). He understands himself totally from the viewpoint of God, to whom he is completely open. John legitimately allows Jesus to say: "I can do nothing by myself . . . because my aim is to do not my own will, but the will of Him who sent me" (John 5:30).

His intimacy with the Father was so profound that the same John could let Jesus say: "I and the Father are one" (John 10:30). Because he opened himself to and gave himself over to God with absolute confidence—and this is his typical way of being, which is also faith's way of being—Jesus does not possess what the Council of Chalcedon taught: He was lacking a "hypostasis," a subsistence, enduring in himself and for himself. He was completely emptied of himself and completely full of the reality of the Other, of God the Father. He realized himself radically in the other; he was not anything for himself, but all for others and for God. He was, in life and death, the grain of wheat that dies to give life, he who lost his own life in order to gain it (cf. Matt. 10:39). The absence of a human personality (hypostasis or subsistence) does not constitute an imperfection in Jesus but rather his highest perfection. Emptying himself means creating interior space to be filled with the reality of the other. It is by going out of oneself that human beings remain profoundly within their own selves; it is by giving that one receives and possesses one's being.

Hence Jesus was the human being par excellence, *ecce homo:* because his radical humanity was achieved not by anarchy and an ontological affirmation of the "I," but by surrendering and communicating his "I" to others and for others, especially for God, to the point of identifying with others and with God. From Jesus' way of being—as being-for-others—we learn our own true way of being and existing. Human existence has meaning only if understood as a total opening of oneself, as a focal point of relationships branching out in all directions to the world, the other, and God.[18] True living means "living with." Hence it is only by means of the "You" that the "I" becomes what it is. The "I" is an echo of the "You" and in last analysis, a resonance of the divine "You." The more human beings relate to others and go out of themselves, the more they grow and become human. The more they are in the other, the more they are in themselves and become themselves. The more Jesus existed in God, the more God resided in him. The more the man-Jesus dwelled in God, the more he was divinized. The more God existed in Jesus, the more God was humanized. The man-Jesus was in God in such a way that they became identified: God made himself human so that the human could become God.

If we accept in faith that Jesus was a human being who could relate to God and be in God to the point of being his Son (i.e., the personal identity of Jesus with the eternal Son), and if we accept in faith that God can empty himself of his own self (cf. Phil. 2:7) in such a way that he fills the complete openness of Jesus to the point of becoming himself human, then we accept and profess what Christians profess and accept as the Incarnation: the unconfounded, immutable, indivisible, and inseparable unity of God and humanity in one and the same Jesus Christ; God remains God and the human being radically human. Jesus was the creature that God wanted and so created that he could exist totally in God, so created that the more he became united to God, the more he became himself, that is, human.

Hence, Jesus is truly human and also truly God. The inverse is also valid: Just as the creature Jesus becomes more himself the more he is in God, in an analogous way God becomes more himself the more he is in Jesus and assumes his reality. God and the human being constitute a unity in Jesus. When confronted with Jesus believers stand before God and the *ecce homo* in a fundamental immediacy. The man-Jesus is not God's exterior receptacle, like a fragile vase about to receive its precious essence, God. The man-Jesus is God himself who enters the world and becomes history: "The word was *made* flesh, he lived among us" (John 1:14). God undergoes *becoming* while losing nothing of his being. When God *becomes* and makes himself history and becoming, there appears the one we call Jesus Christ, Word Incarnate.

Most Christians are not as yet accustomed to this idea: The God experienced and lived by Christianity is not only the transcendent, infinite God called Being, or Nothing, but the God who made himself lowly, who made himself history, who gave us love, who emptied himself even to the point of accepting death (cf. Phil. 2:7–8), who knows good health, the joy of friendship, the sorrow of separation, ardent hope and faith. God, however, could be all this only because he is really infinite, absolute love and self-communication, who created the whole cosmos and history to make possible his entry into them. Hence we can see that creation ought to be thought of with Christ as our starting point. He was the first thought of God, the one who envelops within himself the very cosmos.[19]

Jesus' complete laying open of self to others and to the Great Other was revealed not only during his earthly existence, where "he went about doing good" (Acts

10:38). The resurrection manifested the full depths of Jesus' communion and openness. The earthly Jesus, before the resurrection, was a prisoner to the coordinates of space and time, the limitations of a carnal body. Now, by means of the resurrection, the new man emerged, no longer carnal but pneumatic, for which the body is no longer a limit but total cosmic presence and communion with all reality. The resurrected Christ fills all reality, thus realizing to a maximum degree his being-in-others and his being-for-others. The Incarnation ought not to be thought of only in the light of Jesus of Nazareth participating in all our limitations and weaknesses. It ought to be contemplated also in the light of the resurrection, where what had been hidden in Jesus of Nazareth was revealed in its full clarity and transparency: a universal and maximum openness to all cosmic, human, and divine reality, which was so great that Paul could confess Jesus resurrected saying, "He is everything and is in everything" (Col. 3:11).

THE SINLESSNESS OF JESUS; HE CONQUERED THE SINFUL HUMAN CONDITION FROM WITHIN

These reflections allow us to comprehend the Incarnation in a dynamic manner. The Incarnation was not over when the Word was conceived in the womb of the Virgin. There the Incarnation erupted, to increase according as life increased and was manifested. We ought to take Luke's testimony seriously: Jesus "increased in wisdom, in stature, and in favor with God and men" (Luke 2:52). God did not assume an abstract humanity, but rather a concrete, individualized, and historically conditioned man, Jesus of Nazareth. If this man is historical and he experiences development, phases of life with proper characteristics and perfections, then nothing could be more natural than to understand the Incarnation in a dynamic manner. A truly incarnating process exists. God went on assuming the human concrete nature of Jesus according to how this manifested itself and developed. The inverse is also true: The human nature of Jesus revealed the divinity according to how it increased and matured.

At each phase of his life Jesus revealed God under a new aspect because each phase presented a corresponding development. The child Jesus revealed God within the possibilities of perfection that pertain to a child.[20] As a child he was open to God and others in as perfect and complete a manner as a child can realize. As a young man he concretized the perfection of a young man and so revealed the divinity in a manner possible to that phase of juvenile life. The same can be said of the remaining phases of Jesus' life, especially his adult phase, witnessed to in the Gospels. There, as we related above, appeared the man in full human vigor, a man of sovereignty, of creative imagination, of originality, of commitment to his cause, of total openness to whoever approached him, of virile courage in polemical confrontation with his ideological adversaries (Pharisees, scribes, and Sadducees), and of a mature relationship with God.

The highs and lows natural to a human life served as ways for Jesus to perfect and purify himself, to penetrate the meaning of man and God. The temptations referred to in the Gospels allow us to affirm that Jesus also passed through a number of crises that mark the difficult phases of human life. As in all crises, this implied a painful passage, even if a purifying one, from one level of life to another, with new possibilities of understanding and living life in its entirety.[21] In the gospel accounts one never perceives Jesus complain about the difficulties of existence. He never asks why evil exists side by side with a God who is Father and Love. It is clear to Jesus: Evil does not exist to be understood but to be fought and conquered by love.

Jesus was a person continually rewarded with the grace of God, which made him perfect before God and human beings in each phase of his life, within the possibilities permitted by the situation. He was a person with extreme sensitivity to God's will. But at the same time he was so favored, he corresponded with an adequate response. In Jesus the proposal of God and the human response arrived at a perfect correspondence. The more God communicated himself, the more Jesus gave himself to God.

The maximum in self-giving took place on the cross, where he emptied himself and lost his life for God and human beings. There, too, in a corresponding way God's greatest communication took place. And God's greatest communication is called resurrection. Hence we can say that Jesus' resurrection occurred at the moment of his death, though it was manifested three days afterward with Jesus' carnal body transformed into spiritual body. The incarnating process is completed and ends with the resurrection. Here, matter and spirit, man and God, arrive at an unspeakable unity and a full interpenetration. Only with the resurrection as our point of departure can we in some manner represent to ourselves the real meaning of the humanization of God and the divinization of man in an unconfoundable and indivisible unity.

With this reflection we can now begin to situate and understand the meaning of the sinlessness of Jesus. The New Testament texts witness to the faith of the primitive church that Jesus, though he lived in our mortal flesh (Gal. 3:13; 4:4; 2 Cor. 5:21; Rom. 8:3; 1 Pet. 2:22) and was tempted like us (Heb. 4:15; cf. 7:26; 9:14), remained nevertheless without sin (2 Cor. 5:21; 1 John 3:5; John 8:46; cf. 14:30). He was equal to us in all things except sin. He assumed the human condition characterized by the fundamental alienation that is sin (John 1:14). Paul well says that Jesus was born of a woman under the law (Gal. 4:4), made sin for us (2 Cor. 5:21). He explains this in Romans 8:3 saying: "God dealt with sin by sending his own Son in a body as physical as any sinful body, and in that body God condemned sin."

Nevertheless he was without sin. This is a fact. The tradition of the first two centuries argued like Paul that the sinlessness of Christ came not from a special quality of his nature, but from an intimate and uninterrupted union with God.[22] Only from the time of St. Augustine did they begin to argue in the light of the virginal conception of Jesus: Not only did he not sin; he could not sin since, from the first moment, he was conceived without sin by the work and power of the Holy Spirit. Moreover, the hypostatic union, according to which the divine Person of the Word is the bearer of Jesus' human acts, excludes any shadow of imperfection and sin.

But then how can we explain Jesus' temptations? How do we comprehend Jesus' faith and hope? What is the meaning of his increase and growth in favor and wisdom? A Christology based on the humanity of Jesus, in which the divinity is perceived, can illumine for us the permanent value of the traditional truth concerning the sinlessness of Jesus. Sinlessness is our negative way of expressing Jesus' union with God and God's union with Jesus. Jesus was continually centered in God. Holiness is the quality of one who is-in-God, united to him and penetrated by him. Sin is the inverse: It consists in closing in on oneself to a point where one excludes God, in a centering of the "I" on itself, an incapacity to love without egoism. Because Jesus was emptied of his own self and completely centered in God, he was without sin; because he persevered in this fundamental attitude not only did he not sin but he could not sin. Therefore the sinlessness of Jesus does not consist so much in the purity of his ethical attitudes, in the rectitude of his individual acts, but in the fundamental situation of his being in God's presence and united with God.

Original sin in human beings consists in the schizophrenia of our historical existence which makes us incapable of love, incapable of decentering ourselves radically; it ontologically distorts us even in our ultimate biological roots and places us in a bent position before

God. We can say that Jesus was totally free of original sin. He always stood erect before God. He assumed our human condition characterized by sin, but by the grace and work of the Holy Spirit the degenerating nucleus of all human acts was absent in him.

To say that he assumed the sinful human condition means that he assumed the history of human sin. The human being is a knot of relationships that branch out in all directions, a knot that is twisted and distorted in its personal and collective conscious and unconscious life. And this has its own history. Jesus, though he was without sin, assumed all this; and during his life, by means of his love and his comportment before God and human beings, he gradually overcame the history of sin in his own flesh (cf. Rom. 8:3). He gradually unravelled the knot of human relationships within each phase of human life to the point of being able to relate adequately to the world, the other, and God. The resurrection represents our definitive liberation from the sinful structure of human existence and the full realization of the possibilities of relating the personal "I" with the totality of reality.

Jesus redeemed human beings from within. He conquered temptations, alienations, and the qualities that sin in history had imprinted on human nature. Hence, he can be an example and prototype-archetype of the true human being that each of us ought to be but is not as yet. According to Jung's psychology, each person summarizes and carries in the unconscious the whole history of successful and frustrated experiences made by the human psyche since its most primitive animal and cosmic origins.[23] Each person in our own way is the totality. Admitting the reasonableness of such a hypothesis may help us to illuminate the most profound recesses of the reality of the Incarnation. The Word, humanizing itself, assumed all this reality contained in the collective and personal human psyche, both positive and negative, thereby touching all humanity. The nega-

tive tendencies that created an anti-history were un-
wound from within and the archetypes of positivity,
especially the archetype Self (*Selbst:* the archetype of
God), were activated, allowing the human being who is
really image and likeness of God to emerge. Thus, by yet
another route Jesus touches all humanity, assuming
human nature in order to liberate it for itself and for
God.

WE ARE ALL DESTINED TO BE IMAGES
AND LIKENESSES OF JESUS CHRIST

What we have just said and professed in faith *about*
Jesus and with Jesus as *starting point* has enormous
relevance. If Jesus is a truly human being, consubstantial with us, as asserted in the dogmatic formulation of
Chalcedon, then that which is asserted of him must also
be affirmed in some manner of each person. Having
Jesus, the most perfect of all human beings, as our starting point we can see who we are and how we are. Like
Jesus, all human beings find themselves in a situation of
openness to all of reality. We are open not only to the
world or culture, but also to the Infinite. We can glimpse
it in the experience of love, happiness, hope, and feeling;
in the experience of wanting and knowing that yearns
for eternity and totality. We do not want merely this or
that; we want everything. We not only want to know God
but ardently desire to possess and enjoy God and be
possessed by God.

"The human being is capable of the Infinite," according to the classical formula of medieval thinkers, especially the Franciscans. Jesus realized in an absolute and
full manner this human capacity to the point of being
identified with the Infinite. The Incarnation signifies
the exhaustive and total realization of a possibility that
God placed in human existence by the act of creation.
This is the basic thesis of the wisest and most subtle of
all medieval theologians, the Franciscan Duns Scotus

(d. 1308).[24] Through love we can open ourselves in such a way to God and others that we completely empty ourselves and fill ourselves in the same proportion with the reality of others and God. It is precisely this that occurred in the case of Jesus Christ. In other human beings, sisters and brothers of Jesus, we have received from God and Jesus the same challenge: to open ourselves more and more to everything and to everybody so that we can be the fulness of divine and human communication like Christ.

In our alienation and sin, we realize in a deficient way that relationship which Jesus of Nazareth concretized in an exhaustive and absolute fashion his terrestrial and pneumatic life. The human being that each of us is ought to be interpreted not so much in the light of our biological past, as in the light of our future. This future was manifested in Jesus, incarnate and resurrected. The future of each person is certainly not on earth, but in death and beyond death; our future consists in realizing the capacity for the Infinite that God placed in our being. Only then will the image and likeness of Christ that characterizes all human beings be realized in a complete manner.

Therefore the Incarnation contains a message that concerns not only Jesus Christ but also the nature and destiny of every person. By means of the Incarnation we come to know who in fact we are and what we are destined for. We come to know the nature of God, who in Jesus Christ comes to our encounter with a face like ours—respecting our otherness—in order to assume human nature and fill it with his divine reality.

11

Where Can We Find the Resurrected Christ Today?

The resurrection opened up a new dimension of reality and traced a new horizon for understanding it. The goal toward which human beings and the cosmos itself marched was manifested in Christ: total cosmic-human-divine realization and fullness. We discover in him, glorified in his material reality, the future destiny of human beings and matter. In overt or covert form he is present in cosmic reality and human realities, both personal and collective. This presence culminates in the church, primordial sacrament of the presence of the Lord. Being a Christian means continously trying to reproduce in our lives that which emerged in its maximum intensity and became a historical phenomenon in Jesus, the incarnate, resurrected Word.

CHRISTIANITY DOES NOT LIVE ON NOSTALGIA, BUT CELEBRATES A PRESENCE

Christianity did not present itself to the world as a religion that lives on the nostalgic memory of a happy event in the past. It emerged as an announcement and a joyful celebration of a presence, that of Christ resurrected. Jesus of Nazareth, dead and buried, does not merely live on by means of his remembrance and his message of liberation for the oppressed conscience. He himself is present and lives a way of life that has already surpassed the limitations of our world of death and realized every dimension of all its possibilities. Hence resurrection is not synonymous with resuscitation, the resuscitation of a body as was the case with Lazarus (John 11) or Jairus' daughter, both of whom had need of food (Mark 5) and eventually died once again. Resurrection must be understood as a total, exhaustive realization of human reality in its relationship with God, with others, and with the cosmos. Resurrection is therefore the eschatologization of a human being who has arrived at the end of the evolutionary process and been inserted into the divine reality.

Christ did not leave this world with the resurrection. He penetrated it in a more profound manner and is now present in all reality in the same way that God is present in all things: "I am with you always, yes, to the end of time" (Matt. 28:20). Christian faith lives on this presence and has developed a viewpoint that allows it to see all reality as penetrated by the reverberations of the resurrection. Owing to Christ's resurrection, the world became diaphanous and transparent.

UNDERSTANDING THE WORLD
IN TERMS OF ITS FUTURE ALREADY MANIFEST

The resurrection opened up a new dimension of reality and traced a new horizon of comprehension.[1] The goal of human beings and the very cosmos was revealed in Christ: total cosmic-human-divine realization or fullness. The ascending dynamics of reality found their point of convergence in the resurrected Jesus (cf. Eph. 1:10). The new future creation has already been initiated in him (2 Cor. 4:6). He is the new Adam and the new humanity (Rom. 5:14; 1 Cor. 15:21,45; cf. Col. 1:15,18), the Z-point and the end already achieved (Rev. 1:17; 21:6). With the already accomplished goal as our point of departure, the meaning of the whole process of creation and liberation can be seen. Hence, to a Christian comprehension of the world, not only the beginning and the past are determining factors in the discovery of the meaning of evolution and of totality; the future, especially as revealed in the resurrection, takes on a very specific illuminating and heuristic function.

We discover in Jesus, glorified in his material reality, the future destiny of human beings and matter. Consequently, Jesus Christ transfigured possesses an inestimable and absolute anthropological cognitive value. He brought a revolution in the interpretation of reality: We can no longer be content with analyzing the world with creation *in illo tempore* as our starting point; we must comprehend it with eschatology, the future present in Jesus resurrected, as our point of departure.

In him that which for us will take place only at the end of the world took place in time. He is the anticipated goal. We ought to understand the beginning with the end as point of our departure. God's plan becomes transparent and comprehensible only when considered with its realization and its final goal as our point of departure. Then one can see that the beginning (the creation of the world) and the middle (the creation of human beings) were stages in a vast plan that arrived at its culmination in the resurrected Jesus. With these reflections as our starting point we can better understand the reality of Christ's presence within the world today and also try to articulate some of the ways in which that presence is verified.

WAYS IN WHICH THE RESURRECTED CHRIST IS PRESENT TODAY

There are various ways in which Christ is present within the reality we live. There are different types of reality: the cosmic, the human (personal and collective), the reality of psycho-social evolution, of the church as community of faith, of the sacraments, etc. For each of these ways of being there are corresponding ways by which the resurrected Christ is present, within and through them. We will analyze here, briefly, the most general articulations.

The Cosmic Christ: "History Is Pregnant with Christ"

The Incarnation, which is no myth but a historical fact known through faith, signifies that Jesus was inserted into humanity. Through his human being as body, Jesus assumed a vital part of matter. Consequently, his relationship to our world is one of cosmogenesis.[2] Jesus-human being is the result of a long process of cosmic evolution. As body-spirit, Jesus of Nazareth was also a nexus of relationships with the totality of the human and cosmic reality that surrounded him. Hence he lived, to use the Semitic language of the Scriptures, in a "fleshly" (*sarkikos*) manner: limited by space to Galilee, Palestine, and by time to Judaic culture under Roman domination. It was a sacred agrarian society of primary relationships, with a prescientific comprehension of the world. Jesus himself was subject to the human weaknesses of pain and of death, confined in terms of knowledge and the possible interrelationships which that epoch offered.

Since he lived this corporeal condition (*sarx*=flesh, fragile human condition), the presence of Jesus in this world was necessarily circumscribed within the limitations proper to our terrestrial condition. The resurrection, nevertheless, accomplished the total openness of the man-Jesus to the proportions of the God-Jesus. By the glorification and transfiguration of his corporeal conditions, he did not abandon the world and the body: He assumed it in a fuller and more profound manner. His capacity for communion and communication with worldly matter was completely realized, in such a way that now he is not only present in Palestinian space and time, but in global space and time. The *homo absconditus* (the man hidden) in Jesus was, by the resurrection, transformed into *homo revelatus* (the man completely revealed).

Paul expresses this truth when he says that the resurrected Christ now lives in the form of Spirit (cf. 2 Cor. 3:17; 1 Cor. 6:17; 15:45; 2 Cor. 3:18; Rom. 8:9), and that his fleshly body was transformed into a spiritual-pneumatic body (cf. 1 Cor. 15:44).[3] In saying that Christ glorified is spirit, Paul is not yet thinking of Spirit in terms of the Third Person of the Trinity. Rather he wants to express the way of being of the resurrected Jesus and so reveal the real dimensions of the good news of the resurrection: He overcame all the limitations of space and earthly time and already lives in the divine sphere; his is a full and total presence in all things.[4]

Just as the Spirit fills the universe (Ps. 139:7; Gen. 1:2), so too now does Jesus resurrected. The resurrection made patent what had been latent: Christ-Spirit was acting in the world from the very beginning (Gen. 1:2); he was the creating force in nature (John 37:10; cf. Gen. 2:1) and in human beings (Gen. 2:7; Ps. 104:30; John 27:3); he was the power of God, creator of the spiritual functions of wisdom, intelligence, artistic sensitivity and ability (Exod. 31:3; 35:31; Isa. 11:2); it was he as Spirit who gave rise to extraordinary corporeal force (Judg. 14:6,19; 15:14), to words of enthusiasm (1 Chron. 12:19; 2 Chron. 15:1; 20:14), and especially to prophetic words (2 Sam. 23:2; 1 Kings 22:24; Ezek. 61:1; 11:5; Zech. 7:12; Mic. 3:8; Neh. 9:30) and directed and brought all things to salvation (Ezek. 32:15; Ps. 143:10; Neh. 9:20; Ezek. 63:11,14).

The one who thus revealed himself in a hidden manner now manifests himself openly by the resurrection like an unimaginable explosion. Hence the resurrection revealed the cosmic dimension of Christ, filling the world and human history from its very beginnings.

From this one can understand why Paul was not so much interested in the Christ of flesh (limited and fragile:Christ *kata sarka)* but almost exclusively in the Christ of Spirit (Christ *kata pneuma,* open to the dimensions of God and all reality: 2 Cor. 5:16).

Reflecting on the cosmic dimensions of the fact of the resurrection and seeing in this the goal of God's plan for the world and human beings already achieved, the authors of the New Testament elaborated the first elements of a cosmic and transcendental Christology.[5] If the resurrection revealed the goal of God's paths and clearly demonstrated the action of the Spirit initiated in the creation of the world, then they could say: All reality has moved in the direction of Christ as toward its point of convergence (cf. Eph. 1:10); he constitutes the fullness of time (Gal. 4:4) and the fullness of all things (Eph. 1:22–23; 4:10; Col. 2:9–10; 1:19); everything was created for and by him (Col. 1:16; 1 Cor. 8:6; Heb. 1:2,10; John 1:13; Rev. 3:14), and in him all things have their existence and consistence (Col. 1:17–18).

Affirmations of such grave theological import are possible and comprehensible only if we admit, with the New Testament, that the resurrected Jesus revealed in himself the anticipated goal of the world and the radical meaning of all creation. If Christ is the end and the Omega Point, then everything began in function of him and because of him everything was created. Hence the first human being was not Adam but Christ; when he created Adam God was thinking of Christ. But this was revealed to the awareness of faith only after the resurrection, when what had been latent in Jesus of Nazareth emerged in a patent manner. The Synoptics express this faith by showing in Jesus' genealogy that all history since Abraham, or rather since Adam (Luke 3:23–38), moved in his direction (Matt. 1:1–17).[6]

John will go one step further and say that the very history of the material world depends on him because "not one thing had its being but through him" (John 1:3).

John uses a word that for his listeners had a cosmic, mediating, revealing, and salvific function: *Logos*. He announces that Jesus is the Logos (Word, Meaning) and with this preaches to those listening to his Gospel that the secret meaning which pervades the whole universe and hides in each being and in each fact did not remain an abstract idea but one day made itself flesh and dwelt among us (John 1:14).[7] The one who introduced a new creation must also have collaborated in the creation of the old. Hence he was and is created as the first and the last (Rev. 1:17). The beginning and end, creation and consummation must correspond to one another: "Behold I make the first as well as the last."[8]

Cosmic Christology, like speculation and faith, basically professes that Christ is the beginning, the middle, and end of God's paths and the measure of all things. Hence it is said in the epistle to the Ephesians that in Christ the cosmic totality is summarized and placed under one head (1:10). In this sense, the *agraphon* (a saying of Christ not contained in the canonical Gospels) in logion 77 of the apocryphal Gospel of St. Thomas truly expresses the faith of the primitive community, which is also our faith. There the resurrected Christ says: "I am the light which is above all things. I am the universe. The universe parted from me and the universe returned to me. Cut open a piece of firewood and I am there within; raise up a stone and I am underneath it."[9] Here the cosmic ubiquitousness of the resurrected Jesus is professed.

The senses do not sense, the eyes cannot capture the heart of things. Faith opens up an illuminating access to the ultimate innerness of the world, where it reveals itself as the temple of God and of the transfigured cosmic Christ. The Lord is not far from us. The material elements are sacraments that put us in communion with him, because they, in the most intimate part of their being, pertain to the very reality of Christ. Matthew also expressed this with other categories when he had the resurrected Jesus say: "I am with you always, yes, to the end of time." And St. Augustine, with typical realism, commented: "History is pregnant with Christ."

Is Christ of Importance to the Earth Alone or to the Whole Cosmos?

Having concluded these reflections a modern reader might inquire: Perhaps this whole reflection concerning the cosmic Christ is merely a consequence of our Ptolemaic conception of the cosmos, in which the earth or our solar system is the center of everything. Modern sciences have now taken into account all the undefined dimensions of our universe. Closed systems are relative to our point of view. The reality of stellar space peopled with millions and millions of galaxies obliges us to think in terms of open systems where practically nothing is a priori impossible.

This has its effects on our religious affirmations, even more so when these present themselves with a dogmatic, infallible, and irreformable character. Might there not be other spiritual beings inhabiting other planets in other systems?[10] What is their relationship to Jesus of Nazareth and the resurrected Christ? Are they too in need of redemption? And if they have no such need, how are we to understand the function of God's incarnation? Is it the case that the Word or another divine person communicated himself in an incarnate manner to them also? Can we still speak of a unity in the divine plan of creation, redemption, and consummation?

Some people say that these are idle questions and have no meaning since we are without the necessary conditions to respond adequately to them. We believe that no one has the right to limit the human capacity to ask questions, especially in the field of religion where we touch on the absolute mystery of God, which can never be imprisoned by any definition and made completely harmonious within any system of comprehension. This problem already preoccupied the young Paul Claudel, Teilhard de Chardin, and the great Austrian writer and lay theologian Reinhold Schneider, who in his old age transformed such inquiries into a personal drama.[11] Desperate, he asks: "If we recognize the signs of Christ in history, can we also recognize them in the cosmos? It is much too daring if we invoke the cosmos as a witness to Jesus Christ. The Lord lived and travelled the narrow path of human beings. Like Socrates, he sought out only human beings; he responded to their existence by offering them a personal opportunity; the enigma that the cosmos poses—this he did not perceive."[12]

Teilhard answered the question by introducing a new line of reflection, taken from his ideas on the process of growing consciousness and complexity in the evolutionary curve. Infinitely great stellar space exists. Confronted with this, the human being indeed appears as a *quantité négligeable*, lost as an errant atom in the infinity of empty space. Moreover, there exists the infinitely small microcosmos, probably structured the same as the macrocosmos. But beyond this another great reality exists, the infinitely complex human consciousness, which knows that it exists and takes its littleness into account—which is precisely the basis of its greatness. It is very small and quantitatively unimportant. But it possesses a new quality that makes it greater and nobler than all physical and mathematical magnitudes imaginable: It can think, and especially it can love. A single act of love, noted Pascal, is worth more than the whole physical universe. It is in this new quality of self-consciousness that the cosmos finds its highest unity and convergence. Hence it is in the human being that the meaning of the totality is to be found. And Teilhard drew the following conclusion: The world cannot have two heads; Christ alone can be its center, its motor force, its Alpha and Omega.[13]

Using this Teilhardian perspective we can develop his intuition and ask: In what way can Christ be present and fill the whole cosmos? The following reflection may perhaps throw some light on the question. More and more the totality of reality, in terms of what we perceive and our research instruments reveal, does not present itself as chaotic but as profoundly harmonious. There is a radical unity that transcends and joins all beings one to another. Things are not merely thrown helter skelter. The world is fundamentally a *cosmos*, as the genial intuition of the Greeks well perceived. What is it that makes the world a unity and a totality? What is the principle that unifies beings in being and an invisible totalizing structure? The problem transcends the limits of the sciences, which study specific aspects of reality, and calls for a metaphysical reflection that asks questions about the whole as such. What is it that makes all things, even the most distant in the cosmos, a whole? Leibnitz, who also saw the problem, answered by suggesting the theory of the "substantial bond" that pervades all, joining one being to another. For him as well as for Blondel, who adopted Leibnitz's theory, the resurrected Christ would be the substantial bond, "the supreme lover who attracts and unites *par en haut*, level by level, the whole hierarchy of distinct and consolidated beings. . . . He is the one without which everything that has been created would return to nothing."[14]

Evidently, a Christ conceived in this manner cannot be represented as a cosmic human being, imprisoned within our categories and spatial-temporal coordinates. It is the resurrected Christ who overcame these limitations and is now present, not physically, but pneumatically. That is, he is present in the heart of things, in that transphysical reality that forms a unity of all beings and is comparable to the presence and ubiquity of the divine spirit (*pneuma*). The Spirit which fills everything and constitutes the most profound core of each being, without, however, detracting from its creational otherness. As is evident, this is metaphysical speculation. We must avoid representing it in categories of the imagination so we do not create unnecessary myths and monsters.

Nevertheless, it is worthwhile to ask: Do other rational beings exist in the cosmos? Faith finds nothing repugnant about such an existence. On the contrary, because of the unimaginable immenseness of the universe and the failure of human beings as cosmic priests giving glory to God, one can postulate that there are other spiritual beings who carry out this sacerdotal function better than human beings. As we shall see later, if we say that the incarnation of the eternal Logos pertains to the sphere of creation, which God made the receptacle of his entrance into the world, then we can say: Just as the eternal Logos, which fills all reality, appeared in our flesh and assumed the evolutionary coordinates of our galaxy, nothing prohibits this same eternal Logos from having appeared and assumed the spiritual and evolutionary conditions of other beings in other systems.

St. Thomas Aquinas said: "By the fact of the Incarnation, the power of the Father and the Son was in no way diminished; thus it seems that the Son can assume another human nature" *(Summa Theologica*, III, 3,7 sed contra: III Sent. dist. 1,2,5). In this way Christ would realize the mission of assuming and divinizing creation, for which he was destined from all eternity. The way redemption was realized here on earth would be merely *one* concrete form among many others by which the Word of God relates to creation. Moreover, there is nothing repugnant about the other divine Persons being incarnated. The mystery of the Triune God is so profound and so immense that it can never be exhausted by a single concretization like that which was realized within our earthly system. The Bible witnesses merely to human salvation. It does not speculate about other possibilities because when it was written these problems were simply nonexistent. Today, however, we are confronted with such questions. The possible answers ought to be taken from a more ample horizon, having the very mystery of God and his relationship with creation as point of departure.

Attempting to answer the question raised above—Is Jesus of importance to the earth alone or to the whole cosmos?—we would hypothetically say: Jesus, insofar as he is a human being like us, and insofar as he is the Logos who assumed our human condition, is of interest to our history alone. Nevertheless, Jesus of Nazareth is not only a human being. He forms an unconfusable and indivisible unity with the eternal Logos of God, the Second Person of the Blessed Trinity. In this sense he is of interest to the totality of reality. The Logos, who pervades all things and who could have assumed other conditions different from ours in other systems, was here called Jesus of Nazareth. In the resurrection the reality of Jesus took on the dimensions of the whole cosmos.

Nevertheless we must still make the following restriction: Certainly the cosmos has other dimensions and consequently allows for relationships with God and his Word different from that realized in Jesus of Nazareth. However, this was the form with which God favored us; for this he created us, redeemed us, and glorified us in Jesus Christ. If this need not be God's absolute mode of communication with his creation, this does not take away its value for us. It means merely that we should keep ourselves open to the infinite possibilities of the mystery of God so that, groping, we can catch a glimpse of them and therefore praise and celebrate.

The Human Being: Christ's Greatest Sacrament

If everything has been created by, for, and in Christ in such a way that everything shows traces of the face of Christ, then human beings, his brothers and sisters, are especially marked by his humanity. The human being is not merely the image and likeness of God (Gen. 1:26), but also the image and likeness of Christ (Rom. 2:29; cf. Col. 3:10).[15] First, Christ is par excellence the image of God (2 Cor. 4:4; John 6:15; Col. 1:15; Phil. 2:6; Col. 3:9–10; Eph. 4:24; Rom. 8:29; 1 Cor. 15:49; 2 Cor. 3:18) and only after-

wards are we the image of God insofar as we were
thought of and created in and by him. This has been
especially accentuated by Tertullian and Origen.[16]
Hence it is by the simple fact of creation that the human
being is constituted image and likeness of Christ. The
Incarnation and resurrection revealed this greatness in
a more profound manner. Each person is actually a
brother or sister to Jesus and in some way participates
in his reality. The resurrection perpetuates and deepens
Christ's participation in each human being. He, as
glorified and present in each being and in each person, is
acting and fermenting the goodness, humanity,
brotherhood, communion, and love in all human beings.

But in what sense can we say that each human being
is the locus where we can find God and Jesus Christ? The
other, when loved and accepted, in greatness and small-
ness, reveals a palpable transcendence. No one can be
defined by or framed within one situation. This "something more," which forever escapes us, which makes
each person an intimate mystery, constitutes transcendence, and, moreover, the living and concrete presence
of transcendence. We call this trancendence God.

God is, therefore, not far from us. He is our greatest
depth. In Jesus, God appeared in a concrete form, assuming our human condition. Hence each human being
reminds us of the *human being* who was Jesus. To accept
a poor person as poor is to accept the poor Jesus. He
hides himself, he is incognito, behind each human face.
Faith demands that we look profoundly into the face of
our brothers and sisters; love them; give them food,
drink, and clothing; visit them in prison. For in so doing,
we are being host to and serving Christ himself. Hence
the human being is the greatest manifestation not only
of God, but also of Christ resurrected in our world. Whoever rejects his brother or sister rejects Christ himself,
because whoever rejects the image and likeness of God
and Christ rejects God and Christ himself (cf. Gen. 9:6;
Matt. 25:42–43).

Without the sacrament of brother and sister no one can be saved. Here the indentification of love of the neighbor and love of God becomes transparent.[17] We have the same possibility as that realized in Christ, and this is the basis of our radical dignity and ultimate sacredness penetrated by no other than God (cf. Rev. 2:27). Now we know, only through faith, that the Lord is present in each human being. With our own resurrection, which will be like that of Christ, we will see and enjoy, enjoy and love, love and understand our brotherhood with Jesus incarnate and resurrected (cf. 1 John 3:2).

The Presence of Christ in Anonymous Christians

The resurrected Jesus is present and active in a special way in those who in the vast ambit of history and life carry forward his cause. This is independent of their ideological colorings or adhesion to some religion or Christian belief. Wherever people seek the good, justice, humanitarian love, solidarity, communion, and understanding between people, wherever they dedicate themselves to overcoming their own egoism, making this world more human and fraternal, and opening themselves to the normative Transcendent for their lives, there we can say, with all certainty, that the resurrected one is present, because the cause for which he lived, suffered, was tried and executed is being carried forward. "Whoever is not against us, is with us" (Mark 9:40; Luke 9:50), said the historical Jesus. He thus knocked down the sectarian barriers that divide people and make us see only those who adhere to our own creed as brothers and sisters. All who adhere to Jesus' cause are his brothers and sisters and he is acting in them so that there might be greater openness toward others and more human space for God.

Christ did not come to found a new religion. He came to bring a new human being (cf. Eph. 2:15), one who is defined not by the established criteria of society (cf. Gal.

3:28) but by the option for the cause of love, which is the cause of Christ.[18] As spirit, the resurrected Christ acts wherever he wishes. In the fullness of his human and divine reality, he transcends all possible barriers to his action: both sacred and profane, of the world and of the church, of space and time. He touches all, especially those who by their lives struggle for what Jesus himself struggled and died for even though they do not make explicit reference to him and to his universal salvific meaning.

The Presence of Christ in Avowed Christians

The resurrected Christ is present in a more profound manner in those who have opted to follow him and imitate him in faith, love, and explicit adhesion to his divine reality and absolute meaning for our existence before God.[19] In a word, Christ is present in a specific manner in Christians. Fundamentally a Christian is a person who has opted to imitate and follow Christ. Baptism is a symbol of this decision. The meaning of the imitation of Christ is in itself simple: trying to act in our existential situation in the same way Christ acted in his situation. Thus, the maltreated slave suffers like Christ, who when unjustly treated did not retort with insults and when tormented did not threaten (1 Pet. 2:23). To imitate Christ does not mean to copy or even imitate his gestures: It means having the same attitude and the same spirit as Jesus, incarnating it in our concrete situation, which is different from that of Jesus.

To imitate is "to have the same sentiments as Christ" (Phil. 2:5); to be, like him, unselfish; to feel with others and identify with them; to persevere until the end in love, in faith, in goodness of the human heart.It is not to fear being critical, challenging a religious or social situation that does not humanize human beings nor make them free for others and for God. It is to have the courage to be liberal and at the same time maintain good sense; to use creative imagination; be faithful to the laws that foster an atmosphere of love and human comprehension. A more radical form of imitation is to follow Jesus. At the time Jesus lived, to follow him meant to walk with him, to help him announce the Good News to the world that we have a future totally reconciled with God, with human beings, and with ourselves (cf. Mark 1:17; 3:4–15; 6:7,13; Luke 9:1–6; 10:1–20); it meant to participate in his destiny, including the risk of a violent life and death (Mark 8:34; Matt. 16:24; Luke 9:23; 14:27).

After the resurrection one could no longer speak in the strict sense of following Christ because he has gone from earth to heaven, from visible to invisible. The expression was translated or given a new meaning: To follow Christ and be his disciple became synonymous with being Christian (Acts 11:26). Christians attached themselves to Christ through faith, hope, love, the Spirit (1 Cor. 6:17) and the sacraments (Rom 6:3ff.; 1 Cor. 11:17–30). Thus they would be in him and form one body with him (1 Cor. 12:27; Rom. 12:5).

This following of Christ must not be reduced to a moral category. It attaches us profoundly to the resurrected Christ and allows him to act in us. It inserts us into his new reality. Within the old human being characterized by the ambiguity of grace-sin, justice-injustice, the new person begins to grow (cf. 2 Cor. 5:17; Eph. 2:15; 4:22–24), the one who in death will be freed for the resurrection (cf. 1 Cor. 6:14; 2 Cor. 5:8; Phil. 1:20–23). The resurrected Jesus is present in all sincere Christians, even those who are not in full communion with the Catholic church; hence they "are properly regarded as brothers in the Lord by the sons of the Catholic Church."[20]

The Church: The Primordial Sacrament of the Presence of the Lord

The resurrected Christ—who fills the whole cosmos, who is present in a concrete form in each human being, who is seen by faith in all those who carry forward his cause, and who is visible in explicit Christians— achieves his highest level of historical concretion in the church, the community of faith, the body of Christ resurrected. It is a body not like the carnal body of Jesus but in the likeness of his pneumatic body.[21] Therefore, this body is not limited to a determined space; it is now liberated and relates to the totality. The local church, where one hears the word of God, where the community gathers around the eucharistic table to celebrate the presence of the resurrected Jesus and live the bond of faith, hope, and charity, gives concrete form to the Lord who is present. Since it is pneumatic, the Lord's body is not restricted to the church alone, but in it he becomes present in a unique manner: "I am Jesus whom you persecute," the resurrected Christ would say to Paul, who hunted Christians in order to kill them (Acts 9:5).

Christ is made present through the magisterium, through the sacraments, and through church government and preaching; It is he who baptizes, consecrates, forgives. It is he who teaches when the church in a solemn and irreformable manner establishes orientations for the universal church in matters of faith and morals. It is he who governs when the church, in its universality and collegiality, makes decisions that concern all God's people. In this way the church is constituted the primordial sacrament of the presence of the resurrected Lord.

In the word, especially in the prayer and mediation of his ministers, the Lord is present just as he promised (Matt. 18:20): "In the liturgy, God speaks to His people and Christ is still proclaiming His gospel," says the Constitution on the Sacred Liturgy of Vatican II (no. 33). And, in fact, the liturgical acts, gestures, words, and sacred objects assume a symbolic character: They symbolize the resurrected Christ's encounter with his faithful and make him mysteriously present in the old world.[22] In them and through them Christ communicates himself and people experience his proximity.

It is nevertheless in the Eucharist that the resurrected Lord achieves the maximum degree of density and presence. The transubstantiation of the bread and wine localizes the resurrected Christ under species that are circumscribed in space: *Here* he is, in the totality of his mystery and the reality of his transfiguration. The bread and wine *exhibit* and *contain*, under fragile material reality, the Lord himself in the full realism of his transfigured humanity, giving himself to everyone, just as he had always done during his carnal existence and now, in a definitive manner, does in his pneumatic existence. Eating and drinking his body and blood expresses the radical meaning of his gift of self: To insert us into his very own life, entering our lives because "the partaking of the Body and Blood of Christ does nothing other than transform us into what we consume" *(Lumen Gentium,* no. 26).

It is by eating the body of Christ in the Eucharist that God's people also become the body of Christ. The eucharistic presence is not an end in itself but the means whereby Christ wishes to live in the midst of his own. The Eucharist celebrates the giving and self-communication of the Lord: "This is my body (I) which is given for you. . . . This is the chalice of my blood (life) which is shed for you and for all peoples for the forgiveness of sins." Whoever partakes of the Eucharist ought to live the "giving" and "opening of oneself" to others. The Eucharist is a plea for reciprocity lived outside the sacrament in daily life, so that Christians may be, in truth, a sacrament and sign of the presence of the resurrected Christ in the world.

CONCLUSION: THE PRIDE OF THE CUP
IS IN THE DRINK, ITS HUMILITY IN THE SERVING

If the transfigured Lord is present in all human beings, we Christians have a mission to them: to be his signs in the world and to reflect him. Many times we become countersigns of the Lord and his cause by our mode of being and acting. Instead of being a *syn-bolon* of Christ (a sign that speaks of and brings people to Christ) we transform ourselves into *dia-bolon* (a sign that separates and divides). At other times, the churches fall before temptation and instead of representing Christ substitute themselves for him.[23] Instead of bringing people to Christ, we attract them only to ourselves. At other times, we do not create the silence necessary if his voice is to be heard. The words of John the Baptist apply especially to the churches: "He must grow greater, I must grow smaller" (John 3:30).

Christians ought to live the meaning of the chalice: The pride of the cup is in the drink, its humility in the serving—the words written in the private diary of Dag Hammarskjold in 1954.[24] The meaning of being a Christian consists in always trying to reproduce within our lives that which emerged in Jesus Christ, to create space so that through our existence and comportment he can appear and invite. All Christians and the church ought to be like the husband's friend: "The bride is only for the bridegroom and yet the bridegroom's friend, who stands there and listens, is glad when he hears the bridegroom's voice" (John 3:29). Can we say with John: "This same joy I feel, and now it is complete"?

You are not the oil, you are not the air—merely the point of combustion, the flash-point where the light is born. You are merely the lens in the beam. You can only receive, give, and possess the light as a lens does. If you seek yourself, your rights, you prevent the oil and air from meeting in the flame, you rob the lens of its transparence. Sanctity—either to be the Light, or to be self-effaced in the Light, so that it may be born, self-effaced so that it may be focused or spread wider.[25]

Christ's resurrection brought new light for our vision of the world. Only through faith do we discover the secret in things, how they rejoin God and the cosmic Christ, who, now resurrected, penetrates the heart of all creation. At present in our terrestrial situation, as wanderers and gropers in the realm of definitive realities, we feel little of all this. Nevertheless, we can console ourselves with Peter's words: "You did not see him, yet you love him, and still without seeing him you are already filled with joy so glorious that it cannot be described, because you believe; and you are sure of the end to which your faith looks forward, that is, the salvation of your souls" (1 Pet. 1:8).

What Name Can We Call
Jesus Christ Today?

Faith in Christ is a continuing process of insertion into what he signifies, insofar as our understanding of life, of human beings, and of the world allows. How shall we express our faith? By means of forms that are intelligible to us and represent our contribution to the deciphering of the mystery of Christ? In this chapter we emphasize how the humanity of Christ, which revealed both God and the response to human longings, is the bridge that gives us access to Christ. Admiration for him is the origin of all Christology, both yesterday and today. Then we will review some titles and names by which we today can understand Christ: Jesus as homo revelatus, *as the future already present, as the reconciliation of opposites, as revolutionary, as archetype of the most perfect individuation, and as the God of human beings. Jesus-man is the ongoing critical memory of what we ought to be and as yet are not, and a permanent call that we be daily more so.*

In previous reflections we tried to articulate the principal lines of the so-called christological process. Each cultural group, the Jewish Palestinians, the Jews of the diaspora, and the Greeks, attributed to Jesus the greatest and most perfect titles of honor and glory that their milieu offered in an effort to decipher the richness revealed in the life, death, and resurrection of Christ. The New Testament knows some seventy titles or names conferred on Jesus. The following centuries added still more. People with faith confronted life in its totality with the mystery of Christ and inserted him into human existence in such a way that he in fact emerges as a liberator, the meaning of life and the world, the one who points out our final destiny with certainty, offering harmony, coherence, light, and meaning for human beings.

IN CHRISTOLOGY, IT IS NOT SUFFICIENT
TO KNOW WHAT OTHERS HAVE KNOWN

Faith in Christ is a continuing process of insertion into what he signifies, insofar as our comprehension of life, human beings, and the world allows. Up until now a sacred perspective dominated Christology. Most of his titles were proclaimed in the cultic sphere of the liturgy. Some of his titles, however, are eminently secular, like those in the letters to the Ephesians and Colossians, where Christ is praised as the head of the cosmos and the church, as he who confers existence and consistence on all reality. These titles have not been adequately exploited in theology and the concrete living of the faith.

If we look at the liturgical formulations, the manuals of Christology, and books concerning Christ in general, we note a sad predominance of historicist thinking and an absence of creative imagination. We know in minute detail what others have known in the past, how they tried to integrate Christ into their horizons of comprehension. But we are very poorly informed as to how we should carry on this same process and what precisely it is we are doing. What are we to call Christ today? What contribution shall we make, given the riches our world has to offer, to deciphering his mystery? What titles will we confer that express our love and adhesion to his person and message? In what sense is our life the hermeneutic locus that can bring out the deepest meaning of traditional titles?

Young people say: "Jesus is salvation; Jesus is my Lord; we are all brothers and sisters in the Body of Christ," or, "Latch on to Jesus, my friend! You don't need uppers. Take a little Matthew, Mark, Luke, and John. Christ is an eternal trip."[1] Is it not possible that such titles and terms "salvation," "Lord," "Body of Christ," and "following Jesus," assume a richer and more concrete content that our generation alone lives and can witness to, and that this is our collaboration in the task of revealing who Jesus is?

Faith in Christ Cannot Be Reduced
to Archaic Formulas

The figure of Christ comes loaded down and surrounded by so many titles and dogmatic statements that he is almost inaccessible to the ordinary person. His attractiveness, his vigor, and his challenge all come to us encased within a comprehension that tends, when the meaning of the formulas is not understood, to obscure his originality, hide his human face, and remove him from history; he is hypostasized as a demi-God, outside of this world. Faith ought to liberate the figure of Jesus from the fetters that diminish him. Hence to proclaim Jesus as Messiah, Lord, Son of David, Son of God, etc., does not mean one already has faith, unless one is concerned about what these names mean for our lives. What meaning have the names "Messiah," "Son of David," "Lion of the Tribe of Judah," for people like us who are not Jews? Faith in Christ cannot be reduced to archaic formulas, venerable though they be, nor to biblical archeology.

To believe in Christ as an existential act and way of life is to confront the totality of my personal, social, ecclesial, and cultural life with the reality of Jesus. Faith is realized in the encounter of allowing life and its problems to be interrogated and questioned by Christ and his message. On the other hand, we interrogate Christ, we go to him with our problems and we seek in him an answer for the human condition. It is in this dialogue that faith is strengthened and Christ inserted into the general context of existence. To have faith signifies having the capacity to listen to his voice, which speaks within our situation. Every true encounter with Christ brings us to a crisis that acts as a purifying and refining crucible (the Greek word *krisis* means "turning point," "decision"). In him we find a human depth that challenges us. The root structures of humanity are made tangible in his life and words; his relationship with the Absolute awakens the memory of what we all should be.

The norm that emerges in our contact with Christ takes on a double function: First, there is a critical-judgmental function relative to whatever is not in accord with the criterion by which Christ lived; we are judged and feel the distance and immenseness of the road still to be travelled. Second, there is a critical-refining-saving function: The absolute reference point that we discover in Christ gives us a new impulse, an opportunity for conversion, and the certainty that with him we can achieve the goal. In this sense Christ is a permanent crisis in human existence, but a crisis that operates like a crucible that purifies, refines, and saves.

Faith Does Not Permit an Ideologization of Jesus' Titles

There is a danger that Christology may assimilate the biblical titles of Christ *uncritically*, without an awareness of their historical relativity.[2] It is inevitable that cultural elements enter into the christological process.

We already noted how Christ's Incarnation is prolonged throughout history by assimilating human values to the mystery of Christ. Nevertheless the danger remains that such a process may degenerate into an ideologization of a social or religious status seeking its justification in Christology. Thus, popes and kings find an ideological base in the title "Christ the King" to justify their own power, which is not always exercised according to the message of Christ and at times is even contrary to it. Without much self-criticism they identify themselves as Christ's representatives in the world. Thus, for example, the title "Christ the King" was understood in terms of the image of the feudal kings and absolute Roman and Byzantine monarchs. Later, during the crisis of absolute monarchy, Christ the King was understood as the bearer of powers of legislation, execution, and judgment. Again, Christ was understood as the legitimator of the ecclesiastical system.

The norms of Christ's mystery were simply identified with the church's intervention and Christ was encased within the limits imposed by a type of official theology. It was said that only through the church can one arrive at Christ. In this way important elements of history and life that were not tied to the ecclesiastical structure were placed outside the reach of Christ's mystery. It was customary to teach that Christ—the prophet, master, king, Lord, etc.—continues to live in the ecclesiastical hierarchy, bearer of a prophetic, organizing, and teaching function. There is a great deal of truth in all this but not the whole truth. That Christ, prophet and master, could not adjust to the status quo and was opposed, imprisoned, and killed precisely by the masters of his day was far too easily forgotten.

No concrete historical reality can exhaust the riches of Christ. Hence no title conferred on Christ can be absolutized. Nor can the kingdom of God be privatized and identified purely and simply with the church or a Christian regime. The titles and message of Christ cannot be ideologized to legitimate or sacramentalize the prevailing situation. The inverse is also true. While the dominant classes have understood Christ in terms of themselves, the suffering and oppressed classes have understood him and the preaching of the kingdom in terms of a social revolution. Those who had no social or religious opportunity began to be important and have value before God in Christ. It was to them that he announced the good news of total liberation.

But we have here a reduction of Christ to only one aspect of his message: love of neighbor. We believe that love is central and also essential to Jesus' preaching. His message, however, is much wider and promises the total liberation of human beings and the cosmos for God. Love is the atmosphere in which this is hoped for, lived, proclaimed. We would, however, prefer to be on the side of the oppressed, who at least learnt this from the Gospel, than to be on the side of those who fanatically affirm the totality of orthodoxy but tolerate the injustices and barbarities that surround them and have lost the capacity to hear Christ's words: When you have done this to one of these little ones, you have done it to me.

The important thing is not to do Christology, but to follow Christ. In both cases a true knowledge of Christ is missing because there is no authentic encounter with him, in which we interrogate but also allow ourselves to be interrogated. To understand Christ we must go to him, not with our answers, but with our questions. And the encounter is not to legitimate our solutions, but for him to question and criticize so that we are enriched with his light and can speak and answer the questions raised in our situation. This is valid for all modern attempts to carry the process of deciphering the reality of Christ ahead.

In spite of these dangers we are not dispensed from giving our collaboration, in faith, to Christology as it is lived. Each generation ought to confront itself with the mystery of Christ and try to give him the names that correspond to our living experience of his inexhaustible reality. Basically, the adult faith of each Christian is challenged to speak about him and with him as starting point, well or badly, according to the talents of each one. What does he really mean for us today, especially in our Latin American and Brazilian situation? Before answering this, we should clarify a very important point.

THE BRIDGE BETWEEN CHRIST AND US

If Christ is a determining value in our existence it is because in him we find the response to our problems and hopes for the human condition, a response that involves God and human beings. And we find it in the very reality of Christ. Faith has seen the Man-God in him. We profess that in Christ we have the way and at the same time the goal of our journey: Through human beings we go to God, and through God we understand who human beings really are. We have already seen how it was through his humanity that faith discovered the divinity. Therefore both yesterday and today his humanity is the bridge that joins us with Christ: not a humanity understood as static, clearly definable, categorizable, but humanity as mystery. The more it is known, the more it opens to unlimited knowledge until it is lost (and this we contemplate in the Incarnation) in the mystery of God.

But in what sense is the humanity of Christ a bridge between him and us, in what sense are we in community and solidarity with him? In Christ's humanity, in his creative imagination, in his enormous good sense, in his originality, in his sovereign way of speaking and acting, in his unique relationship with the Father, and in his love dedicated to all, there emerged a reality that all human beings hope for: The fundamental conflicts of life, alienation, sin, hatred, and death are resolved. Reality receives a new meaning: communion with God in the intimacy of the Father with the Son, which envelops and reconciles even his persecutors and killers.

A new situation was created by Christ: The parousia (coming) takes place in him as well as the epiphany (manifestation) of a liberation of the human condition in all its relationships with God, the other, and the cosmos.

The resurrection confirmed that with the coming of this person, history achieved its end. This is not true in the chronological sense, because history continues today. But it achieved its end in the sense of goal and summit: In Christ history attained its Z-point toward which it had strived. Death was overcome, all the latent capacities in being and human beings were realized, and the human person was inserted into the divine sphere. Christ became the new being, the new Adam, the new heaven and the new earth, the realization of human hopes for total, human-divine liberation and realization.

Christ assumed a unique function in history: He became a reality-symbol and a *Gestalt* (type, profile) for us.[3] He continues to speak and to spark the same fascination as in those first moments of the resurrection. Yesterday as well as today, admiration for Jesus is at the basis of Christology. It pertains to the gestalt to activate human forces and to make fundamental structures of human reality visible; we encounter ourselves in the gestalt and the symbol-reality. Many, many, appeared before Christ (cf. Heb. 1:1; 11:1–40 and the genealogies of Luke and Matthew); they also manifested in their own way the new reality. In Christ all its vitality and originality broke through for the first time in history, crystal clear as mountain streams and so profound that only the incarnation of God himself can adequately explain it.

We today, like people of all ages, search for this reconciling and totalizing reality. Christians find it in Jesus. Hence we call him the *Christ*, the awaited, the anointed, the promised one. We find realized in his life, death, and resurrection what the human heart seeks and what God promised would be our future. Because we believe this we can say: We know no one so well as we know Jesus. We know him not so much through sources handed down from the past as through those deep structures of our being which in him, Jesus, received a divine fullness. It is because of this that he is our gestalt, reality-symbol, the way, the light, the truth. How can we express the encounter between the hopes of today and the reality of Jesus? We will try to offer a few suggestions, though they may be fragmentary.[4]

ELEMENTS OF A CHRISTOLOGY IN SECULAR LANGUAGE

Christ as the Omega Point of Evolution,
the Homo Revelatus, *and the Future as Present*

In spite of many unresolved difficulties, our conception of the world today is evolutionist. This view affirms that the world is the product of a long process wherein imperfect forms gradually converged on one another to form ever more perfect ones up to the present stage. Looking back we detect a meaning in the evolution of reality. Although the explanation for isolated phenomena may be obscure, and chance and the absurd seem to prevail, we cannot deny that the totality has been oriented by an entelechy, a latent meaning: Cosmogenesis gave rise to biogenesis, anthropogenesis emerged from biogenesis, and from anthropogenesis there emerged Christogenesis, a major breakthrough in the eyes of Christian faith. The reality that surrounds us is not a chaos but a cosmos, a harmony. The more it progresses the more complex it becomes; the more complex it becomes the more it is unified, the more it is unified the more it becomes conscious of itself. The spirit is, in this sense, not an epiphenomenon of matter but its highest realization and concentration upon itself. The earth is the prehistory of the Spirit. In this perspective, the human being does not emerge as an error in calculation, or as an abortive being in the evolutionary process, but as its fullest meaning, as the point where the global process becomes conscious of itself and begins to direct itself.

The primitive community saw Jesus as the highest revelation of humanity, so human that his humanity totally revealed the most intimate and profound mystery: God. Christ, therefore, in our evolutionary perspective, is the Omega Point, that point where the whole process finds its goal in a personal being and hence is extrapolated into the divine sphere.[5] In him God is already all in all (1 Cor. 15:28) and the center between God and creation. The human being whom God sought and who is fully his image and likeness (Gen. 1:26) is not so much that first man who emerged from the animal, but the eschatological human being who broke through to God at the end of the whole creational-evolutionary process. Christ, incarnate and resurrected, has the characteristics of the ultimate human being. The human being latent in the ascending process became patent in him: He is the *homo revelatus.* Hence he is the anticipated future, the end manifesting itself in the middle of the journey. Because of this he assumes a determining, motivating, integrating, orientating role and is the magnet that attracts those who are still in a painful and slow ascent toward God.

Christ is an absolute within history. Two affirmations are implied by this. He is absolute because he realized the messianic aspirations of the human heart. Human beings have a hope-principle that makes them dream of total liberation. Many people have appeared and have helped us to travel in the direction of God, whether in the religious, cultural, political, or psychological dimension. But no one succeeded in showing us a radical liberation from all alienating forces, ranging from sin to death. This became apparent in the resurrection, at least for the figure of Jesus. A qualitative *novum* took place in him and this sparked an unextinguishable hope: Jesus' present existence is our future. He is the first of many brothers (Rom. 8:29; Col. 1:18). In this sense Christ is an absolute within history. He does not thus diminish his predecessors or followers such as Buddha, Confucius, Socrates, Gandhi, Martin Luther King, and others, but rather gives full and radical form to what they lived and carried forward.

Nevertheless when we affirm that Christ is an absolute *within* history, because he realized the dynamism of history in an exhaustive manner, we imply a second assertion: Because he is absolute, Christ is outside our kind of history. He surpassed it and founded another history in which the ambiguities of this historical process, of grace-sin, of integration-alienation, have been surpassed. The new being is inaugurated with him, polarized only in positivity, love, grace, total communion. As an absolute within and outside history, he is a permanent crisis for all gestalts and reality-symbols of absolute and total liberation within history. Thus he was transformed into a norm by which we can measure all things without diminishing or degrading them. We do not establish Christ's greatness by making little of others; rather we see the reality of Christ realized in the nobility of the great liberating figures and personalities in human history.[6]

Christ as Conciliation of Opposites, Divine Milieu, and a Tremendous High

The growing unification of the world through all channels of communication is forming a planetary, ecumenical, and communal consciousness among people in search of a new humanism. The encounter of cultures and the various interpretations of oriental and occidental worlds generate a crisis in all traditional humanisms, ranging from the classical Greco-Roman, the Christian, and Renaissance, to the technological and Marxist. In this fermentation and confrontation of horizons and models, a new comprehension of human beings and their function in the world will be born.

Jesus Christ can play a determining role in this process because his gestalt is the reconciliation of human and also divine opposites. First, he presents himself as mediator between God and human beings, in the sense of realizing the fundamental hope among people to experience the inexperienceable and the ineffable in a concrete manifestation. As mediator he is not a third reality formed of human being and God. This would make Christ semi-God and semi-man, and hence he would neither represent God nor human beings. In order to represent God before human beings and human beings before God, he must be wholly God and wholly human. When exploring the meaning of the Incarnation we saw how it is through a concrete human existence centered not in itself but in God that the man-Jesus manifests and represents God. The more human he is, the more he reveals God. In this way he can represent both God and human beings without being alienated from either. One who succeeded in being as human as Jesus, to the point where he simultaneously manifested God, gives meaning to human history and will be raised up as the gestalt of the true and fundamental human being.

Christ also represents the conciliation of human opposites. Human history is ambiguous, made of peace and war, love and hatred, liberation and oppression. Christ assumed this human condition and reconciled it. Persecuted, contested, rejected, imprisoned, tortured, killed, he did not pay back in the same coin. He loved the persecutor and redeemed the torturor, assuming them before God: "Father, forgive them, they do not know what they are doing" (Luke 23:34). He did not simply suffer the cross. He assumed it as a form of love and faithfulness to human beings. Hence he conquered alienation and schisms between peoples with the power of the new being revealed in him.

The cross is the symbol of the reconciliation of opposites: the sign of human hatred and love of God. By the cross Christ created the new humanity, a *milieu divin*, a reconciled world within the divided world, with a dynamism and historical activity that touches us today and will endure forever. When by faith, discipleship, hope, love, and the sacraments we become participators in this conciliating and reconciliating focus, at that precise moment we also become new creatures and experience the force of the future world.

Young Jesus people say this in their characteristic language: Jesus is a *tremendous high.* A typically Christian way of life is articulated in this description of Christ. For Jesus is the conciliator of existential opposites and integrator of all human dimensions searching for meaning and light. This is also the human content behind the classical formulas of Christology: Son of Man, Suffering Servant of God, rejected Messiah.[7]

Christ the Dissenter, the Reformer, the Revolutionary, the Liberator

The last three centuries have been characterized by great social mobility. A scientific mentality and technical possibilities have transformed the natural and social conditions of the world. Forms of society succeed one another. Legitimating ideologies of a social or religious status are submitted to rigorous criticism. If they are not overthrown they are at least unmasked. Today people define themselves more in terms of the future than the past. For the sake of the future they elaborate new models of scientific domination of the world, project new forms of social and political organization, and even create utopias in the name of which they contest the sociologically given situation. Thus reformers, dissenters, and revolutionaries appear.

Christ is held in high regard by many and followed as a dissenter, a liberator, a reformer, a revolutionary. Up to a certain point, there is much truth in this.[8] However, we should not confuse the terms. Christ is not to be defined by an "against"; he is not a complainer. He is *in favor of* love, justice, reconciliation, hope, and total realization of the meaning of human existence in God. If he is *against*, it is because he is *in favor of*, in the first place. He preaches, to use the terminology of today, an authentic global and structural revolution: the kingdom of God. It is not liberation from Roman subjugation, nor a shout of rebellion by the poor against Jewish land-owners. It is total and complete liberation from all that alienates human beings, including sickness, death, and especially sin. The kingdom of God cannot be reduced to a single dimension of the world. It is the globality of the world that must be transformed in the direction of God. Jesus is a dissenter and a revolutionary in that specific sense, which excludes violence. In the name of this kingdom Jesus contests legalism, the hard-heartedness of the Jewish religion, and the socio-religious stratification of his time which categorized people in terms of pure and impure, accursed walk of life, neighbors and non-neighbors, etc.

We should, however, make clear what we mean by "revolutionary" and "reformer."[9] Reformers want to better their social and religious world. Reformers do not seek to create something absolutely new. They accept the world and its social and religious form and try to improve it. In this sense Jesus was also a reformer. He was born a Jew and adapted to the customs and rituals of his people. However he tried to improve the religious value system. He made harsh demands. He radicalized the commandment not to kill, demanding the eradication of the cause of killing, which is sin. He radicalized the commandment of not lusting after one's neighbor's wife, postulating custody of the eyes. He deepened the love of the neighbor, commanding that we love our enemies. As is evident, Christ was a reformer in this sense.

Nevertheless he went beyond this. He did not merely repeat the past in an effort to perfect it. He said new things (Mark 1:27) and in this he was a great revolutionary, perhaps the greatest in history. Revolutionaries, in contrast to reformers, do not merely want to improve the situation. They envisage the introduction of something new, the changing of the social and religious game rules. Christ preaches the kingdom of God, which is not an improvement of any particular part of the world but a global transformation of the structures of this old world; it is the good news and joy of God reigning over all things. To be a Christian is to be a new creature (2 Cor. 5:17), and the kingdom of God, in the words of Revelation, is the new heaven and the new earth (Rev. 21:1): "There will be no more death, and no more mourning and sadness. The world of the past has gone" (21:4). Since Christ preaches and promises this good news for human beings he announces an authentic revolution. But it is only in this exact sense that he can be called a revolutionary. He is not a revolutionary in the emotional and ideological sense of violent and rebellious reaction against the socio-political structure. Perhaps a suitable description of Jesus would be Liberator of a consciousness oppressed by sin and all alienations and Liberator of the sad human condition in its relationships with the world, the other, and God.

Jesus Christ, Archetype of the Most Perfect Individuation

One of the most fundamental desires of human beings is to achieve the integration of all the dynamisms in their conscious, subconscious, and unconscious life. The human being is a nexus of relationships going in all directions. The integration of all the pulsations of human life is a painful process, not always free from conflicts and existential dramas. The longest and most perilous journey made by human beings in search of the center that attracts, polarizes, and harmonizes all is not the one to the moon, but the journey within ourselves.

We call this incessant search, to use Jung's language, the process of individuation.

The process of individuation is realized by our capacity to increasingly appropriate the symbol, or archetype, of God—*Selbst*, self—which is constituted in the center of our psychic energies. The archetype of God (*Selbst*) is responsible for the harmony, integration, and assimilation of the conscious ego and its dynamisms. In particular it is responsible for the integration of the unconscious, which is formed by the ponderous and unfathomable inherited mass of experiences of our primitive vegetable, animal, and human ancestors, of our people, nation, and clan; of our family, and other differentiations of a collective and individual nature. The more we succeed in creating an interior, integrating, and assimilating nucleus, the more we are individualized and personalized.

Religion that adores a divine God, and not simply an infinite Being necessary to metaphysical systems, plays a decisive role in this process. People of extraordinary integration, such as the mystics, the great founders of religions, and other personalities of admirable humanity, constitute the archetypes and symbols of the *Selbst*. Jesus Christ, as presented in the Gospels and believed in by the community of faith, is the most perfect and completed concretization of the *Selbst* (archetype of God).[10] He emerges as the consummate stage in the process of individuation; indeed he is identified with—not merely nearer to—the archetype *Selbst* (God).

Hence Christ assumes a transcendental meaning for humanity. We experience ourselves as mystery, as infinitely surpassing ourselves, as a configuration of unlimited possibilities and at the same time limited and imprisoned in the narrow confines of historical conditionings. But we perceive, now that Jesus has died and risen from the dead, that at least in one human being humanity emerges crystal clear and diaphanous as the light on the first morning of creation. Our longings are not merely a possibility, a hope of total realization never realized. Because we are in solidarity with one another, we have the hope that the reality present in Christ will become a reality also in all who open themselves to the Absolute. He now goes ahead of us as way, light, symbol, and archetype of the most integrated and perfect being. He plunged into the hidden mystery of God and identified himself with him.

Jesus Christ, Our Elder Brother

The absolute integration of Jesus with himself and with God (Incarnation) was not realized in the form of a spectacular life, but in a day-to-day life with its ups and downs. By the Incarnation God assumed the totality of our precarious human condition with its anxieties and hopes, with its limitations (the death of God) and desire for the infinite. This is the great theological meaning of the hidden years of Jesus' infancy and adolescence.[11] He is a human being like everyone else in Nazareth, neither a superhero nor a saint who calls attention to himself. He is in solidarity with the mentality of the population of the village and participates in the destiny of a nation subjugated by foreign occupation forces. He left nothing in writing. He is literally lost in the nameless mass. By the Incarnation God so humbled himself that he remained hidden when he appeared here on earth. Hence, Christmas is a feast-day of secularization. God did not fear matter and the ambiguity and littleness of our human condition. It was precisely through this humanity, and not in spite of it, that God revealed himself. Any human situation is sufficiently good for us to plunge into ourselves, mature, and encounter God.

Christ is our brother since he participated in the anonymity of almost all human beings and assumed the human situation that is identical for all. Life is worth living just as it is, with its monotonous day-to-day work and the demands of living together with others, listening to them, understanding and loving them. Nevertheless Jesus is our *elder* brother, since within this human life, assumed both in obscurity and publicly, he lived in such a human manner that he revealed God and, by his death and resurrection, realized all those dynamisms of which we are capable. As one theologian has said: "Christianity does not proclaim the death of God, but the humanity of God."[12] This is the great meaning of the terrestrial life of Jesus of Nazareth.

Jesus, God of Human Beings and God with Us

The discussion so far should have made this very clear: "God or man?" is a false alternative. Equally false is the alternative "Jesus or God?" God reveals himself in the humanity of Jesus. The Incarnation can be seen as an exhaustive and radical realization of a human possibility. Therefore, Jesus, Man-God, is manifested as the God of human beings and God with us.[13] With this understanding as our starting point we ought to demythologize our common conception of God that prevents us from seeing Christ as Man-Revealer-of-the-God-of-humankind in his humanity. God is not competing with us nor vice versa.

We discover in Jesus Christ a side to God that was unknown in the Old Testament. This is a God who can make himself other, who can come to meet us in the weakness of a child, who can suffer, who knows what it means to be tempted, who suffers disappointments, who weeps at the death of a friend, who is concerned about the nobodies who have no chance in this world and announces to them the good news of God's total liberation. God is not distant from human beings. God is not a stranger to human mystery. On the contrary, the human being always implies God as the supreme one, the ineffable mystery who envelops human existence.

The meaning of this mystery cannot be captured by any concept or symbol. When revealed in its maximum manifestation in the humanity of Jesus, it cannot be exhausted by any name or title of greatness. But this is the human God who reveals the divinity of the human being and the humanity of God.

We cannot think of the human being without necessarily thinking also of God. *In the concrete*, we cannot think of God without relating him to human beings—because of Jesus Christ, Man-God. The way to God goes through human beings and the way to human beings goes through God. The religions of the world experienced God, the *fascinosum* and the *tremendum*, in nature, in the power of cosmic forces, in the mountains, in the sun, in springs, etc. The Old Testament discovered God in history. Christianity sees God in the human being. It became clear in Jesus that the human being is not merely the place where God manifests himself. The human being can be God's very way of being. The human being can be an articulation of God's history. This was the case at least in Jesus of Nazareth.

The consequences of such a conception are theologically speaking of extreme seriousness: The vocation of the human being is divinization. In order to become human we must go beyond ourselves and assume that God will humanize himself. If we can be an articulation of God's history, this is possible only in liberty, in giving, in the spontaneous opening of self to God. When liberty appeared it provoked a rupture, overcoming cosmic necessity and mathematical logic. It was the inauguration of the unpredictable, the spontaneous, the creative. Undecipherable mystery made its entrance. All is possible with liberty: the divine and the satanic, the divinization of human beings and absolute human frustration as a consequence of rejecting God's self-communication. In Jesus we perceive the undecipherable human depths that reveal the mystery of God, and we catch a glimpse of God's proximity—so near that he identifies with us. St. Clement of Alexandria (d. 211 or 215) said: "If you have really found your brother, then you will have found your God as well" (*Stromateis* 1,19).

CONCLUSION: CHRIST, THE MEMORY AND
CRITICAL CONSCIOUSNESS OF HUMANITY

Christology has always tried to answer the question "Who is Jesus?" To ask "who are you?" is to ask a question concerning a mystery. People cannot be defined and framed within any situation. To ask "who are you, Jesus Christ, for us today?" means confronting our existence with his and being challenged by his person, message, and the meaning we discover in his comportment. To feel oneself touched by Christ today is to place oneself on the path of faith, which understands who Jesus is, not so much by giving him new titles and different names but by trying to live what he lived. It means always trying to get outside ourselves, seeking the center of the human being not in the self, but in the other and in God, having the courage to leap into the breach in the place of another. It means being a harlequin-Christ,[14] or Dostoyevsky's idiot-Christ,[15] who never abandons human beings, who prefers the marginalized, who knows how to bear with others and has learned how to forgive, who is a revolutionary but never categorizes, who fits in wherever human beings may find themselves, who is jeered and loved, who is thought to be mad but manifests a wisdom that astonishes all.

Christ knew how to put an *and* where we normally put an *or;* hence he succeeded in reconciling opposites and being the mediator of human beings and all things. He is the permanent and disturbing memory of what we ought to be and are not, the critical consciousness of humanity that can never be content with that which it is or may have achieved. Rather we must journey on and realize that reconciliation and attain that degree of humanity which manifests the unfathomable depths of God, who is everything and in everything (cf. 1 Cor. 15:28). In the meantime, as long as this is not the case, Christ, as Pascal used to say, continues to be offended, to agonize and die for each one of us (cf. *Pensées*, no. 553). It is in this sense that we can recite a creed for secular times:

> I believe in jesus christ
> who was right when he
> like each of us
> just another individual who couldn't beat city hall
> worked to change the status quo
> and was destroyed
> Looking at him I see
> how our intelligence is crippled
> our imagination stifled
> our efforts wasted
> because we do not live as he did
> every day I am afraid
> that he died in vain
> because he is buried in our churches
> because we have betrayed his revolution
> in our obedience to authority
> and our fear of it
> I believe in jesus christ
> who rises again and again in our lives
> so that we will be free
> from prejudice and arrogance
> from fear and hate
> and carry on his revolution
> and make way for his kingdom[16]

13

Jesus Christ and Christianity: Reflections on the Essence of Christianity

Jesus Christ is not an aberration within history. He represents the highest emergence of the dynamism that God himself placed in creation and especially in human beings. This dynamism is the basis of a Christianity prior to Christ and independent of an explicit profession of faith in Jesus Christ. Christians are not simply ones who profess Christ with their lips but ones who, yesterday and today, live the structure and the comportment that Christ lived: love, forgiveness, complete openness to God, etc. Religions that teach and live this are the concrete forms that universal Christianity can take. The church institutionally is a special historical articulation of Christianity. As long as human beings and the world have not achieved the fullness in God, Christ continues to hope and still has a future.

At the conclusion of our christological reflections, a more universal consideration concerning Christianity and some of its fundamental structures is appropriate. "Christianity" comes from "Christ" which originally did not designate a proper name of a person but a title. The primitive community, by predicating the title "Christ" of the crucified and resurrected Jesus of Nazareth, expressed their faith that in this man were realized the radical expectations of the human heart for liberation from the ambiguous human and cosmic condition and for closeness to God. He is the *ecce homo*, the new and exemplary man who revealed in all its depth what the human being is and what is now possible: to open oneself to God in such a way as to identify with God.

The Incarnation designates precisely the absolute and exhaustive realization of this possibility contained within the horizons of the human being, concretized for the first time by Jesus of Nazareth. His personal history revealed a type of human being, a form of acting, of speaking, of relating to God and others that broke through the ordinary criteria of religious interpretation. His profound humanity allowed anthropological structures to reveal God with a clarity that surpassed everything that had emerged in religious history up to that moment. Only God could be as human as Jesus. Hence Jesus of Nazareth was justly designated "Christ." Jesus Christ is at the basis of Christianity. And at the basis of Jesus Christ is a way of living, a comportment, a way of being human, a structure which when radically lived by Jesus of Nazareth demanded that he be designated as the Christ. Hence a christic structure exists within human reality, which is manifested in an absolute and exhaustive manner in the life, death, and resurrection of Jesus of Nazareth.

CHRISTIANITY IS AS EXTENSIVE AS THE WORLD

The christic structure is anterior to the historical Jesus of Nazareth. It pre-exists within the history of humanity. Every time a human being opens to God and the other, wherever true love exists and egoism is surpassed, when human beings seek justice, reconciliation, and forgiveness, there we have true Christianity and the christic structure emerges within human history. Thus Christianity could exist before Christianity. Moreover, Christianity can exist outside Christian limits. That is, Christianity not only exists where it is explicitly professed and lived in an orthodox manner but emerges wherever a human being says "Yes" to goodness, truth, and love. Before Christ, Christianity was anonymous and latent.[1] Though it existed and was lived by people, it did not yet have a name. With Jesus Christ Christianity received its name. Jesus Christ lived it so profoundly and absolutely that his surname became Christ.

The fact that nothing was called Christianity does not mean it did not exist. It existed, but in a hidden, anonymous, and latent manner. It achieved its highest revelation, explicitness, and patency in Jesus. The earth was always round, even before Magellan demonstrated it. South America did not begin to exist when discovered by Christopher Columbus. It already existed, though it was not explicitly known. It is likewise with Christianity and Christ. Christ revealed the existence of Christianity within human reality. Hence he gave Christianity its name just as Amerigo Vespucci, the second discoverer of America, gave his name to the discovered continent. St. Augustine, who well understood this reality, could say: "The substance of what we today call Christianity already existed in ancient times and was present ever since the beginnings of humanity. When Christ finally appeared in the flesh, what always existed was called the Christian religion" (Retr. 1,12,3). Hence we can assert that Christianity is as extensive as the human world. It could exist before Christ and can still exist today outside of "Christian" limits, where the word "Christianity" is neither used nor known. Moreover, Christianity can exist even where, because of erroneous consciousness, it is combatted and persecuted.

Christianity is not simply a more perfect worldview or

a more sublime religion, much less an ideology. Christianity is concrete and consistent living in a christic structure, a living of that which Jesus of Nazareth lived: total openness to others and the Great Other, indiscriminate love, unshakeable fidelity to the voice of conscience, and the overcoming of whatever chains human beings to their own egoism. The first great Christian philosopher, Justin (d. 167), has truthfully said: "All who live according to the Logos are Christians: Socrates, Heraclitus, and others among the Greeks, and among the non-Greeks, Abraham, Elijah, Hananiah, Azariah, Mishael, and many others, the citation of whose names would take far too much time" *(Apologia* 1,46). Thus, Christianity can be articulated either in sacred or profane worlds, either in this culture or in any other culture, either yesterday, today, or tomorrow.

Jesus lived the christic structure in his humanity with such radicality that he must be regarded as the best fruit of human evolution; as the new Adam, in the words of the apostle Paul (1 Cor. 15:45); as the human being who reached the goal of the process of humanization. Hence the true Christian is not simply one who is denominated as such and affiliated with the Christian religion, but rather one who lives (naturally in a deficient and partially developed manner) that which Christ lived, that for which he was imprisoned, condemned, and executed. This was well expressed by Ratzinger: "The true Christian is not the confessed member of a party, but one who became truly human by Christian living; not one who observes a system of norms and laws in a servile manner, merely thinking of himself, but one who became free for simple human goodness."[2] To be a Christian is to live human life in that profundity and radicality where it opens itself to and communicates the mystery of God. It is not those who are Christian who are good, true, and just. Rather the good, the true, and the just are Christians.

THE FULL HUMANIZATION OF THE HUMAN BEING
PRESUPPOSES THE HUMANIZATION OF GOD

Can we describe what the christic structure is in a more comprehensible manner? The christic structure is a possibility of human existence. The human being is defined, in contrast to the animal, as a being open to the totality of reality, as a nexus of relationships going in every direction. The human being will be realized only if we are kept open to and in permanent communion with global reality. By being in the other, we are within ourselves. By going out of ourselves we arrive at ourselves. It is only by ex-isting (going outside of self) that we become. The "I" does not exist except when created and nourished by a "you." It is by giving that we possess. Hence we must always transcend ourselves. Through our thought we plunge into the infinite horizon of being. The more we open ourselves to being, the more we can know and the more we become human. Giving not only signifies transcending ourselves and going outside of ourselves but also the capacity to receive the gift of the other. It is by loving and allowing ourselves to be loved by others that we discover our true depth and its mystery. The more we are oriented to the infinite and the other, the greater our likelihood of being humanized, that is, of realizing our human essence.

The most perfect, complete, definitive, and finished human being is one who is one with the Infinite. Jesus of Nazareth was the human being who realized this human possibility to its maximum and thus succeeded in achieving the goal of humanization. It is because he was open to God to the point of being completely filled by him that he ought to be called God incarnate. In the light of this one should understand the profound words of Ratzinger: "The complete humanization of the human being presupposes the humanization of God."[3] That is, in order to become truly ourselves, we must be capable of realizing the possibilities inherent in our nature, especially this power to be one with God. When we achieve communion with God to the point of forming a oneness with him, without confusion, division, and change, then we have attained our maximum degree of humanization. When this occurs, God is humanized and the human being divinized, and Jesus Christ emerges in history. Hence we can complete Ratzinger's thinking by saying that the complete humanization of human beings implies their divinization. We are infinitely surpassed in this event, not by the annihilation of our being but by the complete realization of our unlimited capacity for communion with God, a capacity with which human nature comes equipped. The end of anthropogenesis resides in christogenesis, that is, in the ineffable unity of God and the human being in one being, Jesus Christ.

Christianity is concretized in the world whenever people open themselves like Christ to the totality of reality and especially to "that ultimate and unutterable mystery which engulfs our being and whence we take our rise and whither our journey leads us,"[4] that is, God. This opening of self, as we shall see later, can be articulated with great variations in the sacred and profane worlds. It is not any particular articulation that is decisive, but that there be articulations and that we be ever open to perfecting them. What was realized in an absolute and irreversible manner by Jesus of Nazareth ought to be realized according to the measure of each and every human being. Wherever the christic structure thrives, there humanization reigns and is in process. Wherever it expires because human beings are closed in on themselves, there the humanizing growth of human beings is impeded and blocked.

Openness to the other is such a determining factor that the salvation or absolute frustration of human beings depends on it. According to the so-called parable of the Anonymous Christians (Matt. 25:31–46), the divine

Judge will measure all human beings by their capacity for loving others. Whoever received the traveller, clothed the naked, fed the hungry, and gave drink to the thirsty received not only that human being but unknowingly received God himself. Basically this says that union in love and openness to a human "You" ultimately implies opening oneself to a divine and absolute "You." Where there is human love, solidarity, union, and true growth God is always present. One who lives the christic structure is saved, not one who merely belongs to a Christian sect, not one who says, "Lord! Lord!" and constructs a whole worldview. One must act in conformity with christic reality. Here, Christian labels or models are of little value. What counts is the concrete and consistent living of a reality that Jesus of Nazareth thematized, radicalized, and exemplified. Christianity consists fundamentally in this.

THE CHRISTIC STRUCTURE
AND THE MYSTERY OF THE TRIUNE GOD

If the christic structure consists essentially in giving and knowing how to receive the gift of the other, then we can see that it has intimate reference to the very mystery of God. The essence of God, if we can use such human language, is realized in love, in giving, in knowing how to receive: "God is love" (1 John 4:8,16). God exists only by communicating and subsisting as Father, Son, and Holy Spirit. God is Father because he communicates and gives himself. This communication is called Son. In turn, the Son gives himself and goes completely outside of himself and hands himself over to the Father, who fully receives him. This mutual love and gift of the Father to the Son is called Holy Spirit, who proceeds from the Father and the Son. The Father does not exist without the Son nor the Son without the Father, nor the Holy Spirit without the Father and without the Son. The triune God eternally realizes its infinite being in the total, complete, absolute gift of one to the other.

The structure which is contained in all creation, especially in human reality, and which achieved its maximum visibility in Jesus of Nazareth, was created as an analogy to the very structures of the mystery of the Triune God. But it was through Jesus Christ that this was revealed to human awareness in an explicit manner, not so much through words but in the way in which he lived his human existence—a transparent, limpid, and complete openness and giving to God and others. Hence it was only with Jesus Christ that revelation and theology came to the knowledge of the one and triune God. Jesus not only revealed himself to be the Son of God incarnate, but also revealed the filial nature of all human beings (Rom. 8:14).

CHRISTIANITY: A RESPONSE TO A PROPOSAL

If we wish to formulate the christic structure in other words, we can say that it consists in a response to a divine proposal, given with responsibility.[5] God gives himself to human beings: He makes us a proposal of communion, of love, of union with him. To this divine proposal human beings must give a response. Reciprocity demands that love received be repaid with love. This internal exigency does not arise in the one who gives and loves but in the one who allows himself to be loved and is loved. To accept another's proposal of love is already a giving of love and a response. Hence knowing how to receive is one form of giving, perhaps the most original form of giving, because it creates the atmosphere indispensable for encounter, dialogue, and the growth of love.

God's proposal emerges within the human conscience, the place where God speaks to each person. Whenever conscience feels responsible and experiences a challenge to go outside of itself, to accept the other, to assume the task, there God is making a proposal. The proposal may emerge within life, in the signs of the times, in the exigencies of the concrete situation. Whenever we are called to grow, love, get outside ourselves, open ourselves to others and God, to assume responsibility before our conscience and others, there we have a proposal that demands a faithful response. If we open up and love, we have the concretization of a christic structure. The history of humankind can be seen as the history of the success or failure of the christic structure. It can be analyzed as the happy or unhappy response that human beings, within the historical and social conditionings proper to each epoch, gave to God's proposal, that is, to what extent they created structures that facilitated and realized the fundamental values of love, fraternity, understanding between people, and conscious openness toward God. Hence the whole expanse of human history can be regarded as a history of human damnation or salvation.

Experience has taught us that the human response can never exhaust the divine proposal. Moreover, human experience is characterized by a fundamental ambiguity: It is simultaneously the history of human openness and closure, of positive and negative response to the divine proposal. The history of human salvation is a vast harvest where weeds and wheat grow at the same time. The history of the Old and New Testaments are an example of how a whole people for more than two thousand years, growing more and more, continued to give a positive response to the divine proposal. However, in one person a perfect match between divine proposal and human response was achieved. One person was open to God in the same proportion as God's ineffable communication. Jesus of Nazareth realized the christic structure in an absolute manner; his response was one with the proposal. As we have already seen often enough, it is precisely in this unchangeable, indivisible, and unconfoundable union that the Incarnation of God and the subsistence of man and God in the one same Jesus Christ consists. In this sense, Jesus of Nazareth is humanity's greatest gift to God and at the same time God's most excellent gift to humanity. In this way, he emerges as the sacrament of the encounter between God and humanity,[6] as that focus where everything, creation and Creator, achieves a unity and so attains the ultimate goal of creational history.

THE CHURCH AS A SPECIAL INSTITUTIONAL ARTICULATION OF CHRISTIANITY

If Christianity fundamentally consists in a response to the divine proposal, then let us note that the human response can, historically, be articulated in many different ways. In their responses human beings assume their culture, history, understanding of the world, and past, in a word, their whole world. The religions of the world, both in the past and today, in spite of questionable and even, from the Christian point of view, condemnable elements, represent in themselves the religious response and reaction of human beings confronted with God's proposal and action. Hence, religions can and ought to be regarded as articulations of the christic structure, and in some way they concretize the very church of Christ.[7] In this sense there is no such thing as a natural religion. All have their origin in a reaction to the salvific action of God, which is offered to all without discrimination.

The diversity of religions resides in the diversity of cultures and worldviews that characterize the response to God's proposal. But the proposal transcends all responses and is directed equally at each and every one. Hence we can say that religions are the ordinary ways by which human beings travel to God, experience God, and receive salvation from God. Insofar as religions are human responses to the divine proposal they may contain errors and interpret God's proposal in an inadequate manner. Hence, when we say that religions articulate and concretize the christic structure, we do not mean to legitimate every aspect of their existence. Even religion ought to keep itself open, criticize itself, and develop an ever more adequate response to God's proposal. The Old Testament itself gives us an exemplary lesson: From primitive forms of religiosity and overly anthropomorphic and even demoniacal representations of God,[8] its people developed ever more pure forms until they achieved a conception of a transcendent God, revealer and creator of all things.

The church, because of its strict and unbroken link with Jesus Christ whom it preaches, preserves, and lives in its sacraments and ministries, and to whose criticism it subjects itself, can and ought to be regarded as a special *institutional* articulation of Christianity.[9] Though it be sinful and on route, still far from the paternal home, nevertheless it is committed to bring Christ and his cause forward without substantial error. The church does not exhaust the christic structure, nor can the church be identified purely and simply with Christianity. But it is a special *institutional* objectification and concretization.

When we say this, however, we are not denying the religious and salvific value of other religions. Undoubtedly they retain their legitimacy, but they ought to allow themselves to be interrogated by the church, so that they may open out their horizons and grow to an ever more adequate openness to God's proposal as manifested in Jesus Christ. In turn, the church must not become proud; it must also be open to God who is revealed and manifested in other religions. The church must learn from them those facets and dimensions of religious experience that have been better thematized in other religions, for example, mysticism in India, interior divestiture in Buddhism. Only then will the church be truly catholic, that is universal, because it will also know how to see and capture the reality of God and Christ outside its own articulation and outside the sociological limits of its own reality.

JESUS CHRIST, "ALL IN ALL"

The christic structure is a fact of history, an anthropological structure that must be realized in every human being who is to be saved, a structure fully concretized by Jesus of Nazareth. But we still have a final question to ask: Where does the christic structure originate? What is its ultimate and transcendent foundation? Traditional theology put this question in other terms: What is the reason for the Incarnation, the redemption of sin, or the perfection and glorification of the cosmos? Dominican Thomists and Franciscan Scotists debated this question for centuries. The Thomists cited phrases from Scripture and the formula of the creed that "for our salvation he descended from heaven and was conceived by the Holy Spirit"; they said that the Incarnation took place because of the sin of humankind. The Franciscans cited other texts, taken from the epistles to the Ephesians and the Colossians; they said that Christ would have become incarnate even if sin did not exist because everything was made by and for him.[10] Without Christ something would be missing in creation and human beings would never achieve complete humanization. The assertion that humanity lived in expectation of the Savior ought to be understood ontologically and not chronologically. That is, human beings desire to be ever more themselves and to realize themselves totally. Therefore they desire their divinization, not only before Christ, but also after him. This is the very dynamic of all creation, which converges and arrives at a decisive culmination in the human being. What Christ realized will also be realized in his brothers and sisters.

From the reflections made up to this point, our position should be clear. Christ is not an aberration in the history of humankind but its meaning and culmination.

He is the One who first arrived at the terminus of the journey to give us hope and certainty that we too are destined to be what he has become; if we live what he lived, we too will have a similar end. Christ's perfection is not historical chance nor merely an anthropological success. From all eternity, he was predestined by God to become the human being who could realize all the capacities contained in human nature, especially the capacity of being one with God. Jesus, Word Incarnate, has a unique relationship with God's plan. He constitutes a moment of the very mystery of God. God's plan, insofar as can be discerned from revelation and theological reflection, is oriented to God's glory, which is realized by making all creation participate in his life, love, and mystery. God's glory also consists in the creature's glory.

All creation is inserted into the very mysterious depths of the Triune God. Creation is not exterior to God, but one moment of his complete manifestation. God totally communicates himself and generates the Son and in the Son the infinite likenesses of the Son. The Son, or the Word, is the eternal infinite and consubstantial thought of God the Father. All creation is God's thought that can be created and realized, thus giving origin to creation from nothing.[11] Insofar as it is God's thought, it is generated in the same act of generation as the Son; because it is produced actively by God in the Son, it reflects the Son and is in his image and likeness. The most perfect image and likeness of the eternal Son is the human nature of Christ. Hence, already in the heart of the Holy Trinity, all things carry in their intimate being the marks and signs of the Son. So that the human nature of Christ might be truly the most perfect image and likeness of the Son and might have and give the highest glory to God "outside" of God, God decreed its union with the Eternal Person of the Son. That is, God desired that Jesus of Nazareth should live his humanity with such intensity and profundity that he would become one with God and be simultaneously God and man.

If God created all things in the Son and this Son became flesh, then everything reflects the eternal Incarnate Son.

The christic structure possesses a trinitarian origin. All things are open to infinite growth because God's being is love, communication, infinite openness. And God's total communication is called "Son" or "Word." Hence all creation possesses the structure of the Son insofar as everything communicates itself, maintains an external relationship, and realizes itself by self-giving. Therefore the Son was always acting in the world from the very first moment of creation. Afterward his action was concentrated when he became flesh in Jesus of Nazareth and finally spread over the dimensions of the cosmos by means of his resurrection. Hence Christ, in the words of Paul, "is everything, and he is in everything" (Col. 3:11).

The christic structure that pervades all reality took concrete form in Jesus of Nazareth because he, from all eternity, was thought of and loved as *the* focal being in which the total manifestation of God within creation would take place for the first time. This manifestation signifies the finished interpenetration of human beings and God, unconfoundable and indivisible unity, the goal of creation now inserted into the trinitarian mystery. Jesus Christ thus is constituted the paradigm and exemplar of what will happen to all human beings and the totality of creation. In him we see the future realized. History and the cosmic evolutionary process can assume an ambiguous and often dramatic character. Nevertheless, it is revealed to us in Jesus that the end will be good and has been guaranteed by God in our favor. Hence Jesus takes on an interpretive, determinant, and elucidating value for all past, present, and future reality. Through him it became clear to us that the cosmos and especially human beings can never fully develop themselves and achieve complete perfection unless they be divinized and assumed by God. Christ is the last link in this immense process. In him, what will come to pass in all reality was realized in an exemplary manner: while preserving the otherness of each being, God is "all in all" (1 Cor. 15:28).

CONCLUSION: THE HOPE AND FUTURE OF JESUS CHRIST

As long as "Christian pantheism," that is, "God, all in all" (1 Cor. 15:28) has not yet taken place, Jesus Christ continues to hope and have a future.[12] His brothers and sisters and the human homeland (the cosmos) have not yet been transfigured like him. They are still on the way, living the ambiguity that characterizes the kingdom of God as manifested in this world: in weakness, ignominy, sufferings, and persecutions. Jesus is not only an individual, but a person. And as a person he lives with others; he has a mystical body with which he is in solidarity. The resurrected Jesus, though he realized the kingdom of God in his life, nevertheless hopes that what was concretized and begun with him may have a happy conclusion. Like the saints of heaven who, in the words of Revelation (6:11) must wait "until the number of their fellow servants and their brethren should be complete," Jesus awaits his own. Glorified at the side of God, "he is living forever to intercede for all" (Heb. 7:25), for their salvation and the transformation of the cosmos.

Thus the resurrected Jesus continues to live in hope. He continues to hope for the growth of his kingdom among human beings, because his kingdom does not begin to exist after death; it is already initiated in this world wherever greater justice is established, greater love reigns, and new horizons that capture God's word and revelation within life are opened up. Jesus continues to hope that the revolution that he started—revolution in the sense of real understanding between human beings and God, indiscriminate love for all, and continuous openness to the future when God will come with his definitive kingdom—will penetrate more and more the human structures of thought, acting, and planning.[13] He continues to hope that the image of the future human being, veiled in the present human being, may be more and more unveiled or revealed. Jesus continues to hope that God's *pro-missio* (promise) of a happy future for human beings and the cosmos may be transformed into a human *missio* (mission) of hope, joy, and living a radical meaning of life in the midst of existential absurdities.

While all this has not been completed, Christ continues to hope. Hence the resurrected Jesus also has a future. He has already come, but for us he is still the one who has yet to come. Christ's future not only consists in his parousia and the total apocalypse (revelation) of his divine and human reality. Christ's future realizes something more, not yet fully concluded and realized: the resurrection of the dead, his brothers and sisters; the reconciliation of all things with themselves and with God; and the transfiguration of the cosmos. John could truly say: "What we are to be in the future has not yet been revealed" (1 John 3:2). The former world has not yet passed and the following words have not yet been heard: "The world of the past has gone. . . . Now I am making the whole of creation new" (Rev. 21:4,5). All this is yet in the future for Christ also. Nevertheless, the future will be the future of Jesus Christ. What has already taken place with him, will take place in an analogous manner in his brothers and sisters and the rest of reality.

Hence the end of the world ought not to be represented as a cosmic catastrophe, but as a consummation and achievement of the end as goal and fullness. What is already fermenting in creation will be fully realized. What is now latent will be completely transparent and operative. We will see "the homeland and hearth of oneness" (E. Bloch), the unification of all with all, including God, without indiscriminate homogeneity. The situation of exodus, which is permanent evolutionary process, will be transformed into a situation consisting of a paternal home with God: "There it will never again be night, and they will not need lamplight or sunlight, because the Lord God will be shining on them. They will reign for ever and ever" (Rev. 22:5). Then the true Genesis will take place.[14] The human being and the world that God really and in a definitive manner wanted and loved will explode inward and outward. We have this hope and also this certainty through Jesus Christ, because "however many the promises God made, the Yes to them all is in Him" (cf. 2 Cor. 1:20).

While we are journeying we look to the future, to the Lord who comes, repeating the words of infinite longing prayed by the primitive church: "May your grace come and pass through this world! Amen. Hosanna to the house of David! If any be a saint, draw near! If any not be, do penance! *Maranatha.* Come, Lord Jesus! Amen!"[15]

Epilogue

A Christological View
from the Periphery

RELEVANCE OF THE SOCIAL SETTING
AND LIBERATION FOR CHRISTOLOGY

When we talk about Jesus Christ the Liberator, we are presupposing certain preliminaries that must be noted. Liberation is the opposite correlate of domination. To worship and proclaim Jesus Christ as the Liberator is to ponder and live out our christological faith within a socio-historical context marked by domination and oppression. This faith seeks to grasp the relevance of themes that will entail structural changes in a given socio-historical situation. It explores this relevance analytically and produces a Christology centered around the theme of Jesus Christ the Liberator. Such a Christology entails a specific socio-political commitment to break with the situation of oppression.

To properly understand the articulation of such a Christology, we must first consider two preliminary data: (1) the relevance of socio-political liberation for

264

Christology; (2) the social setting that is the point of departure for this christological reflection.

By "relevance" here I am referring to the importance that a particular set of historical circumstances has for reflection on our faith in Jesus Christ. Those circumstances pose numerous basic questions to us: e.g., in the face of a given situation and its exigencies, how are we to ponder, preach, and live Jesus Christ in such a way that he appears as the Savior, as that which our faith proclaims him to be? Looking at it from the other side, we can say that the relevance has to do with the connection between a particular theological theme and a particular set of historical circumstances. That is to say, in what way does the former help to explain, maintain, or transform the latter? For whom is a particular image of Christ relevant? Who is helped by a particular theme or a particular type of Christology? What interests does it represent and what concrete projects does it support?

These questions make it clear that any such relevance is always quite ambiguous. It always brings us back to a deeper underlying issue: i.e., the social setting or context (concrete practices, commitments, and stances) in which our faith in Jesus Christ is elaborated.[1]

Theologians do not live in the clouds. They are social actors with a particular place in society. They produce knowledge, data, and meanings by using instruments that the situation offers them and permits them to utilize. Their findings are also addressed to a particular audience. Thus theologians are framed within the overall social context. The themes and emphases of a given Christology flow from what seems relevant to the theologian on the basis of his or her social standpoint. In that sense we must maintain that no Christology is or can be neutral. Every Christology is partisan and committed. Willingly or unwillingly christological discourse is voiced in a given social setting with all the conflicting interests that pervade it. That holds true as well for theological discourse that claims to be "purely" theological, historical, traditional, ecclesial, and apolitical. Normally such discourse adopts the position of those who hold power in the existing system. If a different kind of Christology with its own commitments appears on the scene and confronts the older "apolitical" Christology, the latter will soon discover its social locale, forget its "apolitical" nature, and reveal itself as a religious reinforcement of the existing status quo.

Every given type of Christology is relevant in its own way, depending on its functional relationship to the socio-historical situation; in that sense it is a committed Christology. So let us set down this basic affirmation: As an ordered and elaborated knowledge of the faith, Christology takes shape within the context of a particular moment in history; it is produced under certain specific modes of material, ideal, cultural, and ecclesial production, and it is articulated in terms of certain concrete interests that are not always consciously adverted to. Hence the real question is who or what cause is served by a given Christology.

A Christology that proclaims Jesus Christ as the Liberator seeks to be committed to the economic, social, and political liberation of those groups that are oppressed and dominated. It purports to see the theological relevance of the historic liberation of the vast majority of people on our continent. Such a Christology believes that its thinking and practice should be centered on such liberation. It seeks to create a style and to develop the content of Christology in such a way that it can bring out the liberative dimensions present in Jesus' historical course.

In other words, it is the overall context of dependence and oppression at every level of life that prompts Christology in Latin America to ponder and love Jesus Christ as Liberator. The theme was not willed into being by a few theologians trying to find interesting topics for discussion. It arose as a concrete demand of faith for Christians who felt summoned by their consciences to help wipe out the humiliating condition imposed on their fellow human beings. In Jesus Christ they found motives and stimuli for the cause of liberation.

This brand of Christology presupposes and depends on a specific social practice designed to break with the existing context of domination. The social setting of this Christology is the setting of those social groups for whom a qualitative change of the social structure would represent an opportunity to liberate themselves from existing forms of domination. Taking a clear social stand in favor of the oppressed has entailed a real hermeneutic conversion for many. They have turned to the new questions now posed to them for reflection and they have been forced to consider what sort of style is needed to serve as a vehicle for them.

It should be realized, of course, that this commitment does not guarantee the intrinsic quality of any Christology. Considerations of relevance and social setting seek to point up the inevitable link between practice and theory, politics and Christology; they shed light on the basic underlying conditions that enable a Christology to define its thematic object and its mode of treatment.

Here we must carefully distinguish between the area of autonomy and the area of dependence in any Christology or theology.[2] The former has to do with epistemology (the epistemic setting); the latter has to do with the sociology of knowledge (the social setting). Christology enjoys autonomy in elaborating its discourse in line with its own methodology. It has its own mode of theoretical praxis, and it does not have to justify itself before some outside tribunal. It possesses its own inner laws and the criteria to determine its own internal truth.

In this epistemological realm it makes no sense to talk about a "Latin American" as opposed to a "North Atlantic" Christology, or about a Christology of the oppressed as opposed to a Christology of the oppressors. In its internal regimen such designations are not theoretical tools enabling us to pass judgment on the value of a given christological production. A Christology is not better or worse epistemologically because it was produced in the metropolitan center of power or in the dominated periphery. The same holds true when a Christology is designated as "traditionalist" or "progressivist" or "liberation-oriented." None of these adjectives can determine the correctness or "truth" of a Christology. They point outward to the social reference of a given Christological production. They help us to realize that a given Christology entails a given social commitment and can reinforce one or another group in society.

On the other hand Christology (and all theology) is subject to external dependence as well. Its selection of topics and its emphases are dependent on the social position of the theological actors and what they see as the relevance of christological reflection vis-à-vis the social, historical, and religious context. I have made this point already above. It is a complex task to establish the different levels of relationship between the social setting and the epistemic setting, and I do not purport to do that here. I simply want to point up the fact that such an intimate connection does exist.

TWO LEVELS OF SOCIAL AWARENESS AND THEIR CORRESPONDING LIBERATION CHRISTOLOGIES

Now it is time to consider the overall context within which the whole theme of Jesus Christ the Liberator arose.[3] The starting point is the brutal reality facing the vast majority of people on our Christian continent. They are living and dying amid inhuman living conditions: malnutrition; a high infant mortality rate; endemic diseases; low income; unemployment; lack of social security; lack of health care, hospitals, schools, and housing facilities. In short, they lack all the basic necessities that might ensure some minimum of human dignity.

Such is the real-life situation of vast segments of our people, which is commonly called underdevelopment.

Alongside this we find another side that is just as much a reality for our people. There is the Christian faith with its broad range of values. There are the many good qualities of our people: hospitality, human warmth, a sense of fellowship, an immense yearning for justice and participation, and a taste for *fiestas*. This cultural ethos is being invaded destructively by the myth of progress in the capitalist mold and its attendant focus on high consumption by small elites.

Confronted with this situation, some groups of Christians have become more consciously aware and have reacted to it, thereby rescuing the practice of the faith on our continent from its traditional historical cynicism.[4] Two basic reactions can be noted here insofar as we are talking about the theological relevance of the social situation; and they have generated two corresponding Christologies centered around the image of Jesus Christ the Liberator.[5]

One effort attempts to work through the sensible realm of lived experience in christological terms; the other effort attempts to deal with the realm of thought and analysis in christological terms. The former effort is born of ethical indignation; the latter is based on rational social analysis. Both are similar in that they represent a second stage of discourse vis-à-vis the first stage: i.e., the real-life situation and its pervasive poverty. Here I should like to discuss these two Christologies briefly.

A "Sacramental" Articulation of Liberation Christology

The real situation with all its contradictions is here perceived by an intuitive and sapiential process of cognition. I call it "sacramental" because in the facts of real life it symbolically intuits the presence of oppression and the urgent need for liberation. On the basis of their faith many Christians have come to realize that this situation contradicts the historical plan of God. Poverty is a social sin that God does not will, and so there is an urgent obligation to change things, to help our fellow human beings, and to act in obedience to God.

This perception generally finds expression in the language of prophetic denunciation and hortatory proclamation. Ethical indignation is transformed into an appeal for changes.[6] This summons is fleshed out in a praxis of committed love. Since this lifestyle does not entail an analysis of the mechanisms and structures that have generated the existing situation, the efficacy of its commitment is short-range and unpredictable. But its underlying posture is clear enough. It insists that the situation cannot go on. There must be a change in social relationships. More power must be given to the groups now suffering from domination so that the revised or newly created structures will be less oppressive.

This line of practice, based on an implicit theory that is not worked out, prompts its own kind of reading and interpretation of Christology and the faith. It examines and gives special emphasis to all the gestures, words, and attitudes of Jesus that have to do with conversion, a change in existing relationships, a rapprochement with those on the outer margins of Jewish society, a predilection for the poor, a willingness to challenge the religious and social status quo of his day, and the political content of his proclamation of God's kingdom. The factors that led to his death also take on special relevance. The result is an image of Christ the Liberator quite different from that of official dogma, that of popular piety centered around the suffering and downtrodden Christ of the passion, and also the image of Christ as the glorious king in heaven.

I do not propose to discuss the traits of this liberator Christ in detail. The point I want to make here is that this liberation Christology is grounded on values, themes, and appeals calling for change and liberation. It does not propose a line of strategy or a set of tactics. It does not offer any concrete definitions of goals because it is not guided by an analysis of the situation or a consideration of viable pathways to liberation. Its praxis is basically pragmatic.

This kind of Christology possesses relative value for several reasons. It points up the inevitable link between Jesus Christ's salvation and liberation efforts in history. It gets us beyond an individualistic and wholly inner-directed conception of the Christian message, pointing up the latter's entanglement with politics. This Christology can also be accompanied by an incisive critical exegesis, a reinterpretation of the basic christological dogmas, and an elaboration of the liberative dimensions to be found in all the joints and sinews of the Christian faith. Sensitized by the existing situation of degradation, it reacts to that situation from within the context of the Christian faith. It attempts to ponder and live the faith in such a way that it will support the whole effort to achieve economic and political liberation for the downtrodden.

From this standpoint one can proceed to criticize the traditional images of Christ that do not foster liberation, that tend instead to prop up the whole process of colonization and domination.[7] The suffering and dying Christs of Latin American tradition are Christs embodying the "interiorized impotence of the oppressed" (Assmann). The Virgin pierced with a sword of sorrow personifies the submission and domination of women; her tears of sorrow are for her children slain in the colonizer's quest for power and gold. Similar criticisms can be made of the imperial and monarchical Christs crowned with gold, or of Christ the warrior king; these images seem to hearken back to the glorious kings of Spain and Portugal.

Unfortunately this type of Christology also possesses certain obvious limitations. Since it does not broach any social analysis, it has little political force or impact. It is quite possible for certain groups to be theoretically revolutionary in their theology while still remaining conservative or only slightly progressive in practice.

A Socio-Analytical Articulation
of Liberation Christology

This approach starts off from the same spiritual experience vis-à-vis the poor. Its ethical indignation is no less than that of the above approach. But its indignation is mediated through an analysis of reality; it attempts to detect the mechanisms that generate such scandalous poverty and to elaborate a praxis that is liberative and effective. It is liberative praxis that counts. It does not simply seek to make one or another improvement while maintaining the same structure of relations based on force (reformism). Striving to be truly revolutionary, it proposes to change the structure itself. Its basic option is clearly for liberation.

If we are to arrive at a praxis that will achieve its goals, there must first be as careful an analysis as possible of the mechanisms that produce social iniquity. Viewed in the light of faith this iniquity is social and structural sinfulness. This second brand of Christology undertakes such an analysis, and hence I consider it liberative in the real and strict sense.

Any liberation Christology is fashioned through two basic mediations on the theoretical level. One is that of *social analysis* concerned with the reality to be changed; the other is *hermeneutics*, which considers the theological relevance of the social analysis. It considers the socio-analytical text in the light of Jesus Christ the Savior and the word of divine revelation, thereby guaranteeing the theological character of liberation theory and praxis.[8]

I am not going to concern myself with the hermeneutics phase here. Its procedures are familiar ones in theology. Instead I should like to dwell on the mediation of social analysis. Here is where the different theological currents diverge, revealing their real rather than their simply imagined social standpoint or setting.

It can be said in general that every intervention of theology in the social arena, be it by theologians or by the hierarchy, presupposes some underlying sociological theory. It may be a theory held unthinkingly or spontaneously; or it may be a truly critical theory. As G. Bachelard informs us, a spontaneous or intuitive reading tends to constitute a basic "epistemological obstacle." It generally tends to reinforce the status quo and to prevent one from articulating a theology or a Christology of liberation. So we are forced to ask ourselves what social theory is to be used to articulate a liberation Christology.

The choice of an explanatory theory of society usually entails criteria that are not exclusively concerned with objectivity and rationality; they also have to do with the basic underlying option of the analysts and their social place or setting. All reflection on human reality is guided by a basic underlying "project," i.e., a "utopia" that some group fashions and then uses to project its own future. Such a project or utopia is not merely ideological; it is also based on social and material conditions. For our purposes here we can identify two such kinds of projects and associate them with two different sets of advocates. One project is that of the dominant classes in society; the other is that of the dominated classes.

The utopia of the dominant classes envisions a straight line of progress without any change in the structural supports of society. It has great faith in science and technology. It is basically an elitist vision of society, which assumes that benefits will trickle down from the top layers to those at the bottom. By contrast the utopia of the dominated classes envisions an egalitarian society. The chasm between the elite groups and the dominated masses is seen as the major obstacle to development; so long as it persists, there will be no real progress or social justice. This view has an imperishable faith in the transforming power of the oppressed, feeling that they are capable of creating a society with less social oppression and injustice.

These two basic conceptions enter into our choice of one kind of analysis over the other. The dominant groups in society prefer the *functionalist* approach to social studies because it stresses the idea of balance and equilibrium and depicts society as an organic whole made up of complementary parts. The dominated groups in society prefer to use the *dialectical* approach because it stresses the notion of struggle and conflict and sees society fraught with contradictions.

One basic orientation is that which has been articulated in history by the liberal tradition. It looks at society from the top down, from a point where everything seems to be in harmony. The other basic orientation is that which has been articulated in history by the revolutionary and Marxist tradition. It looks at society from the bottom up, from a point where society seems to involve struggle and confrontation.

Christian faith (and its ordered expression, theology) respects the autonomy of reason and the rational approach. But its discernment goes further to determine which type of analysis ties in better with the demands of a faith that is to be fleshed out in practice. Faith will guide our choice toward the socio-analytical framework that is best at discovering the mechanisms that generate injustice, that offers us suitable means for overcoming them, and that does most to foster the notions of brotherhood and participation.

Thus liberation Christology presupposes an option for the dialectical approach to social analysis and for the revolutionary "project" of the dominated. To say "liberation" is to express a well defined option that is neither reformist nor simply progressivist. It is truly liberative because it implies a break with the status quo.

What sort of liberation are we talking about? Here we must be careful not to fall into the semantic trap of endowing the same word with several very different meanings. The liberation involved here has to do with economic, social, political, and ideological structures. It seeks to operate on structures, not simply on persons. It proposes to change the power relationships existing between social groups by helping to create new structures that will allow for greater participation on the part of those now excluded. Liberation Christology takes the side of the oppressed, feeling that it is compelled to do this by its faith in the historical Jesus. In our present historical situation noncommitment would signify acceptance of the existing situation and a subtle stand in favor of those already favored.

The option of liberation Christology for the oppressed does not get rid of the ambiguity inherent in any process of liberation. The ambiguity lies in the fact that not every kind of liberation signifies a present anticipation and concretization of the kingdom of God, and also in the fact that no liberation can be absolutized in and of itself. The salvation proclaimed by Christianity is an all-embracing one. It is not restricted to economic, political, social, and ideological emancipation, but neither can it be realized without them. Christian hope and a proper understanding of eschatology assure us that this world is not simply a stage on which the drama of salvation is played out; it, too, is part of the drama. Our definitive, eschatological salvation is mediated, anticipated and rendered concrete in the partial liberations that take place at every level of historical reality. The latter are oriented toward the fullness and totality of liberation that will be attainable only in the realized kingdom of God.

It is important for any liberation Christology to possess a correct interpretation of the basic phenomenon of underdevelopment, which serves as the common denominator on our continent. The functionalist interpretation of liberal social science is incorrect on this score. Underdevelopment is not primarily a *technical* problem, the problem of speeding up the transition from a traditional, pretechnical society to a modern, technical one. Nor is it primarily a *political* problem, the problem of solidifying interdependent relations between the nations caught up in the same system in order to achieve homogenous development for all. Underdevelopment is basically a system wherein some nations are dependent on others. The latter function as metropolitan or imperial centers around which the former gravitate as satellites oppressed by lack of development and kept in that position.[9]

Underdevelopment is the reverse side of the same coin. It is the opposite of development and a consequence of it. It is a product of development as conceived in capitalistic terms. If the developed nations of the center are to keep up their pace of development and their level of goods, they must keep the peripheral nations in a state of dependence in order to extract what they need for their own affluence. There are many reasons for our underdevelopment, of course. Biological factors, sanitary considerations, differences in cultural ethos all play a part. But the decisive factor is the system of dependence, which comes down to oppression and domination. It is internalized in the various peripheral countries with the help of those who represent the imperial center. This dependence leaves its mark on every aspect of our life: on the economic system, on the division of labor, on politics, on education and culture, and even on religion.

Escape from this situation will entail a process of breaking down these ties of dependence and freeing ourselves for a self-maintained national project. Here we must be realistic, however. The break will not be accomplished simply by an act of will. As Comblin points out: "Human beings make only the revolutions that make themselves."[10] We must consider the objective conditions that make such a course viable. The problem is not to be free at any price because not all liberations bring freedom with them. If the process of liberation succeeds, it will undoubtedly lead to independence; but it will not necessarily lead to progress and development. The nations of Latin America have not been able to develop their own technology and no one can undergo development alone. So we are faced with the bitter choice between achieving liberation without development or else choosing development and remaining in submission. The third possibility, as Comblin points out, is simply a compromise between the two. We may limit development to maintain a certain autonomy or else limit dependence by focusing on certain sectors for development. In any case that puts us far beyond "any simple theory of dependence."[11]

There is the added fact that in Latin America the forces of repression have gained the upper hand and blocked any organized liberation movement.

Faced with this insoluble situation, must we desist from the process of liberation? On the theoretical level one need not concede anything or adhere to a negative diagnosis. But on the practical level we must look for courses of action that will allow for a viable and authentic process of liberation even though it may be long and slow. The overall state of affairs obliges us to seek changes *in* the system in order to get to a change *of* system. This does not mean that we give up our option for a liberation project and for a different sort of society. It is simply a strategy for achieving that goal in terms of the historical and conjunctural factors imposed on us by an overall situation of repression and bondage.

This analysis of reality does not operate solely with considerations derived from the social sciences (e.g., sociology, economics, and political science). It also takes in data from anthropology, history, and popular culture. The downtrodden majorities on our continent have created their own culture of silence, their own way of giving meaning to life, their own forms of liberation and resistance to bondage. All over the continent attention is now being devoted to the culture and religious life of the common people as a seedbed of values that have not been tainted by the imperialist ideology. That seedbed may serve as the dynamic basis for an authentic theology of resistance and an authentic process of liberation.

If we wish to grasp the serious nature of development as a process of dependence and domination, we must go beyond merely sociological analyses. We must also go beyond the social and human sciences to consider structural and cultural factors. Capitalism, consumptionism, and the bonds of dependence and oppression are manifestations of a cultural ethos, of a people's whole way of viewing the meaning of life and death and their relationships with each other, with material goods, and with the transcendent. That ethos has its own concrete embodiments in history. The modern mind opted for an ethos centered around knowledge and power over everything offered to it. In particular it opted for power over the world in terms of domination, exploitation, and profit. This ethos is at the basis of our western history and of Marxism. Any revolution that does not change this cultural ethos will be simply a minor variation on the same basic theme. It will never be an authentic liberation, at least as that is envisioned by more serious-minded and reflective groups in Latin America.[12]

This kind of urgent reflection is presupposed in the liberation Christology now being elaborated on our continent. It is rarely written down or presented in theoretical detail; instead it is being bruited about in discussion groups and passed along in mimeographed texts.

That brings us to a basic question. What image of Jesus appears when we examine him in the light of this liberation interest? What interpretation do we get of his message and his salvific praxis? It is impossible to spell out all the ramifications of such a Christology, so I shall next attempt to present some basic theses on the matter.

COMPREHENDING THE HISTORICAL JESUS
IN TERMS OF LIBERATION

The Liberation Relevance of the Historical Jesus

The liberation Christology elaborated from the standpoint of Latin America stresses the historical Jesus over the Christ of faith:

—Because it sees a structural similarity between the situations in Jesus' day and those in our own time. In other words, it sees objective oppression and dependence lived out subjectively as contrary to God's historical design.

—Because the historical Jesus puts us in direct contact with his liberative program and the practices with which he implements it.

—Because the historical Jesus makes clear the conflict that any liberative praxis will provoke and points up the probable destiny of any prophetic bearer of a liberation project.

—Because the historical Jesus sheds clear light on the chief elements of christological faith: i.e., following his life and his cause in one's own life. It is in this following that the truth of Jesus surfaces; and it is truth insofar as it enables people to transform this sinful world into the kingdom of God while also being able to vindicate itself before the demands of human reason insofar as reason is open to the infinite. Jesus does not present himself as the explanation of reality. He presents himself as an urgent demand for the transformation of that reality. It is in that sense that he constitutes its definitive explanation.

—Because the historical Jesus reveals the Father to us insofar as he shows us how to journey to that Father. Only in and through the process of conversion and *practical* change do we have access to the God of Jesus Christ. Abstract reflection (theory) does not provide us with that access.

—Because the historical Jesus fosters a critique of humanity and society as they appear historically. Only through conversion can they anticipate and concretize God's kingdom, which is God's ultimate intention for humanity and the world. The historical Jesus signifies a crisis, not a justification, for the world. He calls for a transformation rather than an explanation of it.

The *full* import of the historical Jesus is not to be derived from mere analysis of history itself. It must be read and interpreted on the basis of the complete revelation of his course that is to be found in the resurrection. The light of the resurrection does not excuse us from considering his concrete history, however. Instead it sends us back to a closer concern for that history, as the Gospels themselves prove.

The Kingdom of God: The Utopia of Absolute Liberation and Its Anticipations in History

Systematically speaking, we can say that the historical Jesus did not preach about himself or the church or God but rather about the kingdom of God.

The backdrop for the idea of the kingdom of God is the eschatological and apocalyptic vision of reality. In its view the world as we find it contradicts the design of God. At this final hour God has chosen to step in and inaugurate his reign in a definitive way. The "kingdom of God," then, is the semantic sign of this expectation (Luke 3:15). It connotes the realization of a utopia involving complete liberation, a liberation that is also structural and eschatological.

The specific quality of Jesus lies in the fact that he does not proclaim that the kingdom will come in the future. Instead he proclaims that it is at hand (Mark 1:15), that it is here in our midst (Luke 17:21) by virtue of his presence and activity! Thus the fundamental project of Jesus is to proclaim and be the instrument of the concrete realization of the absolute meaning of the world: i.e., liberation *from* every stigma (including suffering, division, sin, and death) and liberation *for* real life, for open-ended communication of love, grace, and plenitude in God.

The kingdom of God always retains its characteristic features of totality and universality. It calls into crisis more immediate and regional interests whether they be religious or political or social.

The potential perversion lies in regionalizing the kingdom of God in one way or another. One may localize it in terms of political power, or in terms of religious and sacerdotal power, or even in terms of prophetic and charismatic power. This was Jesus' temptation (Matt. 4:1–11), and it accompanied him throughout his life (Luke 22:28).

In other words, no liberation within history defines the ultimate shape of the world and realizes utopia. Total liberation and its attendant freedom is the essence of God's kingdom, and that is an eschatological favor from God. History is the ongoing process leading toward that goal, and it is up to humans to help the process along. But the kingdom of God basically possesses a future dimension that cannot be attained by human action and that is an object of eschatological hope.

On the other hand the kingdom of God is not wholly a utopia lying in the future. It is a present reality that finds concrete embodiments in history. It must be viewed as a process that begins in this world and reaches its culmination in the eschatological future. In Jesus we find this dialectical tension properly maintained. On the one hand he proclaims a project of total liberation: the kingdom of God. On the other hand he displays mediating gestures, actions, and attitudes that translate this project into the ongoing process of history. On the one hand the kingdom is a future reality yet to come; on the other hand it is present and near at hand.

Jesus' first public appearance in the synagogue of Nazareth has programmatic import. He proclaims the utopia of the Lord's year of grace, which becomes history in concrete forms of liberation for the captives and the oppressed (Luke 4:16–21). In his programmatic proclamation the stress falls on the material infrastructure. The Messiah is the person who effects the liberation of people who are concretely the victims of misfortune. It is the poor, the suffering, the hungry, and the persecuted who are blest, not because their condition itself has value but because their unjust situation is a challenge to the justice of the messianic king. Through Jesus, God has sided with them. A focal point of Jesus' preaching and the witness of the apostles is the kingdom of God as a liberation from sin (Luke 24:47; Acts 2:38; 5:31; 13:38); but this must not be interpreted in a reductionist way so that we lop off the infrastructural dimension, the social and historical dimension, which Luke underlined in connection with Jesus. The historical Jesus took on the project of the oppressed, which is liberation, and also the conflict it entails.

The liberation of Jesus has a twofold aspect. On the one hand he proclaims the total liberation of all history, not just a part of it. On the other hand he anticipates this total liberation in a process embodying partial liberations that remain open to complete fulfillment. If Jesus were to proclaim the utopia of a happy ending for the world without any anticipations of it in history, then he would be nurturing human fantasies that had no credibility. If he were to introduce partial liberations without offering a vision of future completeness, then he would be frustrating people's hopes and falling into an incoherent immediatism. Jesus does not do either. Instead both dimensions are found operating in dialectical tension in Jesus' work.

Jesus' Praxis: A Liberation in Process

The *acta* and *facta* of Jesus (his praxis) are to be seen as historifications of what the kingdom of God signifies concretely, i.e., a liberative change in the existing situation. In that sense Jesus moves toward the project of those who are oppressed.

His miracles must be interpreted in this context. It is not the wonder-working element that is important. Their significance lies in the fact that they are operative signs (*ergon, semeion*) of the presence of the kingdom (Luke 11:20). The stronger has burst into the world to overcome the strong (Mark 3:27). A process of liberation is under way.

In his attitudes Jesus incarnates the kingdom and fleshes out the love of the Father. It is not simply a humanitarian spirit that draws him to those whom no one else will approach: e.g., public sinners, drunkards, the impure, lepers, prostitutes, and all those who are alienated socially and religiously. He draws near to them because he is fleshing out in history the loving attitude of the Father toward the lowly and the sinful. Their present situation is not the last word on their life; it is not their final structure. They are not lost for good. God can liberate them.

Jesus' praxis is eminently social and public in character. It touches upon the *structure* of society and religion in his day. It is not an ascetic reformism like that of the Essenes, nor an observance of the established order like that of the Pharisees. Instead Jesus presents himself as a prophetic liberator.

Jesus' activity is inscribed within the religious realm. But since the religious realm constituted one of the basic pillars of the political realm and its power, any intervention in the religious realm had political consequences.

Jesus' praxis vis-à-vis religion, sacred laws, and tradition is truly liberative rather than merely reformist. "You have heard . . . but I tell you." He relativizes their allegedly absolute value. Human beings are more important than the Sabbath and tradition (Mark 2:23–26); salvation is determined by one's attitude toward other human beings (Matt. 25:31–46). Jesus shifts the center or gravity insofar as the criteria for salvation are concerned. It is not orthodoxy but orthopraxis that counts. He subjects the Torah and the dogmatics of the Old Testament to the criterion of love, thus liberating human practice from necrophilic structures.

The proclamation and practice of Jesus postulates a new image of God and a new approach to God. God is no longer the old God of the Torah. He is a God of infinite goodness, even to "the ungrateful and the wicked" (Luke 6:35). He draws near in grace, going far beyond anything prescribed or ordained by the law. God is not an *en soi*, isolated outside history and revealing himself only by way of sudden epiphanies. Instead God reveals himself in history by realizing his kingdom and thus changing the existing situation. God must be viewed primarily in terms of the future, in terms of the kingdom that he is going to implant. It will be total liberation from the evil mechanisms of the past and a fullness of life never imagined before. Access to God does not come primarily from cultic worship, religious observance, and prayer. They are authentic mediations, but in themselves they are ambiguous. Unambiguous and privileged access to God comes through service to the poor, for in them God lies hidden and anonymous. Liberative praxis constitutes the surest road to the God of Jesus Christ.

The liberative nature of Jesus' activity shows up clearly in his social relations. The society of his day was highly stratified. There were neighbors and non-neighbors, pure and impure, Jews and Gentiles, men and women, observers of the Torah and ignorant people. Some professions had a bad reputation and some people, such as the sick, were regarded as sinners by that very fact. Jesus established fellowship with such people, hence he was accused of being a glutton, a drinker, and a friend of those outside the law (Matt. 11:19). The unsparing attacks of the theologians, the Pharisees, and the Sadducees have a clear and unequivocal social import.

Justice occupies a central place in his proclamation. He declares that the poor are blest, not because he sees poverty itself as a virtue, but because poverty is the result of unjust relationships between human beings, provoking the intervention of the messianic king. The primary function of this king is to do justice to the poor and to defend the rights of the weak. He also rejects wealth, viewing it dialectically as a result of the exploitation of the poor and regarding it as outright dishonest (Luke 16:9). Jesus' ideal is not a society of affluence or one of poverty but a society of justice and brotherhood.

Equally liberative is his criticism of all power exercised as domination over others (Luke 22:25–28). He demythologizes the notion that its efficacy and validity lie in the fact that it is a mediation of the divine. This relativization is also applied to the sacred power of the Roman emperor. He denies its divine character (Matt. 22:2) and its presumption to be the court of last appeal (John 19:11). The *pax romana*, based on domination, does not incarnate the kingdom of God.

Jesus' praxis entails establishing a new kind of solidarity above and beyond class differences and other differences inherent in human life. He seeks to defend the rights of all, but especially the rights of the poor, the lowly, the sick, and the alienated. He opposes everything that divides human beings: envy, greediness, calumny, oppression, hatred, and so forth. He champions the spirit of the Beatitudes as the only one capable of transforming this world into something pleasing to God.

Jesus' stand against vengeance and in favor of pardon and mercy arises from his keen perception of historical reality. There will always be structures based on domination, but that should not dishearten us or lead us to adopt the same approach. Pardon is a necessity. It is the power of love, which is capable of living with contradictions and overcoming them from within.

Despite these liberative practices, which flesh out the reality of the eschatological kingdom in the concrete,

Jesus did not organize to take over political power. He always viewed political power as a diabolical temptation because it implied a regionalization of God's kingdom, which was meant to be universal. The underlying reason for his rejection of political power lay in his awareness of the nature of God's kingdom. Since it is God's, it cannot be fleshed out in history by forced imposition; it can be established only by human freedom (i.e., conversion). Jesus also shared the cultural horizon of his contemporaries with its apocalyptic strain. The definitive breakthrough of God's kingdom will be the gratuitous work of God himself. Human beings should prepare for it in anticipation, but they cannot induce it. This outlook distinguishes Jesus from the Zealots.

If we now see that history still has a future and that the parousia has been delayed, then we can and should relativize this attitude of the historical Jesus and attribute it to the limitations imposed on him by his cultural milieu and its verbal categories. That frees theology to view a takeover of political power as a proper and legitimate way of offering more justice to the alienated and oppressed. Political power can be subordinated to the law of service and thus avoid absolutization. Thus it can be an historical way of concretizing what is implied in the idea of the kingdom. As Sobrino points out, Jesus did not advocate a depoliticized, dehistoricized, destructured love. He advocated a political love, a love situated in a given context and having visible repercussions for human beings.[13]

Conversion: The Demand Imposed by God's Liberation

The conversion demanded by Jesus is not simply theoretical, i.e., a change of convictions. It is primarily concerned with attitudes and concrete practice. It is not concerned solely with human beings as inviolable centers of personal freedom and individuality, which is to say, with their hearts. It is also concerned with human

beings as concrete creatures involved in a whole net-
work of living relationships and activities. Positively
viewed, conversion is the implementation of altered relationships at every level of personal and social reality.
These altered relationships will express concrete forms
of liberation and anticipate the kingdom of God. The
personal and the social stand in a dialectical relationship.

Conversion should not be viewed as a precondition for
the coming of the kingdom. It signifies that the kingdom
is already inaugurated here, that it is present and active
in history. Conversion makes clear the structure of the
kingdom and the kind of liberation intended by God. On
the one hand it is a gift offered freely to human beings.
On the other hand it is their acceptance of that gift. This
acceptance becomes real insofar as human beings col-
laborate in the work of inaugurating the kingdom
through mediations of a personal, social, political, and
religious nature.

The kingdom and the liberation implied by it typify
the power of God. It is not a power seeking to dominate
people's freedoms. It is rather an offer and a summons to
freedom, and to the work of freedom which is love. The
kingdom is something offered, not something imposed.
In the conditions of history, then, the kingdom of God
does not come unless human beings accept it and enter
into the whole process of conversion and liberation.

Proclamation of the kingdom does not invalidate historical struggle. The total liberation proposed by God
must take the pathway of partial liberations. While the
former is not simply the sum of the latter, the latter do
anticipate and pave the way for the former. Human
beings are never mere spectators, and God is not simply
a donor.

Conversion reveals the conflict-laden dimension of
the kingdom. Jesus' good news is good news only for
those who undergo conversion. It is not for the Pharisee
who remains a Pharisee, for those who seek to maintain

the existing situation and its various discriminations between human beings. For all those people it is bad news. Thus Jesus and his message divide people, and that is of the essence of the kingdom. People enter it by breaking with this world and changing it, not by prolonging its existing structure. Jesus was for all. But in the concrete he was for the poor insofar as he was one of them and shouldered their cause; he was for the Pharisees insofar as he unmasked their vaunted self-sufficiency; and he was for the rich insofar as he denounced the mechanisms they used to maintain injustice and worship mammon. Finally, he died so that we might know that not everything is permitted in this world.[14]

The historical Jesus opposed using power to impose the will of God. That would exempt human beings from their liberative task. They would no longer be active subjects of personal and social transformation but mere beneficiaries of God's work. He chose to die rather than to implant the kingdom of God by violence. The latter course would not produce the kingdom of God but a kingdom grounded on human willfulness, power, domination, and an absence of freedom.

The Death of Jesus: The Price for God's Liberation

Jesus' death is intimately bound up with his life, his proclamation, and his practical activities. His call for conversion, his new image of God, his freedom toward sacred traditions, and his prophetic criticism of those holding political, economic, and religious power combined to provoke the conflict that resulted in his violent death.

Jesus did not seek death. It was imposed on him from outside. He did not simply accept it resignedly. Instead he shouldered it as an expression of his freedom and his fidelity to the cause of God and human beings. Feeling isolated, rejected, and threatened, he did not choose to compromise with the powerful and the privileged in order to survive. He continued to carry out his mission of proclaiming the good news to those willing to be converted, and he freely accepted the death imposed upon him by historical circumstances.

The cross is the symbol of the reign of power in its own service, even if it be religious power. The pious people were the ones who slew Jesus. Whenever a situation closes in upon itself, obscures the future, and turns itself into an absolute, the process of liberation is cut short and the mechanisms of oppression are reinforced.

When Jesus embraces death of his own free will, he reveals the total freedom of himself and his projects. He points up one concrete way of fleshing out the reality of God's kingdom when he accepts death out of love, maintains his fellowship with the downtrodden of history, pardons those who have afflicted him, and puts himself into God's hands in the face of historical failure.

The motives behind the assassination of Jesus are two-fold. Both have something to do with the structural level. First of all, Jesus was condemned as a *blasphemer*. He presents a God who is different from the God of the status quo. As Jon Sobrino points out, Jesus unmasked the religious hypocrisy of the standing order and its use of God to justify injustice. In that sense the religious authorities were correct in saying that Jesus was preaching a God opposed to their own.[15]

Secondly, his whole attitude and approach was eminently liberative, as we have already noted. Thus the political authorities accused him of being a *guerrilla fighter* and executed him for that. His preaching and his outlook brought him close to the liberation project of the Zealots. After all, he looked for the imminent arrival of the kingdom; he acted in radical ways; he made inflammatory remarks about the violent bearing away the kingdom; he acted freely vis-à-vis the established imperial authorities; and he clearly exercised leadership over the common people, who wanted to make him their chief. On the other hand Jesus clearly moved away from the spirit and approach of the Zealots. He renounced religious messianism of a political cast. Messianism grounded on the use of force and power would not succeed in concretizing the kingdom, he felt. The kingdom entails a more radical liberation, one that gets beyond the breakdown of brotherhood and calls for the creation of new human beings.

The cross demonstrates the conflict-ridden nature of every process of liberation undertaken when the structure of injustice has gained the upper hand. Under such conditions liberation can come about only through martyrdom and sacrifice on behalf of others and God's cause in the world. That is the route which Jesus consciously chose and accepted.

Jesus' Resurrection: The Foreshadowed Breakthrough of Definitive Liberation

Jesus' resurrection is intimately bound up with his life, death, and proclamation of the kingdom. If "the kingdom of God" is the semantic term connoting total liberation, if Jesus' life was a liberated and liberating life, and if his death was his completely free offering up of that life, then his resurrection realizes and fulfills his program in its eschatological form. Because of its rejection by the Jews, the kingdom could not be fleshed out in its universal, cosmic dimension. Now it finds a personal realization in the resurrection of the crucified Jesus. He is the *autobasileia tou theou* (Origen—the kingdom of God realized in a self).

As such the resurrection is simply the triumph of life and the explicitation of all its latent potentialities. It is the liberation of life from all its obstacles and conflicts in history. It is already an eschatological reality; as such it reveals God's ultimate intention for human beings and the world.

The resurrection unveils the life that was hidden in Jesus and that could not be devoured by the cross. It connotes full liberation as something that is completely a grace from God. The resurrection points to the goal and fulfillment sought by every liberation process: arrival at complete freedom.

The resurrection of the crucified Jesus shows that it is not meaningless to die for other human beings and God. In Jesus' resurrection, light is shed on the anonymous death of all those who have lost out in history while fighting for the cause of justice and ultimate human meaningfulness. As one author suggests, "the question of resurrection is rightly posed from the standpoint of insurrection."[16] The resurrection tells us that the murderer shall not triumph over his victim.[17]

The import of total liberation to be found in the resurrection appears only when we tie it in with Jesus' struggle to establish God's kingdom in the world. Apart from this link it could degenerate into pious cynicism vis-à-vis injustices in this world and an idealism unconnected with history. Thanks to his resurrection, Jesus continues to exist among human beings, giving impetus to their struggle for liberation. All authentically human growth, all authentic justice in social relationships, and all real increase and growth in life represent a way in which the resurrection is actualized here and now while its future fulfillment is being prepared.

The Following of Jesus as the Way
to Actualize His Liberation

The advent of the eschatological kingdom as the full embodiment of liberation has been delayed. In this context human life possesses a paschal structure. This translates into following the crucified and risen Jesus Christ.

The first and primary aspect of following Jesus is proclaiming the utopia of the kingdom as the real and complete meaning of the world that is offered to all by God.

Second, the following of Jesus means translating that utopia into practice. We must try to change the world on the personal, social, and cosmic level. This utopia is not an ideology, but it does give rise to functional ideologies that will guide liberative practices. The following of Jesus is not mere imitation. We must take due account of the differences between Jesus' situation and our own. In his day there was an apocalyptic atmosphere and people were looking for the immediate breakthrough of the kingdom. In our eyes the parousia has been held up and history still has a future. Hence there must be differences in the way we organize love and justice in society.

To be sure, for both Jesus and us God is the future and his kingdom has not yet fully arrived; but our way of shouldering history will vary from his. Jesus did not prescribe any concrete model. Instead he offered a way of being present in every concrete embodiment of the kingdom, though such embodiments will obviously depend on the details of a given situation. What he offers us by way of example is an option on behalf of those who are treated unjustly, a refusal to succumb to the will for power and domination, and solidarity with everything that suggests greater participation in societal living and fraternal openness to God.

Third, God's liberation translates into a process that will entail conflict and struggle. These conflicts must be taken on and understood in the light of Jesus' own burdensome journey. It is a journey of love that sometimes must sacrifice itself. It is a journey of eschatological hope that must go by way of political hopes. It is a journey of faith that must move ahead gropingly; the fact that we are Christians does not provide us with a key to decipher political and economic problems. Cross and resurrection are paradigms of Christian existence.

To follow Jesus means to follow through with his work and attain his fulfillment.

This basic vision, possessing all the limitations of a vision, is meant to be put in the service of the cause of liberation. And here I am referring to the political, social, economic, and religious liberation of our oppressed peoples in Latin America. It is a contribution on the level of theoretical expression that seeks to illuminate and enrich an already existing praxis of liberative faith.

We live in the dependent Third World. If we seek to ponder and live our christological faith in a truly historical way, then we find that it points us toward the ideological option of liberation, a particular type of analysis, and a very definite commitment. We do not think that we can read the gospel message and follow Jesus in some way that is not liberative. To do so would be to turn our christological faith upside down, or to live it in an ideological way that has bad connotations.

We can preach about the kingdom of God in many different ways. We can refer to it as the *other* world, the world that God is preparing for us after death. Or we can equate it with the church, pointing out that the church continues to represent Jesus with its cultic worship, its dogmatics, its institutions, and its sacraments. These two ways of talking about the kingdom bypass commitment as a task of building a more just and equitable world. They alienate Christians from all the questions posed by the oppression of millions of their fellow human beings.

However, there is another way to preach about the kingdom of God. We can present it as the utopia of a fully reconciled world, a utopia that is prepared and begun here and now in history through the committed action of people of good will. It is my belief that this interpretation translates *the very intention of Jesus himself* on both the historical and the theological level. Thus the function of Christology is to shape and work out a Christian option in society.

THE IMPORTANCE OF A LIBERATION CHRISTOLOGY
FOR WORLDWIDE CHRISTOLOGICAL FAITH

It should not be thought that this type of Christology is of interest solely to Latin America because it concretely experiences all the contradictions of underdevelopment and domination.[18] As I pointed out earlier, this situation has been generated by a whole set of relationships between rich countries on the one hand and poor countries on the other. Our nations are simply one pole of the relationship. Hence the theologians living in the rich nations at the other pole are also caught up in this problem. It is a challenge to every Christian conscience, and it forces us to take a definite turn in our way of pondering and living out our christological faith. The way in which theologians in affluent countries articulate their Christology is not a matter of indifference to us. Their approach has a political dimension, for it may either reinforce or call into question the dominant pole that is chiefly responsible for the present imbalance and inequity.

The issue is not one of aid but of justice. The present set of relationships is violating the fundamental rights of certain nations and violently keeping them in underdeveloped molds. But of course this whole mechanism of injustice is concealed under a cloak of progress and friendly relations designed to deceive the Christian churches and disarm the theological intelligentsia.

There are theologians who are very enlightened, critical-minded, secularized, and progressive. Yet all too often it turns out that this is a cover for political positions that are highly conservative and that serve to reinforce the status quo. Other theologians wish to adopt a liberation approach, but for want of more critical analysis of the existing system their practices are structurally supportive of it.

In Latin America the mechanisms of domination are more clear-cut and open to view. It was easier for theology to call itself into question and to look for theoretical and practical ways to support a project of liberation. In Europe the mechanisms were also present because there we find the decision-making centers that determine our economic, political, and cultural situation; but there they are more subtle and refined. Yet theologians can arrive at a stance that is socially and theologically

MILITARY AND/OR DEPENDENT

NAME: _____
Last   First   Mid

Please answer each question below by selecting applic
question:

Are you currently stationed in California on active milit
If "Yes", when did that duty begin? _____
Month

Are you a dependent of active military? (1) YES   (2
If "Yes", what is your relationship to the military perso

When did the military person's current duty begin in Ca

Date of anticipated separation from active duty? _____
Mon

CHILDREN OF MILITARY UNDER 18 YEARS
INFORMATION:

How long have you lived in California? _____
What state does your father regard as his permanent hon
Where is his military home of record? _____

Does he pay state taxes? (1) YES   (2) NO
If "Yes", in what state? _____

liberative by refining their tools of analysis and maintaining a critical distance more consistently.

In Latin America we still cherish a dream, for it is always permissible to dream. We dream of the day when the privileged intelligence of European theology will realize the important role it has to play in the process of liberation vis-à-vis its own churches and its own society. By virtue of its position at the centers of power it can do much to help its fellow Christians on our continent to set out on their path to liberation. The theology of liberation, of Jesus Christ the Liberator, is the pain-filled cry of oppressed Christians. They are knocking on the door of their affluent brothers and sisters, asking for everything and yet for nothing. Indeed all they ask is to be people, to be accepted as persons. All they ask is that they be allowed to fight to regain their captive freedom.

If liberation Christology helps this messianic task, then it will have fulfilled its prophetic mission. It will have proved itself worthy of the sacred name of Jesus Christ, who wanted nothing else in this world but to free all human beings and bring them to complete fulfillment.

January 1978

Notes

Chapter 1

1. See the bibliography on this topic: *Der historische Jesus und der kerygmatische Christus*, ed. H. Ristow and K. Matthiae (Berlin: Evangelische Verlagsanstalt, 1961); R. Geiselmann, *Dei Frage nach dem historischen Jesus I* (Munich, 1965); X. Léon-Dufour, *Les Evangiles et l'histoire de Jésus* (Paris: Ed. du Seuil, 1963); Eng. trans., *The Gospels and the Jesus of History* (New York: Desclée, 1968); W. Trilling, *Jesús y los problemas de su historicidad* (Barcelona, 1970); German original, *Fragen zur Geschichtlichkeit Jesu* (Dusseldorf: Patmos, 1966); idem, "Legitimidade e localização da questão do Jesus historico," in *Actualidades Biblicas*, Melange internacional a Frei João José P. de Castro (Petrópolis: Vozes, 1970), pp. 353–65; U. Zilles, "O Jesus historico e o Cristo da fe," in *Vozes* 62 (1968): 195–222.

2. This affirmation was made for the first time by C.F. Dupuis (1791), later popularized by Bruno Bauer in a posthumous work *Christus und die Casaren* (1877). Cf. O. Rietmuller, *Woher wissen wir, dass Jesus gelebt hat?* (Stuttgart, 1922).

3. Cf. A. Drews, *Die Christusmythe* (Jena: Diederichs, 1924); Eng. trans., *The Christ Myth*, rev. and enl. (Chicago: Open Court Publ., 1911); H. Zimern, *Der Streit un die Christusmythe* (Berlin, 1910).

4. The principal representatives are A. Kalthoff, *Das Christusproblem, Grundlinien zu einer Sozialtheologie* (Leipzig, 1904); and K. Kautsky, *Der Ursprung des Christentums* (Stuttgart, 1908); Eng. trans., *Foundations of Christianity: A Study in Christian Origins* (New York: International Publ., 1925).

5. Cf. P. Alfaric, *Origines sociales du Christianisme* (Paris: Publ. de l'Union Rationaliste, 1959).

6. R. Bultmann, *Jesus* (Berlin: Deutsche Bibliothek, 1926, Munich-Hamburg, 1965), pp. 13–14; Eng. trans., *Jesus and the Word* (New York: Scribner's, 1934).

7. For the sources see C.K. Barrett, *The New Testament Background: Selected Documents* (New York: Macmillan, 1957).

8. W. Trilling, *Jesús y los problemas de su historicidad*, pp. 62–66.

9. Cf. ibid., p. 17.

10. Cf. *Geschichte der Leben-Jesu-Forschung I, II* (Munich-Hamburg, 1966); idem, *Le secret historique de la vie de Jésus* (Paris, 1961).

11. *Geschichte der Leben*, p. 48.

12. R. Bultmann, *Jesus;* idem, *Theologie des Neuen Testamentes*, (Tubingen: Mohr, 1958); Eng. trans., *Theology of the New Testament* (New York: Scribner's, 1965); idem, *Das Verhältnis der urchristlichen Christusbotschaft zum historischen Jesus* (Heidelberg: C. Winter, 1965).

13. Bultmann, *Theologie des Neuen Testamentes*, p. 1.

14. Martin Kähler, *Der sogenannte historische Jesus und der geschichtliche biblische Christus* (Munich: Kaiser, 1961); Eng. trans., *The So-Called Historical Jesus and the Historical, Biblical Christ* (Philadelphia: Fortress Press, 1964).

15. R. Bultmann, *Das Urchristentum im Rahmen der antiken Religionen* (Zurich: Artemis-Verlag, 1949).

16. R. Bultmann, *Verhältnis*, p. 6; W. Kunneth, *Glauben en Jesus? Christologie und moderne Existenz* (Munich-Hamburg, 1969), pp. 79–86.

17. Bultmann, *Verhältnis*, p. 9.

18. Bultmann, *Glauben und Verstehen I* (Tübingen: Mohr, 1933), p. 260; Eng. trans., *Faith and Understanding* (New York: Harper & Row, 1969).

19. Bultmann, *Offenbarung und Heilsgeschehen* (Munich, 1941), p. 61.

20. *Glauben und Verstehen*, p. 263.

21. Ibid.

22. Ibid., pp. 260ff.

23. Despite this, Bultmann understands and knows the historical Jesus, as is demonstrated by his book *Jesus* of 1926.

24. R. Geiselmann, *Die Frage nach dem historischen Jesus*, pp. 51ff.

25. James McConkey Robinson, *Kerygma und historischer Jesus* (Zurich: Zwingli, 1960), p. 114; orig., *A New Quest of the Historical Jesus* (London: SCM Press, 1959).

26. Bultmann, *Verhältnis*, pp. 5–6.

27. For the most recent research see W.G. Kummel, "Jesusforschung seit 1950," in *Theologische Rundschau* 31 (1965/1966): 15–46; 290–315; F. Mussner, "Leben-Jesu-Forschung," in *Lexikon für Theologie und Kirche* 6 (1961): 859–64; J. Roloff, *Das Kerygma und der irdische Jesus. Historische Motive in den Jesus-Erzählungen der Evangelien* (Göttingen, 1970); M. Lehmann, *Synoptische Quelleanalyse und die Frage nach dem historischen Jesus* (Berlin: de Gruyter, 1970); M. Hengel, *Nachfolge und Charisma* (Berlin: Töpelmann, 1968); C. K. Barrett, *Jesus and the Gospel Tradition* (Philadelphia: Fortress Press, 1968); cf. various other authors, "Zur Frage nach dem

historischen Jesus," in *Biblische Zeitschrift* 15 (1971): 271–79; R. Pesch, *Jesus ureigene Taten,* Quaestiones Disputatae 52 (Freiburg, 1970); P. Grech, "Développements récents dans la controverse sur le Jésus de l'histoire, in *Bulletin de Théologie Biblique* 1 (1971): 193–217.

28. Cf. H.R. Balz, *Methodische Probleme der neutestamentlichen Christologie* (Neukirchen: Euziehungsvereins, 1967), pp. 124ff., 218ff.

29. "Das Problem des historischen Jesus," in *Glauben heute* (Hamburg, 1965), pp. 96–112.

30. *Jesus von Nazareth* (Stuttgart: W. Kohlhammer, 1956); Eng. trans., *Jesus of Nazareth* (New York: Harper & Row, 1960).

31. "Der historische Jesus und der Christus des Glaubens," in *Biblische Zeitschrift* 1 (1957): 224–52.

32. *Grundzüge der Christologie* (Gütersloh: Mohn, 1964), pp. 47–60; Eng. trans., *Jesus, God and Man* (Philadelphia: Westminster Press, 1968).

33. *Jesus von Nazareth,* p. 56.

34. Cf. G. Ebeling, "Jesus und Glaube," in *Wort und Glaube* (Tübingen: Mohr, 1960), pp. 203–54.

35. Cf. E. Stauffer, *Jerusalem und Rom im Zeitalter Jesu Christi* (Bern: Francke Verlag, 1957); *Jesus: Gestalt und Geschichte* (Bern: Francke, 1957); Eng. trans., *Jesus and His Story* (New York: Knopf, 1960); *Die Botschaft Jesu Damals und Heute* (Bern and Munich: Francke, 1959).

36. Cf. G.W. Kümmel, "Jesusforschung," seit 1950/11, in *Theologische Rundschau* 31 (1966): 291ff., 296–98; W. Marxsen, in *Theologische Literaturzeitung* 86 (1961): 38–41; E. Haenchen, in *Gnomos* 32 (1960): 552–56.

37. H. Braun, *Jesus: Der Mann aus Nazareth und seine Zeit* (Stuttgart-Berlin: Kreuz, 1969), p. 170; cf. *Post Bultmann locutum, Eine Diskussion zwischen Prof. D.F. Gollwitzer und Prof. D.H. Braun* (Hamburg, 1965), p. 30.

38. Cf. D. Sölle, *Atheistisch an Gott glauben,* Beiträge zur Theologie (Olten/Freiburg: Walter, 1968).

39. *Atheismus im Christentum,* Nur ein guter Christ kann ein Atheist sein. Nurein guter Atheist kann ein Christ sein (Stuttgart, 1969); Eng. trans., *Atheism in Christianity: The Religion of the Exodus and the Kingdom* (New York: Herder, 1972).

40. P. van Buren, "The Dissolution of the Absolute," *Religion in Life,* 1965; "Christian Education," in *Religious Education,* January–February 1965, pp. 3–10; *The Secular Meaning of the Gospel* (New York: Macmillan, 1963).

41. *Post Bultmann locutum,* p. 30.

42. D. Sölle, *Stellvertretung: Ein Kapitel Theologie nach dem "Tode Gottes"* (Stuttgart/Berlin: Kreuz, 1965); Eng. trans., *Christ the Representative* (Philadelphia: Fortress Press, 1967).

43. Cf. D. Bonhoeffer, *Widerstand und Ergebung* (Munich: Kaiser, 1956); Eng. trans., *Letters and Papers from Prison* (London: SCM Press, 1956).

44. See especially K. Rahner, "Jesus Christus," in *Lexikon für Theologie und Kirche* 5 (1960): 953–61; "Jesus Christus," in *Sacramentum Mundi* (1968), 2: 900–57; in his *Schriften zur Theologie* (Einsiedeln: Benziger, 1954), 1: 169–222; Eng. trans., *Theological Investigations; Zur Theologie der Manschwerdung* 4 (1960) 137–55; the articles by E. Paulinas on Christology in *Teologia e Antropologia* (São Paulo, 1969); "Christologie," *Rahmen des modernen Selbst-und Weltverständnisses* 9 (1970): 227–41; H. Küng, *Menschwerdung Gottes*, Eine Einführung in Hegels theologisches Denken als Prolegomena zu einer zukünftigen Christologie (Freiburg: Herder, 1970), esp. pp. 647–70.

45. Cf. L. Boff, *O Evangelho do Cristo cósmico* (Petrópolis: Vozes, 1970); P. Schellenbaum, *Le Christ dans l'énergétique teilhardienne* (Paris: Cerf, 1971).

46. See especially K. Niederwimmer, *Jesus* (Göttingen: Vandenhoeck, 1918); W.W. Meissner, *Foundations for a Psychology of Grace* (Glen Rock, N.J.: Paulist Press, 1966); cf. H. Harada, "Cristologia e Psicologia de C.G. Jung," in *Revista Eclesiástica Brasileira* 31 (1971): 119–44, and the rich bibliography cited there.

47. J.B. Metz, *Theology of the World* (New York: Herder, 1969); idem, *Perspectives of a Political Ecclesiology*, Concilium 66 (New York: Herder, 1971); *Kirche im Prozess der Aufklärung*, Aspekte einer politischen Theologie (Mainz, 1970); J. Moltmann, *Teologia da esperança* (São Paulo: Herder, 1970); Eng. trans., *Theology of Hope* (London: SCM Press, 1967); Germ. orig., *Theologie der Hoffnung* (Munich: Kaiser Verlag, 1966); F. Gogarten, *Jesus Christus, Wende der Welt* (Tübingen: Mohr, 1966).

48. H. Schmidt, "Politics and Christology: Historical Background," in *Faith and the World of Politics*, Concilium Vol. 36. (New York: Paulist Press, 1968) pp. 72–84; W. Elert, "Das Problem de politischen Christus," in *Der ausgang der altkirchlichen Christologie* (Berlin: Lutherisches Verl., 1957), pp. 26ff.

49. R. Hernegger, "Uhnotus in der Kunst der II. Jahrhunderts," in *Macht ohne Auftrag* (Olten: Walter-Verlag, 1963), pp. 103–6; idem, "Die Verschmelzung des Christusbildes mit dem Kaiserbild," *Macht ohne Auftrag*, pp. 267–80.

50. Cf. Hernegger, "Christus in der Kunst," pp. 279–80 and the bibliography cited.

51. See the well documented article of my student Jose Ariovaldo da Silva, "A experiencia de Cristo na juventude de hoje," in *Revista Eclesiástica Brasileira*, 32 (1972): 383–98.

52. Cf. *Jornal do Brasil*, August 22, 1971.

53. Words of a hippy leader: *Jornal do Brasil*, September 9, 1969.

54. The German magazine *Weltbild*, November 20, 1971, "Jugend im Jesusrausch und was dann?" noted that more and more American industrialists approve of the Jesus movement. It is an excellent sedative preventing the youth from rebelling against the established order, where undoubtedly injustices and discrimination have penetrated (p. 26).

55. *O Cruzeiro*, September 15, 1971, p. 286.

56. Cf. "Fatos e Fotos," September 23, 1971; Cf. B. Häring, "Il Gesu degli hippies," in *La Famiglia Cristiana*, September 11, 1971, p. 7.

57. Spoken by a young couple, in *Tribuna Ilustrada*, Campinas (SP), August 1971, p. 4.

Chapter 2

1. See the major bibliography pertaining to our theme: *Die neue Hermeneutik*, Neuland in der Theologie, 2 (Zurich/Stuttgart, 1965); G. Stachel, *Die neue Hermeneutik* (Munich, 1967); R. Marlé, *Le problème théologique de l'herméneutique* (Paris, 1965); H. Cazelles, *Écriture, Parole et Esprit: Trois aspects de l'herméneutique biblique* (Paris: Desclée, 1971); F. Ferré, *Language, Logic, and God* (New York: Harper & Row, 1969); W. Kasper, "Das Verständnis der Offenbarung," in *Handbuch der Verkündigung* I (Freiburg, 1970), pp. 79–96; R. Bultmann, "Das Problem der Hermeneutik," in *Glauben und Verstehen* (Tübingen: Mohr, 1965), 1:142–50; Eng. trans., *Faith and Understanding* (New York: Harper & Row, 1969).

2. Cf. K. Koch, *Was ist Formgeschichte? Neue Wege de Bibel exegese* (Neukirchen: Neukirchener Verl., 1967); H. Zimmermann, *Neutestamentliche Methodenlehre. Darstellung der historisch-kritischen Methode* (Stuttgart, 1968), pp. 128–213.

3. Zimmermann, *Neutestamentliche* pp. 175ff.

4. See the explanations in T. Maertens, J. Frisque, *Guia da Assembleia Cristã* 7 (Petrópolis: Vozes, 1970), pp. 101–2; Eng. trans., *Guide to the Christian Assembly* (Bruges: St. Andrew's Abbey, Biblica, 1965).

5. J. Rohde, *Die redaktionsgeschichtliche Methode* (Hamburg, 1966); Eng. trans., *Rediscovering the Teaching of the Evangelist* (Philadelphia: Westminster Press, 1968).

6. Cf. M. Heidegger, *Sein und Zeit* (Tübingen: Niemeyer, 1963), 31–34, 141–67; Eng. trans., *Being and Time* (New York: Harper & Row, 1962). R. Bultmann, "Das Problem der Hermeneutik."

7. See E. Coreth, "Der Zirkel des Verstehens," in *Grundfragen der Hermeneutik in philosopischer Betrachtung* (Freiburg: Herder, 1969).

8. Cf. J. Moltmann, "Toward a Political Hermeneutic of the Gospel" in *Religion, Revolution and the Future* (New York: Scribner's, 1969), pp. 83–107; J. Blank, "Das politische Element in der historisch-kritischen Methode," in *Die Funktion der Theologie in Kirche und Gesellschaft* (Munich: P. Neuenzeit, 1969), pp. 39–60; R. Alves, *¿Religión: opio o instrumento de liberación?* (Montevideo, 1970); in Eng. see *A Theology of Human Hope* (Washington: Corpus, 1969).

9. Cf. K. Lehmann, "Die Kirche und die Herrschaft der Ideologien," in *Handbuch der Pastoraltheologie* 2:2 (Freiburg: Herder, 1966), pp. 109–202.

10. Cf. A. Darlap, "Os fundamentos da teologia historico-salvifica," in *Mysterium Salutis* 1/1 (Petrópolis: Vozes, 1971), pp. 34–167; W. Kasper, *Das Verständnis der Offenbarung*, pp. 90–96.

11. See my own work, "Tentativa de solução ecumenica para o prob-

lema da inspiração e da inerrancia," in *Revista Eclesiastica Brasileira* 30 (1970): 648–67.

12. Cf. J. Macquarrie, "Religious Language and Recent Analytical Philosophy," in Concilium 46 (New York: Paulist Press, 1969), pp. 159–72.

13. Cf. "Utopia" by the Concilium General Secretariat in *The Problem of Eschatology*, Concilium 41 (New York: Paulist Press, 1969), pp. 149–65; M. Demaison, "The Christian Utopia," in Concilium 59 (New York: Herder, 1970), pp. 42–58.

14. "Christologie," in *Gesammelte Schriften* (1927–1944) (Munich: C. Kaiser, 1958–1961), 3:167.

15. L. Wittgenstein, *Tractatus logico-philosophicus n. 7* (São Paulo: 1967), p. 129; Eng. trans., *Tractatus logico-philosophicus* (New York: Humanities, 1963).

16. *Obras de São João da Cruz* II (Petrópolis: Vozes, 1960), 2:201; in Eng. see *The Collected Works of St. John of the Cross* (Washington: ICS, 1973).

Chapter 3

1. H.D. Bastian, *Theologie der Frage* (Munich: Kaiser, 1969), pp. 18–31; H.D. Gadamer, *Wahrheit und Methode* (Tübingen: Mohr, 1965), pp. 356–57; Eng. trans., *Truth and Method* (New York: Seabury, 1975).

2. See the classic of E. Bloch, *Das Prinzip Hoffnung* (Berlin: Auflau-Verlag, 1954–59); see also J. Moltmann, *Teologia da Esperança*, (São Paulo: Herder, 1971); Eng. trans., *Theology of Hope* (New York: Harper & Row, 1967).

3. See the work of H.R. Balz, *Methodische Probleme der neutestamentlichen Christologie* (Neukirchen: Neukirchen-Vluyn, 1967); he reviews the works of Cullmann, Hahn, Kramer, E. Schweizer, and others.

4. Concerning this theme there exist innumerable studies: see R. Schnackenburg, *Gottes Herschaft und Reich* (Freiburg: Herder, 1959); A. Schweitzer, *Reich Gottes und Christentum*, new edition (Tübingen: Mohr, 1967); E. Staehlin, *Die Verkundigung des Reiches Gottes in der Kirche Jesu Christi*, 7 vols. (Basel, 1951–1964); R. Morganthaler, *Kommendes Reich* (Zurich, 1952); J. Bonsirven, *Le règne de Dieu* (Paris: Aubier, Montaigne, 1957); W. Knorzer, *Reich Gottes* (Stuttgart: Traum, Hoffnung, Wirklichkeit, 1969); H. Flender, *Die Botschaft Jesu von der Gottesherrschaft* (Munich: Kaiser, 1968).

5. Cf. T. Maertens, *C'est fête en l'honneur de Yahvé* (Bruges: Desclée, 1961), pp. 169–79; Eng. trans., *A Feast in Honor of Yahweh* (Notre Dame: Fides, 1965).

6. J. Jeremias, *Paroles de Jésus, le sermon sur la montagne, le Notre-Père* (Paris: Cerf, 1963), p. 122; In English see *The Sermon on the Mount* (Philadelphia: Fortress, 1963).

7. J. Becker, *Das Heil Gottes: Heils-und Sündenbegriffe in den Qumrantexten und im Neuen Testament* (Göttingen: Vandenhoeck, 1964), p. 203.

8. Cf. H.H. Rowley, *Apokalyptik, ihre Form und Bedeutung zur biblischen Zeit* (Einsiedeln: Benziger, 1965), esp. pp. 43–46; Eng. orig., *The Relevance of Apocalyptic: A Study of Jewish and Christian Apocalypses from Daniel to Revelation* (New York: Association Press, 1964); J. Schreiner, *Alttestamentlich—jüdische Apokalyptik* (Munich: Kosel, 1969), esp. pp. 195ff.

9. Cf. M. Hengel, *Die Zeloten; Untersuchungen zur jüdischen Freiheitsbewegungen in der Zeit von Herodes* (Leiden: E. J. Brill, 1961); idem, *War Jesus Revolutionär?* (Stuttgart: Calver, 1970); Eng. trans., *Was Jesus a Revolutionist?* (Philadelphia: Fortress Press, 1971); O. Cullmann, *Jesus und die Revolutionaren seiner Zeit* (Tübingen: Mohr Siebeck, 1970), esp. pp. 40–70; Eng. trans., *Jesus and the Revolutionaries* (New York: Harper & Row, 1970).

10. F. C. Grant, "Economic Messianism and the Teaching of Jesus," *Anglican Theological Review* 12 (1929/1930): 443–47, esp. p. 445; idem, *Antikes Judentum und das Neue Testament* (Frankfurt: Ner-Tamid-Verlag, 1962), pp. 153–56; Eng. orig., *Ancient Judaism and the New Testament* (New York: Macmillan, 1959).

11. Cf. T.W. Manson, *The Servant-Messiah* (Cambridge: University Press, 1953), p. 55; P. Hoffman, "Die Versuchungsgeschichte in der Logienquelle. Zur Auseinandersetzung der Judenchristen mit dem politishen Messianismus," in *Biblische Zeitschrift* 13 (1969): 207–23.

Chapter 4

1. See R. Schnackenburg, "Umkehr-Predigt im Neuen Testament," in *Christliche Existenz nach dem Neuen Testament* (Munich: Kösel, 1967), 1:35–60; Eng. trans., *Christian Existence in the New Testament* (Notre Dame: University of Notre Dame Press, 1968); H. Braun, "Unkehr in spätjudisch-häretischer und in fruhchristlicher Sicht," in *Gesammelte Studien zum Neuen Testament* (Tübingen: Mohr Siebeck, 1967), pp. 70–85; the whole copy of *Lumière et Vie* 47 on "La conversion," April-May 1960; P. Aubin, *Le problème de la conversion* (Paris: Beauchesne, 1962); W. Trilling, "Metanoia als Grundforderung der neutestamentlichen Lebenslehre," in *Einübung des Glaubens*, Fest. f. K. Tillmann (Würzburg: Echter, 1965), pp. 178–90.

2. Cf. M. Hengel, *Nachfolge und Charisma; eine exegetisch religionsgeschitliche Studie zu Mt. 8,21f.* and *Jesu Ruf in die Nachfolge*, (Berlin: A. Töpelmann, 1968), esp. pp. 9–17 and 80–82.

3. See J. Jeremias, *Unbekannte Jesusworte* (Gütersloh: Mohr, 1963), pp. 64–71; Eng. trans., *Unknown Sayings of Jesus* (London: SPCK, 1964).

4. J. Jeremias, *Paroles de Jésus*, see note 6 in Chapter 3.

5. Cf. P. Noll, *Jesus und das Gesetz* (Tübingen: Mohr Siebeck, 1968); W.G. Kümmel, "Jesus und der jüdische Traditionsgedanke," in *Heilsgeschehen und Geschichte* (Marburg: Elwert, 1965), pp. 15–35; H. Braun, *Spätjüdisch-häretischer und früchristlicher Radikalismus. Jesus von Nazareth und die judische Qumransekte*, v. 2 (Tübingen,

1957). Carlos Mesters, *Palavra de Deus na história dos homens* (Petrópolis: Vozes, 1971), 2:135–81; Frei Bernardino Leers, "Jesu Cristo e a Lei," in *Grande Sinal* 25 (1971):491–503; E. Schweizer, "Observance of the Law and Charismatic Activity in Matthew," in *New Testament Studies* 16 (April 1970):213–30; A. Sand, "Die Polemikgegen Gesetzlosigkeit in Evangelium nach Matthäus und bei Paulus," in *Biblische Zeitschrift* 14 (1970):112–15.

6. Matt. 5:17–19 cannot be seen as an objection: "Do not imagine that I have come to abolish the Law or the Prophets. I have come not to abolish but to complete them. . . ." Both Catholic and Protestant exegesis has made it clear that here we are not faced with a "logion" of the historical Jesus, but a construction of the primitive community, and especially Matthew, preoccupied with the antinomists who began to appear in the communities (perhaps under the influence of the theology of Paul concerning Christ as the end of the Law: Rom. 10:4 and Gal. 3). For the theology of Matthew, the Law as well as the Prophets are still places where one can discover the will of God. Nevertheless they are under the criticism of Jesus, who came to reveal and manifest in a definitive form the will of God. For Matthew, the Law is valid only if it assists love. For this see G. Barth, "Das Gesetzverständnis des Evangelisten Matthäus," in *Uberlieferung und Auslegung im Matthäus-evangelium*, ed. G. Bornkamm, G. Barth and J. Held (Neukirchen, 1960), pp. 54–154; G. Strecker, *Der Weg der Gerechtigkeit: Untersuchung zur Theologie de Matthäus* (Göttingen: Vandenhoeck and Ruprecht, 1962), pp. 137–43; H. Schurmann, "Wo fand Matthäus das Logion 5,19?" in *Biblische Zeitschrift* 4 (1960): 238–50.

7. See in J. Jeremias, *Unbekannte*, pp. 61–64; Eng. trans., *Unknown Sayings*.

8. For the question of the Sermon on the Mount, see especially the excellent work of J. Jeremias, *Les paroles de Jésus, Le sermon sur la montagne* (Paris: Cerf, 1963); W. D. Davies, *The Setting of the Sermon on the Mount* (Cambridge: University Press, 1964); R. Schnackenburg, "Die Bergpredigt Jesu und der Heutige Mensch," in *Christliche Existenze nach dem Neuen Testament*, pp. 109–30, see note 1 of this chapter; Carlos Mesters, "O Sermão de Montanha: conselho, lei ou ideal?" in *Deus onde estás?* (Belo Horizonte: Vega, 1971), pp. 133–52.

9. S. Dickey, *The Constructive Revolution of Jesus* (New York: George H. Doran Co., 1923), esp. pp. 85ff; E. Stauffer, *Jerusalem und Rom im Zeitalter Jesu Christi* (Bern: Francke, 1957), esp. pp. 62–73; F. Gogarten, "Jesus Christus Wende der Welt" in *Grundfragen zur Christologie* (Tübingen: Mohr, 1966), pp. 91–100 and 154–71.

10. See the work of W. Beilner, *Christus und die Pharisäer: Exegetische Untersuchung über Grund und Verlauf der Auseinandersetzungen* (Vienna: Herder, 1959), esp. pp. 89–122, 239–47, with its enormous bibliography.

11. For a study of the social relations of the time of Jesus see the classical work of J. Jeremias, *Jerusalem zur Zeit Jesu* (Göttingen: Vandenhoeck and Ruprecht, 1958); Eng. trans.: *Jerusalem in the Time of Jesus* (Philadelphia: Fortress 1969); L. Goppelt, "Die soziölogische

und religiöse Struktur des palästinschen Judentums zur Zeit Jesu," in *Christentum und Judentum in ersten und zweiten Jahrhundert* (Gütersloh: C. Bertelsmann, 1954), pp. 23–30; the whole volume of *Kontexte* 3: *Die Zeit Jesu* (Stuttgart-Berlin, 1966); O. Cullmann, *Jesus und die Revolutionären seiner Zeit*, pp. 40–46, see Chapter 3, note 9; C. Boff, "Foi Jesus revolucionário?" in *Revista Eclesiastica Brasileira* 31 (1971): 97–118, esp. 99–107.

12. Cf. J. Blinzler, *Herodes Antipas und Jesus Christus* (Stuttgart, 1947), esp. pp. 16–20.

13. Cf. K. Rahner, "Bermerkungen zur Bedeutung der Geschichte Jesu für die Katholische Dogmatik," in *Die Zeit Jesu* (Freiburg: Herder, 1970), pp. 273–83.

14. See L. Boff, "Simbolismo dos Milagres de Pentecostes," in *Vozes* 64 (1970): 325–26, as well as "A fe na Ressurreição de Jesus em questionamento," in *Revista Eclesiastica Brasileira* 30 (1970): 871–95.

15. Carlos Mesters, *Palavra de Deus*, pp. 171–72.

16. "The Epistle to Diognetus" from *Ancient Christian Writers*, vol. 6 (Westminster, Md.: Newman Press, 1948).

17. Cf. P. de Labriolle, "Paroikia", in *Recherches de Science Religieuse* 18 (1928): 60–72, esp. p. 61 with the accompanying citations.

18. H. Lietzmann, *Geschichte der alten Kirche* (Berlin/Leipzig: W. de Gruyter, 1932), pp. 156–74; J.-M. Hornus, *Politische Entscheidung in der alten Kirche* (Munich, 1963), pp. 91–117.

19. A fragment cited by Clement of Alexandria in *Stromata*, 6,5; see also Origen, *Contra Celsum*, 8,2.

Chapter 5

1. E. Stauffer, *Die Botschaft Jesu; Damals und Heute* (Bern-Munich: Francke, 1959), pp. 55–56; L.J. Philippidis, *Die goldene Regel, religionsgeschichtlich untersucht*, 1929; J. Jeremias, "Goldene Regel," in *Die Religion in Geschichte und Gegenwart*, 1958, pp. 1688ff.

2. H. Diels, *Die Fragmente der Vorsokratiker, griechisch und deutsch*, 6 vols. (Berlin: Weidmann, 1951–).

3. E. Stauffer, *Die Botschaft Jesu*, p. 59.

4. St. Augustine, "Retractationum," in J.P. Migne, *Patrologiae Latinae* (Paris: Garnier Frères, 1877), 32:602–3.

5. Cf. E. Käsemann, *Der Ruf der Freiheit* (Tübingen, 1968), p. 43; Eng. trans., *Jesus Means Freedom* (Philadelphia: Fortress Press, 1970).

6. C.-H. Hunzinger, "Unbekannte Gleichnisse Jesu aus dem Thomasevangelium," in *Judentum, Urchristentum, Kirche*, Fest. J. Jeremias, ed. W. Eltester (Berlin: Töpelmann, 1960), pp. 209–20, esp. pp. 211–12.

7. Cf. E. Bouet-Dufeil and Jean-Marie Dufeil, "L'amitié dans l'Evangile," in *La Vie Spirituelle*, June–July 1968, pp. 642–60; C. Jean-Nesmy, "Les amitiés du Christ," in *La Vie Spirituelle*, June 1964, pp. 673–86.

8. Cf. D. Sölle, *Phantasie und Gehorsam* (Stuttgart: Kreuz, 1968), pp. 56–71; M. Meschler, *Zum Charakterbild Jesus* (Freiburg, 1916), pp. 95–104.

9. See Boff, "Foi Cristo um Revolucionário?" in *Revista Eclesiastica Brasileira* 31 (1971): 97–118.

10. Cf. J. Jeremias, "Zöllner und Sünder," in *Zeitschrift für die Neutestamentliche Wissenschaft* 30 (1931): 293–300, esp. p. 300.

11. Luke 17:6 does not have a moral context; moreover it represents an editorial revision of Mark 11:23; cf. Matt. 21:23. Matthew's other text (Matt. 18:17) is evidently a theological elaboration of the primitive church. Also Luke 10:20 does not have a moral context. However, see R. Deichgraber, "Gehorsen und Gehorchen in der Verkundigung Jesum," in *Zeitschrift für die Neutestamentliche Wissenschaft* 52 (1961): 119–22.

12. Cf. R. Otto, *Reich Gottes und Menschensohn* (Munich: Beck, 1934), pp. 277–83; Eng. trans., *The Kingdom of God and the Son of Man* (Boston: Starr King Press, 1957).

13. G. Bornkamm, *Die Frage nach dem historischen Jesus* (Göttingen: Vandenhoeck and Ruprecht, 1962); H. Braun, *Jesus. Der Mann aus Nazareth und seine Zeit* (Stüttgart Berlin: Kreuz, 1969), pp. 73ff.; W. Gründmann, *Die Geschichte Jesu Christi* (Berlin: Evangelische Verlagsanstalt, 1961), pp. 261–70; J.R. Geiselmann, *Jesus der Christus* (Munich: Kösel, 1965), 1:218–21.

14. E. Käsemann, "War Jesus liberal?" in *Der Ruf der Freiheit*, pp. 28–58, esp. p. 42; see note 5 of this chapter.

15. Cf. H.E. Brunner, *Dogmatik* II, 1950, p. 263ff; Eng. trans., *Dogmatics* (Philadelphia: Westminster Press, 1950); W. Pannenberg, *Grundzüge der Christologie* (Gütersloh: G. Mohn, 1966), p. 42; Eng. trans., *Jesus, God and Man* (Philadelphia: Westminster Press, 1968).

16. Cf. R. Schnackenburg, "Mitmenschlichkeit im Horizont des Neuen Testaments," in *Die Zeit Jesus*, Fest. for H. Schlier, ed. G. Bornkamm and K. Rahner (Freiburg/Basel/Vienna, 1970), pp. 70–93, esp. pp. 84–86.

17. J. Gnilka, in *Die Zeit Jesus*, ibid., pp. 190–207.

18. Cf. F. Gogarten, *Jesus Christus, Wende der Welt* (Tübingen: Mohr, 1966), pp. 32–39; G. Ebeling, "Die Frage nach dem historischen Jesus und das Problem der Christologie," in *Wort und Glaube* (Tübingen: Mohr, 1960), pp. 300–318, esp. p. 308–11.

19. *Correspondence* I, Calmann-Levy (Paris, 1961), p. 157, writing to Baronesa von Wizine.

Chapter 6

1. See the principal bibliography used by us: J. Blinzler, *Der Prozess Jesu*, 4th ed. (Regensburg: F. Pustet, 1969), esp. pp. 73–100; Eng. trans., *The Trial of Jesus* (Westminster, Md.: Newman Press, 1959); W. Koch, *Der Prozess Jesus* (Munich: Deutscher Tatsachenbuch, 1968); K.

Schelkle, *Die Passion Jesu in der Verkündigung des Neuen Testamentes* (Heidelberg, 1949); H. Conzelmann, E. Haenchen, E. Käsemann, E. Lohse, *Zur Bedeutung des Todes Jesu* (Gütersloh, 1967); P. Benoit, *Passion et Résurrection du Seigneur* (Paris: Cerf, 1961); idem, "La Passion de Christ," in *Exégèse et théologie* (Paris: Cerf, 1961), 1:265–362; Carlos Mesters, "O processo contra Jesus," in *A Palavra de Deus na história dos homens* (Petrópolis: Vozes, 1971), pp. 149–71; cf. also the valuable collection of the best German Protestant theologians and exegetes: *Diskussion um Kreuz und Auferstehung*, ed. B. Klappert (Quppertal, 1968), especially the works of Barth, Zahrnt, Kunneth, Bornkamm, pp. 113–14; 145–58; 183–89.

2. Cf. R. Bultmann, *Das Evangelium des Johannes* (Göttingen: Vandenhoeck & Ruprecht, 1957), pp. 92ff., 113–93ff., 349–72, 436; Eng. trans., *The Gospel of John: A Commentary* (Philadelphia: Westminster, 1971); C.H. Dodd, *The Interpretation of the Fourth Gospel* (Cambridge: University Press, 1953), pp. 354–68; J. Blank, *Krisis; Untersuchungen zur johanneischen Christologie und Eschatologie* (Freiburg: Lambertus, 1964), esp. pp. 53–108.

3. The thesis of R. Eisler, *Jesus Basileus*, 2 vols. (1929–1930), became especially famous; S.G.F. Brandon, *The Fall of Jerusalem and the Christian Church* (London: SPCK, 1951); idem, *Jesus and the Zealots*, (New York: Scribner's, 1967); J. Carmichael, *Leben und Tod des Jesus von Nazareth* (Frankfurt am Main: Fischer Bücherei, 1968); Eng. trans., *The Death of Jesus* (New York: Macmillan, 1963); see also the works of Danilo Nunes refuting the above, especially that of Eisler: *A pascoa de sangue* (Rio de Janeiro: Editora Expressão e Cultura, 1970); idem, *Judas traidor ou traido?* (Rio de Janeiro: Graf. Record, 1968); a basic work concerning the same subject matter was written by M. Hengel, *Die Zeloten, Untersuchungen zu den Jüdischen Freiheitsbewegungen in der Zeit des Herodes* (Leiden: E.J. Brill, 1961); idem, *War Jesus Revolutionär?* (Stüttgart: Calwer Verlag, 1970); Eng. trans., *Was Jesus a Revolutionist?* (Philadelphia: Fortress Press, 1971).

4. Cf. the work mentioned above by Nunes, *Judas, traidor ou traido?*, pp. 177, 189ff., 211ff.

5. See the various theories concerning the reasons for Judas' betrayal in J. Blinzler, *Der Prozess Jesu*, pp. 85–87.

6. Cf. H. Conzelmann, "Historie und Theologie in den synoptischen Passionsberichten," in *Zur bedeutung des Todes Jesu*, pp. 35–54; E. Haenchen, *Historie und Geschichte in den johannesichen Passionsberichten*, pp. 55–78; G. Bornkamm, *Jesus von Nazareth* (Stuttgart: W. Kohlhammer, 1965), pp. 141–54; Eng. trans., *Jesus of Nazareth* (New York: Harper, 1960); E. Stauffer, *Jesus, Gestalt und Geschichte* (Bern: Francke, 1957), pp. 92–108.

7. See the long discussion in J. Blinzler, *Der Prozess Jesu*, pp. 127–53; P. Benoit, "Jésus devant le Sanhédrin" in *Exégèse et théologie* (Paris: Cerf, 1961-), 1:290–311.

8. Cf. W.G. Kummel, *Die Theologie des Neuen Testamentes nach seinen Hauptzeugen* (Göttingen, 1969), pp. 59–65; J. Blinzler, *Der Prozess Jesu*, pp. 188–97; J. Gnilka, "Das Christusbild einer alten Pas-

sionsgeschichte," in *Jesus Christus nach frühen Zeugnissen des Glaubens* (Munich: Kösel, 1970), pp. 95–109.

9. Cf. M. Hengel, *Die Zeloten* (Leiden-Cologne, 1961), pp. 25–76, 316–18, 228–34.

10. Cf. J. Gnilka, "Die Christologie Jesu von Nazareth," in *Jesus Christus nach frühen*, pp. 159–74; F. Hahn, *Christologische Hoheitstitel; ihre Geschichte im frühen Christentum* (Göttingen: Vandenhoeck & Ruprecht, 1963), pp. 159–79.

11. P. Benoit, "Le procès de Jésus," in *Exégèse et théologie*, 1: 281–82; W. Pannenberg, *Grundzüge der Christologie* (Gütersloh: G. Mohn, 1966), pp. 259ff.; Eng. trans., *Jesus, God and Man* (Philadelphia: Westminster Press, 1968).

12. Cf. E. Stauffer, "Die Kreuzesstrafe im antiken Palästina," in *Jerusalem und Rom im Zeitalter Jesu Christi* (Bern: Francke, 1957), pp. 123–27; cf. also D. João Mehlmann, "A Crucificação na Judéia," in *Estudos Historicos* (Univ. Marilia—SP), 3–4, 1965, pp. 113–47.

13. F. Gogarten, "Die Verkündigung Jesu und die bestehende Welt," in *Jesus Christus, Wende der Welt* (Tübingen: Mohr, 1966), pp. 91–110.

14. Cf. J. Alfaro, "Fides in terminologia biblica" in *Gregorianum* 42 (1961): 463–505; P. Antoine, "Foi (dans l'Ecriture)," in *Dictionnaire de la Bible* (Paris: Librairie Letouzy et Ané, 1938), 3:276–310.

15. G. Ebeling, "Jesus und Glaube," in *Wort und Glaube* (Tübingen: Mohr, 1960), pp. 203–54, esp. pp. 241–42; H. Urs von Balthasar, *La foi de Christ; cinq approches christologiques* (Paris: Aubier, Ed. Montaigne, 1968), pp. 13–79, esp. pp. 28–51; P. Charles, "Spes Christi," in *Nouvelle Revue Théologique* (1934), pp. 1009–21; (1937), pp. 1051–75; J. Moltmann, *Teologia da esperança* (S. Paulo: Herder, 1971), pp. 235–68; Eng. trans., *Theology of Hope* (New York: Harper & Row, 1967); P. Schoonenberg, *Ein Gott der Menschen* (Einsiedeln: Benziger, 1969), pp. 185–89; Eng. trans., *The Christ* (New York: Herder, 1971); C. Duquoc, "The Hope of Jesus," Concilium 59 (New York: Herder, 1970), pp. 21–30.

16. Cf. W. Manson, *Bist du, der da kommen soll?* (Zurich, 1952), pp. 154–57; M. Jeremias, *Der Opfertod Jesu Christi* (Stuttgart: Calwer Heute, 1963), pp. 23–30.

17. The position of J. Jeremias is well known; he wants at all costs to have these be the authentic words of Jesus; see "Das Lösegeld für Viele (Mk. 10,45)," in *Abba: Studien zur neutestamentlichen Theologie und Zeitgeschichte* (Göttingen, 1966), pp. 216–232; Eng. trans., *The Prayers of Jesus* (Naperville, Ill.: A.R. Allenson, 1967); however, he is seriously challenged, even by Protestant exegetes. Cf. W. Marxsen, *Anfangsprobleme der Christologie* (Gütersloh: G. Mohn, 1960), pp. 22–31ff.

18. Cf. H. Schürmann, *Der Abendmahlbericht Lucas 22, 7–38 als Gottesdienstordnung—Gemeindeordnung—Lebensordnung* (Paderborn: Ferdinand Schoeningh, 1957); G. Voss, *Die Christologie der Lukanischen Schriften in Grundzügen* (Paris: Desclée de Brouwer, 1965), pp. 99–107.

19. R. Otto, *Reich Gottes, und Menschensohn* (Munich, 1954), pp.

214–30; Eng. trans., *The Kingdom of God and the Son of Man* (Boston: Starr King Press, 1957).

20. W. Manson, *Bist du, der da kommen soll?*, pp. 165–68.

21. Cf. R. S. Barbour, "Gethsemane in the Tradition of the Passion," in *New Testament Studies* 16 (1970): 231–51.

22. Cf. G. Bornkamm, "Kreuz," in *Diskussion um Kreuz und Auferstehung*, pp. 184–89, esp. p. 188, see note 1 above; a good summary of the current debate is by W. Pannenberg, *Grundzüge der Christologie*, pp. 250–257; Eng. trans., *Jesus, God and Man*.

23. Cf. the beautiful reflections of K. Niederwimmer, *Jesus* (Göttingen, 1968), pp. 85–86.

24. D. Bonhoeffer, *Letters and Papers from Prison* (New York: Macmillan, 1953), pp. 347–48.

25. Ibid., pp. 348–49.

Chapter 7

1. See G. Bornkamm, *Jesus von Nazareth* (Stüttgart: W. Kohlhammer, 1956), pp. 159–68; Eng. trans., *Jesus of Nazareth* (New York: Harper, 1960); M. Dibelius, *Jesus* (Berlin: W. de Gruyter, 1960), pp. 117–18; Eng. trans., *Jesus: A Study of the Gospels and an Essay on the Motive for Social Action in the New Testament* (London: SCM Press, 1963); H. Kessler, *Die theologische Bedeutung des Todes Jesu; eine traditionsgeschichtliche Untersuchung* (Düsseldorf: Patmos-Verlag, 1970), pp. 235–36.

2. Cf. L. Boff, "A fé na ressurreição de Jesus em questionamento," in *Revista Eclesiástica Brasileira* 30 (1970): 871–95, where the reader can find this theme dealt with in greater depth.

3. Cf. J. Kremer, *Die Osterbotschaft der vier Evangelien* (Stüttgart: Verlag Katholisches Bibelwerk, 1968); P. Seidensticker, *Die Auferstehung Jesu in der Botschaft der Evangelisten* (Stüttgart: Katholisches Bibelwerk, 1967); Grelot, Delorme, Léon-Dufour, and others, *La Résurrection du Christ et l'exégèse moderne* (Paris: Cerf, 1969); P. Benoit, *Passion et Résurrection du Seigneur* (Paris: Cerf, 1966); Eng. trans., *The Passion and Resurrection of Jesus Christ* (New York: Herder, 1969); F.X. Durrwell, *The Resurrection: A Biblical Study* (New York: Sheed and Ward, 1960); J. Comblin, *A ressurreição* (São Paulo: Herder, 1965); Eng. trans. *The Resurrection in the Plan of Salvation* (Notre Dame: Fides, 1966); P. Benoit and R. Murphy, "Immortality and Resurrection," Concilium 60 (New York: Herder, 1970).

4. See G. Greshake, *Auferstehung der Toten* (Essen: Ludgerus, 1969); F. Mussner, *Die Auferstehung Jesu* (Munich: Kösel, 1969); W. Marxsen, U. Wilckens, G. Delling, and H.G. Geyer, *Die Bedeutung der Auferstehungsbotschaft für den Glauben an Jesus Christus* (Gütersloh, 1968); B. Klappert, ed., *Diskussion um Kreuz und Auferstehung* (Wuppertal, 1968), bringing together the best Protestant essays; F.X.

Léon-Dufour, "Bulletin d'exégèse du Nouveau Testament," in *Recherches de Science Religieuse* 57 (October–December 1969): 583–622; H. Grass, *Ostergeschehen und Osterberichte* (Göttingen: Vandenhoeck & Ruprecht, 1956), pp. 138–86; Carlos Mesters, "Fé na ressurreição: Se Deus esta conosco quem será contra nós?" in *Deus onde estás?* (Belo Horizonte: Vega, 1971), pp. 195–208.

5. P. Gaechter, "Die Engelerscheinungen in den Auferstehungsberichten," in *Zeitschrift für Katholische Theologie* 89, pp. 191–202; J. Kremer, *Die Osterbotschaft der vier Evangelien*, pp. 25–28; L. Boff, "A fé na ressurreição," pp. 886–87.

6. Cf. J. Kremer, *Das älteste Zeugnis von der Auferstehung Christi* (Stüttgart: Katholisches Bibelwerk, 1970), pp. 82–85.

7. Cf. H. Grass, *Ostergeschehen und Osterberichte*, pp. 233–49.

8. John 21 is thought to be a later appendix to the Gospel. The apparition narrated there can be interpreted in a more coherent manner if we admit that it may be a re-elaboration of a pre-paschal tradition concerning the calling of the apostles (Luke 5:1–11), it is now being retold in the light of the good news of the Resurrection and has the clear purpose of relating the ministry of Peter with the power of the resurrected Christ; see P. Benoit, *Passion et résurrection du Seigneur*, pp. 337–53, see note 3 above.

9. Cf. P. Seidensticker, *Die Auferstehung Jesu*, pp. 62–77.

10. The basic kerygma is now expressed thus: "I was dead. But behold, now I am to live forever and ever and I hold the keys of death and of the underworld" (Rev. 1:18; cf. Rom. 6:10).

11. Cf. J. Dupont, "Le repas d'Emmaüs," in *Lumiere et Vie* 31 (February 1957): 77–92; P. Schubert, "The Structure and Significance of Luke 24," in *Neutestamentliche Studien*, Fest. R. Bultmann (Berlin, 1957), pp. 165–86; M. Kehl, "Eucharistie und Auferstehung. Zur Deutung der Ostererscheinungen beim Mahl," in *Geist und Leben* 43 (1070): 00 1D5, cap. pp. 101–5.

12. R. Schnackenburg, "Die Auferstehung Jesu Christi als Ausgangsund Ansatzpunkt der neutestamentlichen Christologie," in *Mysterium Salutis* III/2 (Einsiedeln: Benziger, 1970), pp. 230–347; W. Pannenberg, "Die Bedeutung der Auferweckung Jesu in der traditionsgeschichtlichen Situation des Urchristentums," in *Grundzüge der Christologie* (Gütersloh: G. Mohn, 1969), pp. 61–69; Eng. trans., *Jesus, God and Man* (Philadelphia: Westminster Press, 1968).

13. *Quelle* is a German word meaning "source"; it is a technical term in modern exegesis. The Synoptic texts that are not in Mark but are common to or can be found with small alterations in both Luke and Matthew pertain to the *Quelle* (or simply "Q"). Cf. J. Gnilka, "Das Christusbild der Spruchquelle," in *Jesus Christus nach frühen Zeugnissen des Glaubens* (Munich: Kösel, 1970), pp. 110–26; H. Kessler, *Die theologische bedeutung des Todes Jesu*, pp. 236–39.

14. H. Kessler, *Die theologische Bedeutung*, pp. 227–329, considers with great exegetical erudition the various interpretations of the death of Christ; cf. also W. Pannenberg, "Die ältesten Deutungen des

Todes Jesu und ihre Problematik," in *Grundzüge der Christologie*, pp. 252–57.

15. Cf. E. Peterson, "Die Kirche," in *Theologische traktate* (Munich, 1951), pp. 409–24.

16. Cf. F. Hahn, *Christologische Hoheitstitel* (Göttingen: Vandenhoeck & Ruprecht, 1963), pp. 66ff.; J. Jeremias, *Jesu Verheissung für die Volker* (Stuttgart: Kohlhammer, 1956), pp. 12ff.

17. Cf. E. Bloch, *Das Prinzip Hoffnung*, vol. 2 (Berlin: Aufbau-Verlag, 1959); H. Linding, "Wanderungen der Tupi-guarani und Eschatologie der Apapocuva-guarani," in W. Muhlmann, *Chiliasmus und Nativismus: Studien zur Psychologie, Soziologie und historischen Kasuistik der Unsturzbewegungen* (Berlin, 1964), pp. 19–40.

18. Cf. A. Gélin, *L'homme selon la Bible* (Paris: Ligel, 1968), pp. 9–18; Eng. trans., *The Concept of Man in the Bible* (Staten Island, New York: Alba House, 1968); M. Koennlein, *L'homme selon l'apôtre Paul* (Paris: Neuchâtel, 1951), pp. 9–12 and 38–44.

19. Cf. J.B. Metz, "Caro cardo salutis. Zum christlichen Verständnis des Leibes," in *Hochland* 55 (1962): 97–107, esp. p. 97.

20. Cf. L. Boff, "O homem-corpo e imortal," in *Vozes* 65 (1971): 61–68, with the bibliography cited there.

Chapter 8

1. See the principal bibliography used by us: F. Hahn, *Christologische Hoheitstitel* (Göttingen: Vandenhoeck & Ruprecht, 1966); Eng. trans., *The Titles of Jesus in Christology* (New York: World, 1969); O. Cullmann, *Die Christologie des Neuen Testaments* (Tübingen: Mohr, 1958); Eng. trans., *The Christology of the New Testament* (Philadelphia: Westminster Press, 1959); R. Schnackenburg, "Christologie des Neuen Testaments," in *Mysterium Salutis* III/1 (Einsiedeln: Benziger, 1970), pp. 227–383; V. Taylor, *The Person of Christ in New Testament Teaching* (New York: St. Martin's Press, 1958); C. Duquoc, *Christologie, essai dogmatique* (Paris: Cerf, 1968); H.R. Balz, *Methodische Probleme der neutestamentlichen Christologie* (Neukirchen-Vluyn-Neukirchner Verlag des Erziehungsvereins, 1967); R. Schnackenburg, and F. J. Schierse, *Wer war Jesus von Nazareth? Christologie in der Krise* (Düsseldorf: Patmos, 1970); J. Doyon, *Christologie para o nosso tempo* (São Paulo: Ed. Paulinas, 1970); French orig., *Christologie pour notre temps* (Sherbrooke, Québec: Ed. Paulines, 1968); W. Marxsen, *Anfangsprobleme der Christologie* (Gütersloh: G. Mohn, 1967); K. Berger, "Zum traditionsgeschichtlichen Hintergrund Christologischer Hoheitstitel," in *New Testament Studies* 17 (July 1971): pp. 391–425.

2. Cf. H. Conzelmann, "Jesus Christus," in *Die Religion in Geschichte und Gegenwart*, 2:667; in English see Conzelmann's *Jesus* (Philadelphia: Fortress Press, 1973); W. Künneth, "Die indirekte

Christologie," in *Glauben an Jesus?* (Hamburg, 1969), pp. 88–93.

3. Cf. M. Hengel, *Nachfolge und Charisma: eine exegetisch-religionsgeschichtliche Studie zu Mt. 8,21f.* and *Jesu Ruf in die Nachfolge* (Berlin: A. Töpelmann, 1968), p. 98; W. Pannenberg, *Grundzüge der Christologie*, pp. 47–61; Eng. trans., *Jesus, God and Man;* E. Käsemann, "Das problem des historischen Jesus," in *Glauben heute* (Hamburg, 1966), pp. 113–52, esp. pp. 140–53; Eng. trans., *New Testament Questions of Today* (Philadelphia: Fortress Press, 1969); E. Fuchs, "Die Frage nach dem historischen Jesus," in *Zeitschrift für Theologie und Kirche* (1956), pp. 210–220; H. Braun, *Jesus: Der Mann aus Nazareth und seine Zeit* (Berlin: Kreuz, 1969).

4. J. Jeremias, *Les paraboles de Jésus* (Le Puy-Lyon, 1965), pp. 131ff; *The Parables of Jesus* (New York: Scribner's, 1963).

5. H. Küng, *Was ist die christliche Botschaft?* A Conference of the International Congress of Theology in Brussels, Belgium, September 12, 1970, p. 2.

6. Cf. E. Schweizer, *Jesus Christus im vielfältigen Zeugnis des Neuen Testaments* (Munich: Siebenstern Taschenbuch Verlag, 1968), pp. 34–38; Eng. trans., *Jesus* (Richmond: John Knox Press, 1971).

7. Cf. M. Hengel, "Jesus war kein Rabbi," in *Nachfolge und Charisma*, pp. 46–55; W.G. Kümmel, *Theologie des Neuen Testaments nach seinen Hauptzeugen* (Göttingen, 1969), pp. 57–59.

8. Cf. C. Duquoc, *Christologie*, pp. 131–70; O. Cullmann, *Die Christologie*, pp. 11–41; Eng. trans., *The Christology of the New Testament*.

9. O. Cullmann, *Die Christologie*, pp. 117ff.; F. Hahn, *Christologische Hoheitstitel*, pp. 242–69.

10. V. Taylor, *The Person of Christ in New Testament Teaching;* H. E. Balz, *Methodische Probleme der neutestamentlichen Christologie*, pp. 124–27; H. Conzelmann, *Grundriss der Theologie des Neuen Testaments* (Munich: Kaiser, 1967), pp. 147–59.

11. W. Manson, *Bist du, der da kommen soll?* (Zürich, 1952), p. 130.

12. W. Grundmann, *Die Geschichte Jesu Christi* (Berlin: Evangelische Verlagsanstalt, 1961), p. 270.

13. Cf. H.R. Balz, *Methodische Probleme*, p. 124; G. Bornkamm, *Jesus von Nazareth* (Stuttgart, 1965), pp. 155–63.

14. Cf. H. Braun, *Jesus*, pp. 149–56; O. Cullmann, *Die Christologie des Neuen Testaments*, p. 13; Eng. trans., *Christology*.

15. Cf. the good summary by Bornkamm, *Jesus von Nazareth*, pp. 208–10; H.R. Balz, "Strukturen der spätjüdisch-apokalyptischen Heilserwartung," in *Methodische Probleme*, pp. 48–112.

16. Balz, ibid., p. 124, with the bibliography cited favoring this point of view.

17. Cf. E. Schweizer, *Jesus Christus*, pp. 68ff.

18. F. Hahn, *Christologische Hoheitstitel*, pp. 133–225; O. Cullmann, *Die Christologie*, pp. 109–37; Eng. trans., *Christology*.

19. H. Conzelmann, *Grundriss der Theologie des Neuen Testaments*, p. 143.

20. H.R. Balz, "Die urgemeindliche Christologie im Zusammenhang mit den Gruppen und Schichten der Gemeinde," in *Methodische Probleme*, pp. 129–75.

21. Cf. V. Taylor, *The Person of Christ;* R. Schnackenburg, "Die älteste Christologie in der Urkirche," in *Mysterium Salutis*, pp. 248–71.

22. F. Hahn, *Christologische Hoheitstitel*, pp. 280–333, esp. pp. 319ff.

23. Ibid., pp. 67–125; O. Cullmann, *Die Christologie*, pp. 200–52; Eng. trans., *Christology*.

24. Cullmann, ibid., pp. 245–52.

25. H. Conzelmann, *Grundriss der Theologie*, pp. 97–99.

26. Cf. L. Boff, *O evangelho do Cristo Cosmico* (Petrópolis: Vozes, 1971), pp. 67–82.

27. Cf. R. Schnackenburg, "Johannische Christologie: die Inkarnation des Logos, der Sohn als Offenbarung des Vaters," in *Mysterium Salutis* III/1, pp. 337ff.

28. H. J.Winter, "Der christologische Hoheitstitel 'Theos' im Neuen Testaments," in *Bibel und Liturgie*, no. 3, 1969, pp. 171–90; R.E. Brown, "Does the New Testament Call Jesus God?" in *Theological Studies* 26 (1965): 545–73.

Chapter 9

1. Exegetically speaking we do not want to bring in anything new. We are merely trying to reproduce what serious Catholic exegesis allows one to say. We omit any reference to Protestant exegesis, though in the above case it has arrived at the same conclusions as Catholic exegesis: J. Riedl, *Die Vorgeschichte Jesu* (Stuttgart: Verlag Katholisches Bibelwerk, 1968); A. Heising, *Gott wird Mensch: Eine Einführung in die Aussageabsicht und Darstellungsweise von Mt. 1–2; Lk 1–2; 3,28–38* (Trier, 1967); R. Schnackenburg, *Die Geburt Christi ohne Mythos und Legende* (Mainz: Matthias-Grunewald Verlag, 1969); A. Vögtle, "Die Genealogie Mt. 1,2–16 und die matthäische Kindheitsgeschichte," in *Biblische Zeitschrift* 8 (1964): 45–58; 239–62; and 9 (1965); idem, "Das Schicksal des Messiaskindes. Zur Auslegung und Theologie von Mt. 2," in *Bibel und Leben* 6 (1965): 32–49; idem, "Erzählung oder Wirklichkeit. Die Weihnachtsgeschichte als Frohbotschaft," in *Publik* no. 51/52, pp. 33–34; H. Schürmann, "Aufbau Eigenart und Geschichtswert der Vorgeschichte von Lk 1–2," in *Bibel und Kirche* 21 (1966): 106–11; G. Voss, "Die Christusverkündigung der Kindheitsgeschichte im Rahmen des Lukasevangelium," in *Bibel und Kirche* 21 (1966): 1112–15; idem, *Die Christologie der Lukanischen Schriften in Grundzügen* (Paris: Desclée de Brouwer, 1965), pp. 62–83; M.M. Bourke, "The Literary Genius of Matthew 1–2," in *Catholic Biblical Quarterly* 22 (April 1960): 160–75; R. Laurentin, *Structure et théologie de Luc 1–2* (Paris: J. Gabalda, 1957); A.M. Denis, "L'adoration des Mages," in *Nouvelle Revue Théologique* 82

(1960): 32–39; J. Racette, "L'Évangile de l'enfance selon Saint Matthieu," in *Sciences Ecclésiastiques* 9 (1957): 77–82; S. Muñoz Iglesias, "El género literario del Evangelio de la Infancia in San Mateo," in *Estudios Bíblicos* 17 (1958): 243–73; W. Trilling,*Jesús y los problemas de su historicidad* (Barcelona: Herder, 1970), pp. 85–97; German orig., *Fragen zur Geschichtlichkeit Jesu* (Düsseldorf: Patmos Verlag, 1967); J. Daniélou, *Os Evangelhos da infância* (Petrópolis: Vozes, 1969); Eng. trans., *The Infancy Narratives* (New York: Herder, 1968); A. Läpple, "*A mensagem dos Evangelhos hoje* (São Paulo: Paulinas, 1971), pp. 413–46; U.E. Lattanzi, "Il vangelo dell'infanzia è verità o mito?" in *De primordiis cultus mariani* (Rome: Pontificia Academia Mariana Internationalis, 1970), 4:31–46, a very polemical study; E. Nellessen, *Das Kind und seine Mutter* (Stuttgart: Verlag Katholisches Bibelwerk, 1969); O. Knoch, "Die botschaft des Matthäusevangeliums über Empfängnis und Geburt Jesus vor dem Hingergrund der Christus verkündigung des Neuen Testaments," in *Zum Thema Jungfrauengeburt* (Stuttgart, 1970), pp. 37–60; G. Lattke, "Lukas 1 und die Jungfrauengeburt," in *Zum Thema Jungfrauen-geburt*, pp. 61–90; E. Cywinski, "Historicidade do Evangelho da Infância segundo São Lucas," in *Revista da Cultura Bíblica* 5 (1968): 15–29; D.E. Bettencourt, "Os Magos, Herodes e Jesus," in *Revista de Cultura Biblica* 5 (1968): 30–42.

2. Frei Carlos Mesters, "Origem dos quatro evangelhos: do 'Evangelho' aos quatro evangelhos," in *Deus, onde estás?* (Belo Horizonte: Vega, 1971), pp. 125–28; A. Heising,*Gott wird Mensch*, p. 26.

3. Cf. J. Riedl, *Die Vorgeschichte Jesu*, pp. 12–13.

4. "A concepção virginal de Jesus e a mentalidade contemporânea," in *Revista Eclesiástica Brasileira* 29 (1969): pp. 38–63, esp. pp. 39–40; cf. the excellent book by K. Suso Frank, R. Kilian, O. Knoch, G. Lattke, K. Rahner, *Zum Thema Jungfrauengeburt* (Stuttgart, 1970).

5. Cf. R. Schnackenburg, *Die Geburt Christi ohne Mythos und Legende*, p. 8.

6. Cf. W. Trilling,*Jesus y los problemas de su historicidud*, pp. 88–89; G. Krol, *Auf den Spuren Jesu* (Leipzig, 1963), p. 29.

7. For the parallel see R. Bloch, "Die Gestalt des Moses in der rabbinischen Tradition," in*Moses* (Düsseldorf, 1963), pp. 71–95, esp. pp. 108–110; A. Vögtle, "Das Schicksal des Messiaskindes," in *Bibel und Leben* 6 (1965): 267–70; A. Heising, *Gottwird Mensche*, pp. 48–49.

8. Cf. J. Riedl, *Die Vorgeschichte Jesu*, pp. 42–45.

Chapter 10

1. The christological bibliography is unlimited. We will list the most important works used by us: A. Adam, *Lehrbuch der Dogmengeschichte* (Gütersloh: G. Mohn, 1965); M. Schmaus, A. Grillmeier, *Handbuch der Dogmengeschichte*, vol. 3, no. 1 (Freiburg, 1965); A. Grillmeier, H. Bacht, *Das Konzil von Chalcedon; Geschichte und Gegenwart*, 3 vols. (Würzburg: Echter-Verlag, 1951–54); A. Grillmeier, "Zum Christusbild

der heurigen katholischen Theologie," in *Fragen der Theologie heute* (Zurich, 1951), pp. 266–99; P. Smulders, "Dogmengeschichtliche und lehramtliche Engfaltung der Christologie," in *Mysterium Salutis* III/1 (Einsiedeln: Benziger, 1970), pp. 389–475; C. Duquoc, *Christologie: essai dogmatique* (Paris: Cerf, 1968), pp. 282–99; W. Pannenberg, *Grundzüge der Christologie* (Gütersloh: G. Mohn, 1969), pp. 291ff.; Eng. trans., *Jesus, God and Man* (Philadelphia: Westminster Press, 1968); J. Doyon, *Cristologia para o nosso tempo* (São Paulo: Ed. Paulinas, 1970), pp. 243–68; French orig., *Christologie pour notre temps* (Sherbrooke, Québec: Ed. Paulines, 1968).

2. K. Rahner, "Wast ist eine dogmatische Aussage?" in *Schriften zur Theologie* (Einsiedeln: Benziger, 1964), 5:68; Eng. trans., *Theological Investigations* (Baltimore: Helicon Press, 1961).

3. Cf. J. McIntyre, *The Shape of Christology* (Philadelphia: Westminster Press, 1966); J. Knox, *The Humanity and Divinity of Christ: A Study Pattern in Christology* (Cambridge: University Press, 1967); P. Schoonenberg, *Ein Gott der Menschen* (Zürich: Benziger, 1969), pp. 53–59; Eng. trans., *The Christ: A Study of the God-Man Relationship* (New York: Herder, 1971).

4. Denzinger-Schönmetzer, *Enchiridion Symbolorum: Definitionum et Declarationum de rebus fidei et morum* (Freiburg: Herder, 1964), no. 125.

5. Cf. A. Grillmeier, "Die theologische sprachliche Vorbereitung der christologischen Formel von Chalkedon," in *Das Konzil von Chalkedon* I (1951), pp. 81ff., 77–102.

6. S. Gregory Nazianzen, Epist. 101, "Ad Cledonium presbyterum."

7. Theodore of Mopsuestia, "Homily cat. V, 11," cited by A. Grillmeier, *Vorbereitung*, p. 145.

8. Cf. F. X. Arnold, "Das gott-menschliche Prinzip der Seelsorge und die Gestaltung der Christlichen Frömmigkeit," in *Das Konzil von Chalkedon* III, pp. 287–340, esp. pp. 302–27.

9. Denzinger-Schönmetzer, nos. 301–2. Cf. I. O. de Urbina, "Das glaubenssymbol von Chalkedon—sein Text sein Werden seine dogmatische Bedeutung," in *Das Konzil von Chalkedon* I, pp. 389–418.

10. José I. G. Faus, "Las fórmulas de la dogmática cristológica y su interpretación actual," in *Estudios Eclesiásticos* 46 (1971): 344.

11. W. Pannenberg, *Grundzüge der Christologie*, pp. 349–57; Eng. trans., *Jesus, God and Man*.

12. Cf. A. van de Walle, "Die Person Christi in der heurigen Theologie," in *Wissenchaft und Weisheit* 30 (1967): 44–61; J. B. Libânio, "Modernos conceitos de pessoa e personalidade de Jesus," in *Revista Eclesiastica Brasileira* 31 (1971): 47–65.

13. Duns Scotus, *Opus Oxioniense* III, d. 1.2.1, n. 17.

14. For a critique of the Chalcedonian christological model see José I. G. Faus, "Las fórmulas," pp. 351–56; P. Schoonenberg, *Ein Gott der Menschen*, p. 64–69; Eng. trans., *The Christ*.

15. José I. G. Faus, "Las Fórmulas," p. 353.

16. Following more or less this tendency: K. Rahner, "Zur Theologie der Menschwergung," in *Schriften zur Theologie*, 4:137–55; Eng. trans., "On the Theology of the Incarnation," in *Theological Investigations* (Baltimore: Helicon Press, 1966), 4:105–20; idem, "Jesus Christus," in *Lexikon für Theologie und Kirche*, 5:152ff.; idem, "Jesus Christus," in *Sacramentum Mundi* II, pp. 920–57; Eng. trans., "Jesus Christ," in *Sacramentum Mundi* (Baltimore: Helicon Press, 1967), 3:174–209; idem, "Die Christologie innerhalb einer evolutiven Weltanschauung," in *Schriften*, 5:183–221; Eng. trans., "Christology Within an Evolutionary View of the World," in *Theological Investigations* (Baltimore: Helicon, 1966), 5:157–92; idem, "Christologie im Rahmen des modernen Selbst-und Weltverständnisses," in *Schriften*, 9:197–201; Eng. trans., "Christology in the Setting of Modern Man's Understanding of Himself and of His World," in *Theological Investigations* (New York: Seabury Press, 1974), 11:215–29; idem, "Ich glaube an Jesus Christus," in *Schriften*, 8:213–17; Eng. trans., "I Believe in Jesus Christ," in *Theological Investigations* (New York: Herder, 1972), 9:165–68; P. Schoonenberg, *Ein Gott der Menschen*, pp. 70–111; Eng. trans., *The Christ;* W. Pannenberg, *Grundzüge der Christologie*, pp. 357–61; Eng. trans., *Jesus, God and Man;* F. Gogarten, *Jesus Christus, Wende der Welt* (Tübingen: Mohr, 1966), pp. 190ff., 231ff.; Eng. trans., *Christ the Crisis* (Richmond: John Knox Press, 1970); R. Welte, "Homousios hemin. Gedanken zum Verständnis und zur theologischen Problematik der Kategorin von Chalkedon," in *Das Konzil von Chalkedon* III, pp. 51–80; C. Duquoc, *Christologie, essai dogmatique*, pp. 299ff.; B. Langemeyer, "Was heisst: Gott ist Mensch geworden?" in *Geist und Leben* 43 (1970): 407–21; J. Ratzinger, "Zum Personverständnis in der Dogmatik," in *Das Personverständnis der Pädagogik und ihrer Nachbarwissenschaften* (Münster, 1966), pp. 157–71; idem, *Introdução ao cristianismo* (São Paulo: Herder, 1970).

17. P. Schoonenberg, *Ein Gott der Menschen*, p. 109; Eng. trans., *The Christ.*

18. Cf. L. Boff, "O homen como um nó de relações," in *Vozes* 65 (1971):481–82.

19. Cf. L. Boff, *O Evangelho do Christo cósmico* (Petrópolis: Vozes, 1971), pp. 103–9.

20. "Die Mysterien des Lebens Jesu," in *Mysterium Salutis* III/2 (Einsiedeln: Benziger, 1969), pp. 1–132.

21. Cf. L. Boff, "Elementos de teologia para uma situação de crise," in *Credo para amanhã* 3 (Petrópolis: Vozes, 1972), pp. 169–97; C. Mesters, "A transfiguração de Jesus: O sentido das crises na vida," in *Deus onde estás?* (Belo Horizonte: Vega, 1972).

22. Cf. W. Pannenberg, *Grundzüge der Christologie*, pp. 363–78; Eng. trans., *Jesus, God and Man.*

23. See the bibliography cited in Chapter 9, note 10.

24. Cf. *Opus Oxoniense* III, d.1, question 1, no. 9; XIV 100b; XIV 26b; H. Mühlen, *Sein und Person nach J. D. Scotus* (Werl-West, 1954), pp. 95ff.

Chapter 11

1. This is heavily accentuated by W. Künneth, *Glauben an Jesus? Die begegnung der Christologie mit der modernen Existenz* (Hamburg: F. Witting, 1969), pp. 150–83; R. Schnackenburg, "Die Auferstehung Jesus Christi als Ausgangs-und Ansatzpunkt der neutestamentlichen Christologie," in *Mysterium Salutis* III/2 (Einsiedeln: Benziger, 1970):230–47.

2. This aspect is especially emphasized by Teilhard de Chardin; see C. F. Mooney, *Teilhard de Chardin and the Mystery of Christ* (New York: Harper & Row, 1966), pp. 67–103; E. Rideau, *O pensamento de Teilhard de Chardin* (Lisbon, 1965), pp. 245–50; Eng. trans., *The Thought of Teilhard, de Chardin* (New York: Harper & Row, 1967).

3. Cf. A. Grabner-Haider, "Auferstehungsleiblichkeit," in *Stimmen der Zeit* 181 (1968): 217–22; L. Boff, "O sentido antropológico da morte e da ressurreição," in *Revista Eclesiástica Brasileira* 31 (1971):306–32, and the bibliography cited there.

4. Cf. I Hermann, *Kyrios und Pneuma* (Munich: Kösel Verlag, 1961); H. Mühlen, *Una mystica persona: Eine Person in vielen Personen* (Munich/Paderborn/Vienna: Schöningh, 1968); idem, "Das Christusereignis als Tat des Heiligen Geistes," in *Mysterium Salutis* III/2 (Einsiedeln: Benziger, 1969):513–48; L. Boff, "Die Kirche als Sakrament des Pneuma," in *Die Kirche als Sakrament im Horizont der Welterfahrung* (Paderborn, 1972), Chap. 11.

5. L. Boff, *O Evangelho do Cristo cósmico* (Petrópolis: Vozes, 1971), and the bibliography cited there. Cf. also, K. H. Schelkle, "Die Schöpfung in Christus," in *Die Zeit Jesu*, Fest. H. Schleir (Freiburg, 1970), pp. 208–17; F. Mussner, "Schöpfung in Christus," in *Mysterium Salutis* II (Einsiedeln: Benziger, 1967): 455–63.

6. Cf. J. Daniélou, *Os Evangelhos da infância* (Petrópolis: Vozes, 1969), pp. 7–13; Eng. trans., *The Infancy Narratives* (New York: Herder, 1968); J. Riedl, *Die Vorgeschichte Jesu* (Stüttgart: Verlag Katholisches Bibelwerk, 1969), pp. 14–29; J. A. Heising, *Gott wird Mensch. Eine Einführung in die Aussageabsicht und Darstellungsweise von Mt 1–2; Lk 1–2; 3,23–38* (Trier: Zimmer, 1967), pp. 29–35.

7. Cf. R. Schnackenburg, *Das Johannesevangelium* I (Freiburg: Herder, 1965), pp. 257–69; 290–302; Eng. trans., *The Gospel According to St. John* (New York: Herder, 1968); J. Jeremias, *The Central Message of the New Testament* (London: SCM Press, 1965), pp. 71–90; A. Feuillet, *O prologo do quarto Evangelho* (São Paulo: Ed. Paulinas, 1970); French orig., *Le Prologue du quatrième évangile; étude de théologie johannique* (Paris: Desclée de Brouwer, 1968).

8. Cf. *Barnabas* 6,3; *Apost. Didaskalia* 6, 18, 15.

9. Cf. J. Jeremias, *Unbekannte Jesusworte* (Gütersloh: G. Mohn, 1963), pp. 100–4; Eng. trans., *Unknown Sayings of Jesus* (London: SPCK, 1964).

10. Cf. R. MacGowan, F. Ordway, *Inteligência no Universo* (Petrópolis: Vozes, 1970), pp. 369–86; Eng. orig., *Intelligence in the Universe* (Englewood Cliffs: Prentice-Hall, 1966); P. Dessauer, "Geschöpfe auf fremden Welten," in *Wort und Wahrheit* 9 (1954): 576ff.; D. Grasso, "La teologia e la pluralità dei mondi abitati," in *La Civiltà Cattolica* 103 (1952); E. Bettencourt, *A vida que começa com a morte* (Rio de Janeiro: Agir, 1955), pp. 259–66.

11. Cf. L. Boff, *O Evangelho do Cristo cósmico* (Petrópolis: Vozes, 1971), pp. 55–7; 97–103.

12. R. Schneider, *Verhüllter Tag* (Cologne: J. Hegner, 1956), pp. 220–222; *Winter in Wien* (Freiburg, 1959), pp. 132–241; cf. M. Doerne, "Theologia tenebrarum. Zu Reinhold Schneiders Spätwerk," in *Theologische Literaturzietung* 86 (1961): 401–4.

13. Teilhard de Chardin, *Super-Humanité* (1943), t. 9, pp. 209–10.

14. M. Blondel, *Une énigme historique: le "vinculum substantiale" d'après Leibniz et l'ébauche d'un réalisme supérieur* (Paris: G. Beauchesne, 1930), p. 105.

15. O. Loretz, *Die Gottenbenbildlichkeit des Menschen* (Munich: Kösel Verlag, 1967), esp. pp. 90–95; K. L. Schmid, "Homo imago Dei im Alten und Neuen Testament," in *Der Mensch als Bild Gottes* (Darmstadt: Wissenschaftliche Buchgesellschaft, 1969), pp. 10–48; B. Fraigneau-Juliem, "Présence du Christ glorifié dans le genre humain," in *Revue des Sciences Religieuses* 45 (1971): 305–38.

16. Cf. Tertullian, "De resurrectione carnis," 6; *Patrologiae Latinae* 2, 848; Origen, "In Gen. Hom.," 1,13, *Patrologiae Graecae* 12, 156; cf. also A. Orbe, "El hombre en la teología de San Ireneo," in *Gregorianum* 43 (1962): 449–91.

17. Cf. K. Rahner, "Uber die Einheit von Nächsten-und Gottesliebe," in *Schriften zur Theologie* (Einsiedeln: Benziger, 1965), 6:277–300; V. Warnach, *Agape; die Liebe als Grundmotiv der neutestamentlichen Theologie* (Düsseldorf: Patmos-Verlag, 1951), pp. 367–69, 449ff.

18. Cf. E. Stauffer, *Die Botschaft Jesu; Damals und Heute* (Bern/Munich: Francke Verlag, 1959), pp. 55–67; R. Schnackenburg, "Mitmenschlichkeit im Horizont des Neuen Testamentes," in *Die Zeit Jesu*, pp. 70–92; J. B. Metz, *Befreindes Gedachtnis Jesu Christi* (Mainz: Mathias Grünewald Verlag, 1970).

19. See the most important literature: M. Hengel, *Nachfolge und Charisma* (Berlin: A. Töpelmann, 1968); H. D. Betz, *Nachfolge und Nachahmung Jesu Christi im Neuen Testament* (Tübingen: Mohr, 1967); A. Schulz, *Nachfolgen un Nachahmen*, Studien über das Verhältnis der neutestamentlichen, Jungerschaft zur urchristlichen Vorbildethik (Munich: Kösel Verlag, 1962), and the résumé of this work in *Discipulos do Senhor* (São Paulo: Paulinas, 1969); R. Schnackenburg, "Nachfolge Christi," in *Christliche Existenz nach dem Neuen Testament* (Munich: Kösel Verlag, 1967), 1:87–105; Eng. trans., *Christian Existence in the New Testament* (Notre Dame: University of Notre Dame Press, 1968).

20. *Unitatis Redintegratio*, no. 3.

21. Cf. E. Schweizer, "Kirche als der missionarische Leib Christi," in *Kirche heute* (Bergen-Enkheim, 1965), pp. 26ff; J.A.T. Robinson, *Le corps. Etude sur la théologie de Saint Paul* (Lyon, 1966), pp. 85–103; Eng. orig., *The Body: A Study in Pauline Theology* (Chicago: Regnery, 1952); J. Ratzinger, *Introdução ao cristianismo* (São Paulo: Herder, 1970); Eng. trans., *Introduction to Christianity* (New York: Herder, 1970).

22. See the various works presented in *Acta Congressus Internationalis de Theologia Concilii Vaticani II* (Rome, 1968), pp. 271–338, especially the contribution of K. Rahner, "De praesentia Domini in Communitate cultus: synthesis theologica," pp. 316–338; De Haes, "Les présences du Christ Seigneur," in *Lumen Vitae* 20 (1965):259–74; J. Castellano, "La presencia de Cristo en la Asemblea Litúrgica," in *Revista de Espiritualidad* 30 (1971):222–35.

23. Cf. L. Boff, "Das syn-bolische und das dia-bolische Moment im Sakrament der Kirche," in *Die Kirche als Sakrament im Horizont der Welterfahrung*, Chap. 17.

24. Dag Hammärskjold, *Markings* (New York: Knopf, 1964), p. 95.

25. Ibid., p. 155.

Chapter 12

1. See "The New Cry: Jesus is Coming!" in *Time*, July 21, 1971, pp. 28–37; *O Pasquim* 22 (July 28, 1971), p. 2.

2. Cf. J. Comblin "Os títulos de honra de Cristo, problema teológico," in *Revista de Cultura Bíblica* 5 (1968):103.

3. P. Tillich, *Systematische Theologie* (Stuttgart: Ev. Verlagswerk, 1958), 2:98–106; Eng. trans., *Systematic Theology*, 3 vols. (Chicago: University of Chicago Press, 1951–); Cf. also in the same line W. Rauch, "Gestalt und Person bei Franziskus und Bonaventura," in *Einsicht und Glaube*, Fest. F. Gottlieb Sohngen (Freiburg: Herder, 1962), pp. 200–08; K. Jaspers, *Die grossen Philosophen* (Munich: Piper, 1957): 1129ff.; Eng. trans., *The Great Philosophers*, 2 vols. (New York: Brace & World Inc., 1962).

4. There is hardly any literature on this theme. One can fruitfully consult: J. Comblin, "Cristo en la Iglesia de hoy y de manãna," in *Cristología y pastoral en América Latina* (Santiago de Chile and Barcelona: Dilapsa & Ed. Nova Terra, 1966), pp. 11–48; A. Grillmeier, "La imagen de Cristo en la teología católica actual," in *Panorama de la teología actual* (Madrid: Guadarrama, 1961), pp. 335–76; D. Wiederkehr, "Entwurf einer systematischen Christologie," in *Mysterium Salutis* III/1 (Einsiedeln: Benziger, 1970), pp. 477–648; V. Taylor, *La personne du Christ dans le Nouveau Testament* (Paris: Cerf, 1969), pp. 279–298; Eng. trans., *The Person of Christ in New Testament Teaching* (New York: St. Martin's Press, 1958); D. Bonhoeffer, *Christologie und moderne Existenz: Glauben an Jesus?* (Munich/Hamburg, 1969); K. Niederwimmer, *Jesus* (Göttingen: Vandenhoeck & Ruprecht, 1968),

esp. pp. 80–88; J. B. Metz, *Befreiendes Gedachtnis Jesu Christi* (Mainz: Mathias Grünewald Verlag, 1970); D. Sölle, *Stellvertretung; ein Kapital Theologie nach dem "Tode Gottes"* (Stuttgart: Kreuz Verlag, 1965), pp. 133–295; Eng. trans., *Christ the Representative: An Essay in Theology After the "Death of God"* (Philadelphia: Fortress Press, 1967); F. Gogarten, *Jesus Christus, Wende der Welt* (Tübingen: Mohr, 1966); H. Kung, "Prolegomena zu einer künftigen Christologie," in *Menschwerdung Gottes* (Freiburg: Herder, 1970), pp. 503–610; 647–70; P. Schoonenberg, *Ein Gott der Menschen* (Einsiedeln: Benziger, 1969); Eng. trans., *The Christ: A Study of the God-Man Relationship in the Whole of Creation and in Jesus Christ* (New York: Herder, 1970); J. Doyon, *Cristologia para o nosso tempo* (São Paulo: Paulinas, 1968), pp. 396–421; French orig., *Christologie pour notre temps* (Sherbrooke, Québec: Ed. Paulines, 1968); C. Mesters, "Jesus e o Povo: Qual foi a libertação que Ele trouxe parao povo de seu tempo?" in *Palavra de Deus na história dos homens* (Petrópolis: Vozes, 1971), 2:133–82.

5. This is the Teilhardian perspective: P. Schellenbaum, *Le Christ dans l'energétique teilhardienne* (Paris: Cerf, 1971); K. Rahner, "Die Christologie innerhalb einer evolutiven Weltanschauung," in *Schriften zur Theologie* 5 (Einsiedeln: Benziger, 1964); Eng. trans., "Christology Within an Evolutionary View of the World," in *Theological Investigations* (Baltimore: Helicon, 1966), 5:157–92; U. Zilles, "A cristologie numa mundividencia evolucionista," in *Vozes* 61 (1967): 99–118.

6. Cf. T. Deman, *Socrate et Jésus* (Paris: L'Artisan de Livre, 1944); F. Leist, *Moses, Sokrates, Jesus* (Herder, 1964); G. Mensching, *Buddha und Christus* (Bonn, 1952); H.-R. Schlette, "Der Buddha und Jesus," in *Einführung in das Studium der Religionen* (Freiburg: V. Rombach, 1971), pp. 111–25.

7. Cf. J. Comblin, "Cristo en la Iglesia de hoy y de manãna," pp. 35–45.

8. Cf. L. Boff, "Foi Jesus um revolucionario?" in *Revista Eclesiastica Brasileira* 31 (1971): 97–118; M. Hengel, *Foi Jesus revolucionario?* (Petrópolis: Vozes, 1971); Eng. trans., *Was Jesus a Revolutionist?* (Philadelphia: Fortress Press, 1971).

9. See the lucid exposition of the concepts in P. Demo, "Sociologia da revolução; Reforma ou revolução," in *Vozes* 62 (1968):689–700; 877–85.

10. H. Harada, "Cristologia e Psicologia de C. G. Jung," in *Revista Eclesiastica Brasileira* 31 (1971):119–144; G. Zacharias, *Psyche und Mysterium* (Zürich: Rascher, 1954), pp. 8–22; K. Niederwimmer, *Jesus*.

11. Cf. C. Duquoc, *Christologie* (Paris: Cerf, 1968), 1:39–41; R. Aron, *Les années obscures de Jésus* (Paris: Grasset, 1960); Eng. trans., *Jesus of Nazareth: The Hidden Years* (New York: Morrow, 1962).

12. Duquoc, ibid., p. 41.

13. Cf. P. Schoonenberg, *Ein Gott der Menschen*, pp. 191–203; Eng. trans., *The Christ.*

14. Cf. H. Cox, *The Feast of Fools: A Theological Essay on Festivity and Fantasy* (Cambridge, Mass.: Harvard University Press, 1969).

15. D. Bonhoeffer, *Christologie*, p. 174; M. J. Le Guillou, *Celui qui vient d'ailleurs, l'innocent* (Paris: Cerf, 1971); Dostoyevsky's theme in terms of the suffering innocent is developed on pp. 27–43; 287–98.

16. D. Sölle, in *A Oração no mundo secular* (Petrópolis: Vozes, 1971), p. 110; Eng. trans., *Revolutionary Patience* (Maryknoll, New York: Orbis, 1977).

Chapter 13

1. Cf. the reflections of K. Rahner, "Diė anonymen Christen," in *Schriften zur Theologie* (Einsiedeln: Benziger, 1965), 6:545–54; Eng. trans., "Anonymous Christians," in *Theological Investigations* (Baltimore: Helicon, 1969), 6:390–98; idem, "Der Christ und seine Umwelt," in *Schriften zur Theologie* (Einsiedeln: Benziger, 1966), 7:91–104; Eng. trans., "The Christian in His World," in *Theological Investigations* (New York: Herder, 1971), 7:88–99; A. Roper, *Die anonymen Christen* (Mainz: Mathias Grünewald, 1963), esp. pp. 149ff; Eng. trans., *The Anonymous Christian* (New York: Sheed and Ward, 1966).

2. J. Ratzinger, *Introdução ao Cristianismo* (São Paulo: Herder, 1970), p. 223; Eng. trans., *Introduction to Christianity* (New York: Herder, 1970).

3. Ibid., pp. 189–90.

4. *Nostra Aetate*, no. 1.

5. See our own exposition concerning this subject matter: L. Boff, "Tentativa de solução ecumênica para o problema da inspiração e da inerrância," in *Revista Eclesiastica Brasileira* 30 (1970): 648–67, esp. 658–670.

6. Cf. E. Schillebeeckx, *Cristo Sacramento do encontro* (Petrópolis: Vozes, 1967); Eng. trans., *Christ the Sacrament of the Encounter with God* (New York: Sheed & Ward, 1963).

7. Cf. H.-R. Schlette, *Die Religionen als Thema der Theologie*, Quaestiones Disputatae 22 (Freiburg: Herder, 1963); J. Heilbetz, *Fundamentos teologicos das religioēs nãocristãs*, Questiones Disputatae 33 (São Paulo: Herder, 1970); G. Thils, *Propos et problèmes de la théologie des religions non chrétiennes* (Paris/Tournai: Castermann, 1966), pp. 146–54, 186–96.

8. Cf. P. Volz, *Das Dämonische im Jahwe* (Tübingen, 1924).

9. Cf. L. Boff, "Die Katholische Kirche als Ganzsakrament und die sakramentale Struktur der nichtkatholischen Kirchen," in *Die Kirche als Sakrament im Horizont der Welterfahrung* (Päderborn, 1972), Chap. 14.

10. Cf. "Primogenito da Criação," in *Vozes* 60 (1966):34–39; C. Koser, "Cristo Homem, razão de ser da criação," in *O Pensamento franciscano* (Petrópolis: Vozes, 1960), pp. 37–45. More technical studies: A. Caggiano, "De mente Ioannis Duns Scoti circa rationem Incarnationis," in *Antonianum* 32 (1957):311–34; R. Rosini, *Il cristocentrismo di Giovanni*

Duns Scotus e la Dottrina del Vaticano Secondo (Rome, 1967); R. Nooth, "The Scotist Cosmic Christ," in *De Doctrina Ioannis Duns Scoti* (Rome, 1968), pp. 169–217.

11. See a more detailed discussion in L. Boff, *O Evangelho do Cristo cosmico* (Petrópolis: Vozes, 1971), pp. 103–8.

12. Cf. P. Charles, "Spes Christi," in *Nouvelle Revue Théologique* 61 (1934):1009–12; 64 (1937):1057–75; P. Schoonenberg, *Ein Gott der Menschen* (Einsiedeln: Benziger, 1969), pp. 185–89; Eng. trans., *The Christ: A Study of the God-Man Relationship* (New York: Herder, 1970); J. Moltmann, *Teologia da Esperança* (São Paulo: Herder, 1971), pp. 235–63; Eng. trans., *Theology of Hope* (New York: Harper & Row, 1967); C. Duquoc, "The Hope of Jesus," in *Dimensions of Spirituality*, Concilium 59 (New York: Herder, 1970), pp. 21–30.

13. D. Rougemont, *L'aventure occidentale de l'homme* (Paris: Albin Michel, 1957), p. 104. Note that the idea of revolution is coextensive with the world influenced by Christianity. In Japan, the trade union movement was begun by a Christian called Kagawa. In China, the father of the social revolution was the Christian Sun Yat-sen. Even Gandhi confessed that he thought up the idea of a pacifist revolution while reading the Sermon on the Mount. See also E. Peterson, "Der Monotheismus als politisches Problem," in *Theologische Traktate* (Munich, 1951), pp. 79–80; G. van der Leeuw, *Phänomenologie der Religion* (Tübingen: J.C.B. Mohr, 1956), p. 739; Eng. trans., *Religion in Essence and Manifestation* (New York: Harper & Row, 1963).

14. Cf. Matt. 19:28, which speaks of a palingenesis at the end of the world, i.e., of a new birth and genesis for all things.

15. *Didaqué. Catecismo dos primeiros cristaos* (Petrópolis: Vozes, 1970), p. 22; Eng. trans., *The Teaching of the Twelve Apostles*.

Epilogue

1. A. Vieira Pinto, *Ciência e consciência: Problemas filosóficos de pesquisa cientifica* (Rio de Janeiro, 1969), Chaps. 12–14; C. Boff, "L'engagement social du théologien," in *Théologie et libération: Questions d'épistémologie*, mimeographed, Louvain 1976, pp. 398–435; M. de Certeau, *L'Ecriture de l'histoire* (Paris, 1975), pp. 65–79; P. Blanquart, "L'acte de croire et l'action politique," in *Lumière et Vie* 19 (1970): 12–30.

2. A detailed treatment of this question can be found in C. Boff, *Théologie et libération*, pp. 40–48, 398–435, 465–86.

3. L. Boff, *Teologia desde el cautiverio*, Spanish edition (Bogotá 1975), pp. 13–56; Portuguese edition, *Teologia do cativeiro e da libertacão* (Lisbon: Multinova, 1976).

4. See H. Assmann, *Teología desde la praxis de la liberación* (Salamanca: Sígueme, 1973), p. 40: "The historical situation is that two-thirds of humanity are subject to dependence and domination. Thirty million people a year die of hunger and malnutrition. That situation must become the starting point for any Christian theology

today, even in the dominant, affluent countries. Otherwise theology will not be able to situate and concretize its basic themes in history. Its questions will not be real questions, for they will bypass real human beings. . . . Theology must be saved from cynicism." Portions of this work can be found in H. Assmann, *Theology for a Nomad Church*, Eng. trans. (Maryknoll, New York: Orbis Books, 1976).

5. The following are some of the more important works embodying Latin American Christology: H. Borrat, "Para una cristología de la vanguardia," in *Víspera*, 1970, pp. 26–31; A. Zanteno, "Liberación social y Cristo," in *Cuadernos Liberación*, Ed. Secretariado Social de Mexico, 1971; G. Gutiérrez, "Christ and Complete Liberation," in *A Theology of Liberation*, Eng. trans. (Maryknoll, New York: Orbis Books, 1973), pp. 168–78; F. Bravo, B. Catão, and J. Comblin,*Cristología y pastoral en América Latina* (Santiago-Barcelona, 1965); H. Assmann, *Teología desde la praxis de la liberación*, p. 57f.; idem, "La situación histórica del poder de Cristo," in *Cristianismo y Sociedad* 13 (1975):43–54; J. Sobrino, *Cristología desde América Latina* (Mexico, 1976), Eng. trans., *Christology at the Crossroads* (Maryknoll, New York: Orbis Books, 1978); I. Ellacuría,*Carácter político de la misión de Jesús* (MIEC-JECI, Document 13-14, Lima, 1974), Eng. trans., in *Freedom Made Flesh: The Mission of Christ and His Church* (Maryknoll, New York: Orbis Books, 1976); R. Alves,*Cristianismo opio o liberación?* (Salamanca: Sígueme, 1973), pp. 187–91, Spanish translation of author's*A Theology of Human Hope* (Washington, D.C.: Corpus, 1969); S. Galilea and R. Vidales,*Cristología y pastoral popular* (Bogotá: Paulinas, 1974); J. Miranda, *El ser y el mesías* (Salamanca: Sígueme, 1973); Eng. trans.,*Being and the Messiah* (Maryknoll, New York: Orbis Books, 1977); R. Vidales, "Como hablar de Cristo hoy?" in *Spes*, January 1974, p. 7f.; idem, "La práctica histórica de Jesús," in*Christus* 40 (1975):43–55; the complete issue (nos. 43–44) of *Cristianismo y Sociedad*, 1975, which is devoted to Christology; also some of issue No. 45, especially J. S. Croatto, "La dimensión política del Cristo liberador"; L. Boff, "Salvation in Jesus Christ and the Process of Liberation," Concilium 96 (New York: Herder & Herder/Seabury Press, 1974), pp. 78–91; idem, Statement in *Theology in the Americas*, edited by S. Torres and J. Eagleson (Maryknoll, New York: Orbis Books, 1976), pp. 294–98; idem, "Liberación de Jesucristo por el camino de la opresión," in *Teología desde el cautiverio*, pp. 145–71; idem,*Paixão de Cristo—paixão do mundo* (Petrópolis: Vozes, 1977); S. Galilea, "Jesús y la liberación de su pueblo," in *Panorama de la teología latinoamericana II* (Salamanca: Sígueme, 1975), pp. 33–43.

6. See Merleau-Ponty, *Humanisme et terreur*, Paris, p. 13: "It is indignation, not science, that makes one a revolutionary. Science comes afterwards to fill out the hollow protest and make it precise." Emile Durkheim also maintained that the origin of socialism was to be found in a passion for justice and the redemption of the exploited *(Le socialisme: Sa définition. Ses débuts. La doctrine saint-simonienne*, Paris, 1928).

7. See S. Trinidad, "Cristología—Conquista—Colonización," in *Cristianismo y Sociedad* 13 (1975):12–28. In the same issue see P. N.

Rigol, "Cristología popular: alienación o ironía," pp. 29–34. Also see H. Lepargneur, "Imagens do Cristo no catolicismo popular brasileiro," in *Quem é Jesus Cristo no Brasil?* (São Paulo, 1974), pp. 55–94.

8. See C. Boff, "Teologia e prática," in *Revista Eclesiástica Brasileira* 36 (1976):789–810; also his thesis done at Louvain, *Théologie et libération: Questions d'Epístémologie*, 1976.

9. The bibliography in the field is enormous. A few titles are listed here: F. H. Cardoso, "Desarrollo y dependencia: perspectivas en el análisis sociológico," *Sociología del desarrollo* (Buenos Aires, 1970), p. 19f.; O. Fals Borda, *Ciencia propia y colonialismo intelectual* (Mexico, 1970); T. Santos, *Dependencia y cambio social* (Santiago de Chile, 1970); G. Arroyo, "Pensamiento latinoamericano sobre subdesarrollo y dependencia externa," in *Mensaje*, October 1968, pp. 516–20; P. Negre, *Sociología do terceiro mundo* (Petrópolis, 1977).

10. See J. Comblin, *Théologie de la pratique révolutionnaire* (Paris, 1974), p. 65.

11. Ibid., p. 127.

12. See J. C. Scannone, *Hacia una pastoral de la cultura* (MIEC-JECI 16, Lima, 1976).

13. See J. Sobrino, *Cristología desde América Latina*, p. 297.

14. See J. Miranda, *El ser y el mesías*, p. 9.

15. J. Sobrino, *Cristología desde América Latina*, p. 39.

16. F. Belo, *Una leitura política do evangelho* (Lisbon, 1975), p. 133; French original, *Lecture matérialiste de l'évangile de Marc* (Paris: Ed. du Cerf, 1974); forthcoming in English by Orbis Books.

17. The question about the murderer triumphing over his victim was raised by M. Horkheimer, *Die Sehnsucht nach dem ganz Anderen* (Hamburg, 1972), p. 62.

18. J. Sobrino, "El conocimiento teológico en teología europea y latinoamericana," in *ECA (Estudios Centroamericanos*, San Salvador, 1976), p. 365f; I. Ellacuría, "Tesis sobre la posibilidad y sentido de una teología latinoamericana," in *Teología y mundo contemporáneo* (Madrid, 1975), pp. 335–50.